W9-BIH-695

THE POLITICS OF THE
BUDGETARY PROCESS

THE POLITICS OF THE BUDGETARY PROCESS

Third Edition

AARON WILDAVSKY

Little, Brown and Company
Boston   Toronto

Library of Congress Catalog Card No. 78–71869

ISBN 0-316-940402

9 8 7 6 5 4 3

HAL

Published simultaneously in Canada
by Little, Brown & Company (Canada) Limited

Printed in the United States of America

The author gratefully acknowledges the permission of *New York Affairs*
to reproduce portions of his "Policy Analysis Is What Information
Systems Are Not," IV *New York Affairs* (Spring 1977) No. 2, copyright 1977. The author also gratefully acknowledges the permission of
The American Society for Public Administration to reproduce substantial parts of his "Political Implications of Budgetary Reform," XXI
Public Administration Review (Autumn 1961) pp. 183–190; "The
Political Economy of Efficiency: Cost-Benefit Analysis, Systems Analysis,
and Program Budgeting," XXVI *Public Administration Review* (December 1966) pp. 292–310; and "Rescuing Policy Analysis from PPBS,"
XXIX *Public Administration Review* (March/April 1969) pp. 189–202.

PREFACE TO
THE THIRD EDITION

RANK OBJECTIVES, compare alternatives, choose the highest: *The Politics of the Budgetary Process* was written to show that this accepted paradigm does not describe either how budgetary decisions are made or how they might be made. Sneaking suspicions were voiced in earlier editions that this sequence is also inadequate as a guide to how decisions ought to be made, but, in those editions, there was no direct confrontation with the irrationality of the accepted paradigm of rationality. This third edition claims (how well the reader will have to judge) that putting objectives first, alternatives second, and choices third is inefficient as a method of calculation, ineffective in relating thought to action, and inappropriate as a design for learning.

Our opportunity for rationalizing rationality, so to speak, for observing whether the rational paradigm in action is reasonable, comes from the continuous effort to improve public policy by introducing budgetary procedures — preeminently Planning, Programming, and Budgeting Systems and Zero Base Budgeting (PPB and ZBB) — designed to strengthen policy analysis. Though they go about it in quite different ways, these two procedures for making budgetary choices share four basic premises: that objectives are rational, that calculations should be comprehensive, that power is promises, and that history is irrelevant. I shall argue the opposite. Rational choice (it is always right to be rational) limits calculation so choices can be made, uses history to correct mistakes, harnesses power through organizational incentives, and never, never ranks objectives or resources alone but always together. Just as scientists compare hypotheses containing "if" conditions and "then" consequences, so policy analysts should compare programs containing mixtures of resources and objectives. The title of Chapter 6 may be translated as PPB and ZBB equals IPA, Irrational Policy Analysis.

The related reform (everything we hate today, after all, was once someone's beloved reform) of "Sunset Laws," which require existing agencies to be reevaluated periodically, leads one to wonder whether legislators, who bite, claw, kick, gouge, and otherwise use their hearts, liver, and spleen to create new programs that will last forever, can suddenly, by a flick of the wrist (maybe it wasn't such a wonderful idea?) undo all they have done. The matter is of more than rhetorical interest, for the Congressional budget reform, studied in the last chapter, must soon answer a similar question. Can reform succeed if Congressmen engage in behavior like voting sums that break the ceiling and then (to show they're not such big spenders) voting against raising the same ceiling? The first two years following Congress' budget reform have shown that Congress can make the necessary calculations; their numbers are better and their decisions are being made on time. So far so good. Whether the coalition forged on the anvil of Vietnam and Watergate, which brought high and low spenders together, will remain active no one can say. I hope so, for the fate of Congress as an independent voice in government is tied up with its ability to discipline itself.

Much has happened to the federal budgetary process in the past four years. The new laws and regulations on the impounding of funds by the Office of Management and Budget have made it difficult to slow spending either for bad reasons or for good. The change in the fiscal year from July 1 to October 1 still has accounts confused, but no more than expected. And the size of the budget keeps growing in real purchasing power as well as inflated dollars. The purpose of this preface, however, is not to write about new developments but to complete the old account.

The preface to the second edition mentioned a "major omission," and went on to say that "if the necessary research were done, understanding of *The Politics of the Budgetary Process* would be enhanced by knowledge of how expenditure totals were influenced by (or emerged as by-products of) efforts to manage the economy."[1] Now that John P. Crecine has done the research[2] and Michael Dempster and I have modified and tested it,[3] it is possible to present an abbreviated account of how efforts to increase employment or decrease inflation by using government spending as an instrument of policy affect the process of budgeting.

ECONOMIC MANAGEMENT (FISCAL POLICY) AND BUDGETING

How do the considerations of economic management — employment, inflation, growth — help determine the total federal spending the President will recommend to Congress? One would think that the size of spending enters the budgetary process in the form of expenditure goals designed to smooth out the economic cycle. How?

It is obviously impossible for budgetary totals to be determined entirely by a "bottom-up" process in which all the

[1] Aaron Wildavsky, *The Politics of the Budgetary Process*, 2d ed. (Boston, 1974).

[2] John P. Crecine, "Coordination of Federal Fiscal and Budgetary Policy Processes: Research Strategies for Complex Decision Systems," presented at the annual meeting of the American Political Science Association, September 1977; and John P. Crecine and Glenn W. Fischer, "On the Resource Allocation Processes in the U.S. Department of Defense," Discussion Paper No. 6, University of Michigan, Institute of Public Policy Studies (1969), p. 38.

[3] Michael A. H. Dempster and Aaron Wildavsky, *A Predictive Theory of U.S. Federal Appropriations* (forthcoming, 1980).

spending desires of all the spending agencies are added up. Such a process would require that there be no limits to resources, and we know that there are. By the same token, it is also impossible for spending totals to be determined entirely by a "top-down" process, because that process would require that there be no limits below which governmental spending could be reduced, and again we know that is not true. Both bottom-up and top-down processes must operate simultaneously and within the same environment. The interest for students of budgeting lies in their interaction.

Economic management (or fiscal policy, as it is called) requires a notion of an appropriate level of expenditures either to stimulate or depress economic activity. In that sense it is a top-down process. Those in government, of course, operate in a world they never made, which is only partially subject to their ministrations. Commitments of the past make up the largest part of the budget, and it is either legally or politically impossible to alter them drastically. Considerations of desirable defense and domestic expenditures compete of necessity with optimal fiscal policy, assuming anyone knows what that should be. Among the many constraints within which the makers of fiscal policy operate, the least understood are those imposed by time and by targeting.

There is a prospective fallacy that assumes, by a foreshortening of the future, that fiscal policy goes into effect at the time it is made. If it is the expenditures of fiscal policy we are talking about, that assumption cannot be correct. The most important time, usually, for bringing fiscal considerations to bear on budgetary totals is during the Spring Preview conducted by the Office of Management and Budget (OMB) in April. Suppose this is done in April of 1978. The fiscal policy total is considered along with other matters, and a budgetary target is established and passed down to the spending agencies by the OMB. For the moment, suppose that this total is not challenged by agencies nor revised by the President but goes directly into his Budget in the winter. Even if these contrary-to-fact conditions are met, Congress will not finish acting on appropriations bills until the fall of 1979. It will take spending agencies several months to act on this legislation, so that the impact of these expenditures will not begin to be felt until the winter of 1980. Thus, about two years elapse before the thoughts that went into fiscal policy are reflected in real budgetary behavior. By that time, to be sure, conditions may have markedly changed so that what seemed appropriate then is inappropriate now.

The two years can be shortened to eighteen months by postponing or modifying fiscal policy decisions until November or December. This alternative, however, sacrifices the benefit of considering fiscal policy in the ceilings initially set by the OMB. Renegotiating all the bargains of the prior six months in a few weeks in late November and December is an experience that most of the participants will try to avoid. By late fall, fiscal policy can be fiddled with but the entire orchestral arrangement, insofar as budgetary totals are concerned, is likely to have been settled earlier. Fall fiscal policy is much tighter than what was already an extremely constrained situation the previous spring.

There are more immediate ways of introducing fiscal policy into spending patterns but, resembling as they do the scatter-gun approach, they are likely to miss their target and wound innocent bystanders as they are to hit it. I refer here to speeding up or slowing down the rate of expenditure to coincide with or to counter reported rhythms in the economy. Increases in spending that are temporary are hard to find. In any event, agencies normally cannot gear up quickly for substantially larger rates of spending, and their career administrators are reluctant to do so because of the traumatic effects of equally rapid reductions in personnel when the time comes to return to normal. In sum, it is easy to spend more but not immediately and not necessarily in the desired

amount. Spending less, naturally, is harder. The result is likely
to be an initial increase in spending as employees are given
severance pay and contractors compensated for delay. In
other words, the fine-tuning of spending is a splendid idea in
the abstract, but it is far from practical in application.

There is less to fiscal policy than meets the eye; yet it is
one important consideration among many. It does contribute
to fixing expenditure totals, and we need to know more about
how it is supposed to operate and what it actually does.

During the time of Presidents Truman and Eisenhower,
the operative fiscal rule was a balanced budget. Put (perhaps) too simply, Truman would take existing domestic
spending, add on something he would like or could get
through Congress, add or subtract a little according to the
employment situation, and devote what was left within a
balanced budget to defense. At the same time, of course, he
kept in mind what he considered the minimum necessary to
support national defense. The defense budget rose considerably above his $15 billion level partly because of inflation but
largely because of the Korean War. Eisenhower also worked
within a balanced budget framework except that he was
more concerned with inflation and with the division of the
national product between the private economy and the public sector. Using his own considerable judgment backed by
National Security Council staff papers, he fixed the defense
budget after the Korean War at around $35 billion so that
there would be room for tax reduction within a nearly balanced budget. Because both Truman and Eisenhower believed in balanced budgets, because Truman could not get
expensive spending programs passed and Eisenhower did not
want them, and because both were willing to impose spending ceilings on defense, they were able to keep revenues and
expenditures roughly in line.

Kennedy and Johnson changed all that. The shibboleth
of "balanced budget" held little attraction for them. Kennedy

was mainly interested in economic growth to support his ambitious plans in Space and on Earth. Kennedy's transitional "new economics," under which discretionary deficits were possible and a strong tax reduction stimulus was desirable, opened more room for both defense and domestic spending. Under Johnson, military expenditures rose because of the war in Vietnam, domestic expenditures because of the War on Poverty. The remnants of the balanced budget ideology went down with Johnson's "guns and butter" approach. Under Secretary of Defense McNamara, who spanned the Kennedy and Johnson Administrations, there was more conflict over missions and programs in defense but less over totals because there was more money to go around. There were limits, of course, but these were high.

Among the many surprises of the Nixon Administration was the Keynesian concept of "full-employment surplus," which permitted a deficit so long as its size did not exceed the level of revenues that would have been achieved had the nation been at full employment. Since no one could specify the correct size, there was room to maneuver. Defense was constrained by the rising costs of domestic social programs and by efforts to impose fiscal limits, which were generally nudged upwards at the last moment by President Nixon's and Secretary of State Kissinger's desire to use larger defense totals for bargaining with the Soviet Union.

What can we conclude from this all-too-brief account? Following the rule of a balanced budget was an effective mechanism for keeping expenditures down. The dislike of raising taxes exerted restraint on expenditure. Deficits were tolerated during emergencies, usually in times of war or excessive unemployment. The decline of balanced budgeting has been accompanied by the rise of federal expenditures. The value of a balanced budget was eroded on one side by so-called technical developments: the replacement of the old cash budget with an administrative budget (including a wide variety of transactions, all sorts of trust funds and transfer payments) has made the meaning of a particular level of deficit problematic. The larger the total budget, the more important small differences in estimates (for example, 5 per cent of $600 billion compared to 5 per cent of $100 billion), so that the last $10 to $30 or more billion may be pure guesswork. Technique no doubt follows will, and the desire for high-level spending spawned a variety of devices that would facilitate it. For example, tax expenditures, that is, subsidies given through the tax process, have risen faster than regular budgetary outlays. Because the concept of a full-employment surplus is not overly precise, the question of an appropriate level of spending depends on judgmental variables — on tax estimates, on the velocity with which money moves through the economy, on the impact of deficits spent in different ways, and on more than can be recounted here. One is left with the feeling that there may well be a fiscal limit, but what it should be and, therefore, how much force it can have are increasingly open to question. Perhaps a review of the specific procedures for relating fiscal policy to budgetary totals will help us see what happened.

During the period from 1960 to the present, fiscal policy was essentially made by the President on the advice of his "troika," the Director of the Budget, the Secretary of the Treasury, and the Chief of the Council of Economic Advisors (CEA). The site was the Spring Preview of the OMB. Their analysis consisted of subjecting projected revenues from the Treasury, projected expenditures from the OMB Staff, and data on employment, inflation, and growth from the CEA, to a particular formula. The OMB used its past experience to estimate the likely spending of the thirteen largest agencies (the rest was combined in a single figure) based on Presidential preferences, insofar as these were known, new legislation just passed or likely to be passed, and spending plans as discovered by its examiners. Spending and revenue estimates are tricky, but the OMB must work with what it has. OMB also estimates a total for defense based on past experience and discussion with the Secretary of Defense, the President, and whomever else the budget makers think important. Their idea is to come up with a total that will withstand the shocks of the ensuing months, that will give the domestic economy and the defense establishment livable figures, and that will enable them to proceed in making suballocations within an agreed-upon framework. The Spring Preview is the time for considering not so much the merit of individual programs but the aggregate totals. The value of this process is that everyone starts with a similar target; the difficulty is that the target keeps moving.

At the end of the Spring Preview, the OMB sends appropriations and expenditure targets to domestic agencies. During the Kennedy and Johnson Administrations, apparently, these targets were not sent to Defense but were, in a manner of speaking, kept in Secretary McNamara's head or in some tacit understanding among him, the President, and the troika. Since Nixon's time the military services have been given "fiscal guidance." And that is just what it is — guidance, not ultimate decisions. Bargaining goes on between the Secretary of Defense and others, conditions change, domestic programs show lesser or greater volatility, and fiscal guidance is, as they say, updated. Until recently, the Office of the Secretary of Defense (OSD) reviewed the military budget, and the OMB sent observers but did not participate directly. A final reconciliation of OSD desires and OMB preferences takes place, as usual, at the last minute.

The total for defense was not finally set until the latter part of December when the latest economic forecasts became available. In response to last-minute changes in fiscal policy, as Crecine shows, the government budget was regularly "reopened" during the Nixon Administration. "Budgetary add-ons" and fiscal stimulus (federal spending increases) increased totals at the last minute. Thus, total defense spending is not fixed once and for all. And every time there is a substantial alteration in domestic spending, marginal changes in defense expenditures may also be made.[4]

Early in the fall the Secretary of Defense, the President's National Security Advisor, the Secretary of State, the Director of the OMB, and perhaps the Secretary of the Treasury sit down in an effort to bargain out their differences. Not that they necessarily have to bargain; they can take their disagreements to the President. The record shows that Secretary McNamara won on every occasion he did so, and there is reason to believe that Secretary of State (or National Security Advisor) Kissinger was not far behind. But they had to be careful of the sensitivities of OMB, not necessarily because of its importance, but because any significant change in the defense totals may mean reallocation among domestic agencies, and the President may not wish to suffer the trauma of such change if he can avoid it. The OMB is better off making an agreement instead of being reversed later and is not averse to maintaining a cushion of 2 to 4 per cent so it will have something to give at the appropriate time. The OMB can usually keep its part of the bargain, by whittling down domestic agency requests to agreed target levels and using the "fair shares" approach described in the text,[5] provided others keep their agreements and — a big and — the world does not change too much in the meantime.

It is often said, with reason, that the final decision on the President's Budget is handed to the government printer on the midnight before it is scheduled to be delivered to Congress. What can happen? There may be miscalculation of entitlement programs (direct claims on the Treasury, which do

[4] John P. Crecine, "Defense Budgeting: Organizational Adaptations to Environmental Constraints," RAND Corporation, RM6121 P.R. (1970).
[5] See "fair shares," pp. 16–18.

not go through the appropriations process), so that they grow much more rapidly than anyone thought, or employment may increase faster than the Administration thought possible, or election prospects every two years may look gloomier than the President thinks desirable, or the international situation may deteriorate, or revenues may lag far behind or leap far ahead of predictions, and on and on. Once any major element in the picture begins to change — defense or domestic programs, unemployment, inflation, growth, revenue, or electoral or foreign policy prospects — they can all begin to go at once because they are predicated on some rough relationship to one another. How much better for all concerned if they can agree to live within some approximation of the initial totals they set in April and make minor adjustments in the fall.

Where there's a will, there's also a way to find agreement where it did not exist before. Supplemental appropriations are one such way. Essentially, they put off into the future decisions that cannot be made now. The budget is made in late fall, and then the following spring and summer additional amounts enter, especially in defense. Another method of manufacturing agreement is to blur the relationship between outlays — the amount projected to be spent in a given fiscal year — and budget authority — the legal right of agencies to spend over a number of years. Greater budget authority, which has the effect of authorizing expenditures in future years, can be traded for lesser expenditure in the next fiscal year. Total obligation authority and expenditures can vary one with the other as much as 10 per cent without causing major discomfort. Congress cares about immediate expenditures, as do most of those interested in fiscal policy; they can, in effect, agree to defer decisions or to pass them on to future years and possibly other decision makers.

President Johnson's first budget, for example, involved a fairly explicit deal with Senator Byrd of Virginia to the effect that Johnson could have his tax cut if expenditures did not exceed $100 billion. According to a former Budget Director quoted by Crecine, "It was there that Johnson learned to exploit the ambiguities between expenditures and budget authority. After that, LBJ focussed almost entirely on the expenditures game and gave up easily on agency requests for increases in NOA (New Obligational Authority)."[6] Sufficient until the budget year is the evil thereof!

The evident volatility of these fiscal and budgetary processes, the visible pulling and hauling that goes on, suggests to some an irrational political process in which popular priorities became perverted. The people, it is said, want more social programs and instead they get excessive defense spending. Crecine's investigations cast considerable doubt on this interpretation. This is a case in which volatility hides stability. In the period from 1953 (fiscal 1955), at the end of the Korean War, to the present, defense expenditure has not increased at all in real terms. Crecine has calculated that defense expenditure increased on the average about 5.4 per cent a year, which, until recently, has about taken care of inflation. Decisions about defense, therefore, should not be looked upon as being taken on a once-and-for-all basis. Rather, in response to the inroads of inflation, they are taken over and over again, so that popular preferences reflected in the executive and legislative branches do indeed have an opportunity to make themselves felt. Whether as a proportion of the total budget or as a percentage of Gross National Product, defense has, in fact, declined considerably in relation to domestic social and welfare expenditures.[7]

In summing up his position, Crecine states, "In normal times whatever the government's fiscal policy is (tax revenues

---

[6] Crecine, "Defense Budgeting," Chapter 1, Section 3, p. 27.

[7] See "Coordination without a Coordinator," Chapter 15, in Aaron Wildavsky *Speaking Truth to Power: Policy Analysis as a Problem* (Boston: Little, Brown, 1979).

plus deficit) determines within fairly close tolerances what Defense plus Non-Defense spending must add to." [8] This relationship is, as Crecine says, an identity and not a proposition; it is true by definition. One could as easily say that domestic spending equals tax revenues and a deficit minus defense. I could not agree more when Crecine says, "At any given point in time political and economic limits on defense expenditures exist. The question of whether budget limits drive strategy and force posture, or the reverse, is an empty one when it is recognized that an effective defense strategy must reflect domestic priorities and economic stabilization policy as well as strictly national security consideration." [9] Let's look at it this way: If you are in a spending agency, whether defense or large domestic, and you think that a budget can be made from your bottom-up viewpoint, you must be told that there are fiscal limits placed at the top which effectively limit your discretion. If you sit where the President does or are part of the "troika" that concerns itself with fiscal policy, however, and you think you can impose a fixed ceiling from the top down, then you must be told that the millions below and the multitudes outside have a great deal to say about how far you can go. I cannot argue with those who believe that the budget is made upside-down or downside-up, but I feel secure in saying that it is made top-wise, bottom-wise, and side-wise, as well. Budgets are planned (and this is the theme of the book to follow) by mutual adaptation.

[8] Crecine, "Defense Budgeting," Chapter 1, Section 5, p. 1.
[9] *Ibid.*, Chapter 2, p. 3.

PREFACE TO
THE SECOND EDITION

THIS IS NOT A REVISED, but an expanded edition. I have added this preface and two new chapters — one on program budgeting and one on restoring Congressional control of the budget — and have updated the appendix on formal steps in the budgetary process. Otherwise, not a word of the original edition has been altered. Why not? Anyone can see that if the budgetary process has not changed there is little point in tinkering with a book that is still essentially accurate. And in fact, if one doesn't pay too much attention to passing fancies, like program budgeting or super-cabinet-secretaries or a flurry of Presidential impounding in 1973, one finds very little break in continuity with the recent past. The relation between the OMB and the Department of Defense, for instance, which has undergone several structural changes in the last twenty years, is now about back to where it was in the late 1950's.

Selective inattention would become inappropriate, of course, if a real break with the past should occur. Congress is now seriously considering making fundamental changes in the way it goes about making the federal budget. As my father would say, there are basically only two things that can happen: either it will work or it won't. If it fails, then there is no need to consider it further. If the reform succeeds, then it will take at least a couple of years to see what difference it will make. There is no point in revising *The*

Politics of the Budgetary Process right now, therefore, because I don't know whether a minor facelifting or major plastic surgery will be required.

One subject that unquestionably deserves attention in this new edition is program budgeting, and I have added an entire chapter on this phenomenon. Increasingly PPBS has come to represent pretension in social science and public policy alike. Now PPBS is succeeded (if I may use that word to refer to a technique that has failed everywhere it has been tried) by a motley band of similar-sounding initials — PERT (Program Evaluation and Review Technique), MIS (Management Information Systems), TA (Technology Assessment), SI (Social Indicators), MBO (Management by Objectives) — all singing the same song about improving policy through analysis of better information. Upon investigation, it turns out that the bureaucratic client doesn't know what he wants, the social science expert doesn't know what he is doing, and the (by now) poorer citizenry has been had again. In social research (indeed, more in social action) it is as important to know what can't be done as what can. For the acceptance and use of constraints (on knowledge, time, manpower, data, support) distinguishes the responsible adult from the willful child, ("Why can't I have . . . ?"). Without constraints, in fact, it is impossible to do creative work. Still, program budgeting, though it has finally been abandoned by the federal government, deserves study as the major budgetary phenomenon of our time.

The second major addition to this second edition deals with restoring Congressional control of the appropriations process. My analysis of what led to the current difficulties — declines in the norms of guardianship and reciprocity — and my suggestion for remedying them — the Annual Expenditure Increment — are found in the last chapter.

The perspicacious reader will have noticed that I exhort no one to study budgeting or acknowledge its importance.

The time for that was a decade ago when the first edition came out. Now a great deal more study has been done,[1] and the importance of the subject, both in its own right, narrowly confined to financial administration, and more broadly construed, as a (never, *the*) key to political life, is widely recognized.

In the light of the availability of these outstanding works, the reader has a right to know why he is not offered comparisons among different budgetary processes. The simple answer is that I do this in a book called *Budgeting* (Boston, 1975). In that volume I compare rich and poor countries; the United States, Britain, France, and Japan; and city, state, and federal budgeting in America. Some idea of the value of wide-ranging comparison, not only for descriptive but also for prescriptive purposes, may be had, however, by consulting the section in the final chapter that shows how the institutionalization of incremental budgeting in France, Britain, and Japan suggests comparable changes in the American context.

[1] Among the recent works on the subject are: Thomas J. Anton, *The Politics of State Expenditure in Illinois* (Urbana, 1966); Naomi Caiden and Aaron Wildavsky, *Planning and Budgeting in Poor Countries* (New York, 1974); John Creighton Campbell, *Contemporary Japanese Budget Politics* (Ph.D. Dissertation, Columbia University, 1973); John P. Crecine, *Governmental Problem-Solving: A Computer Simulation of Municipal Budgeting* (Chicago, 1969); Richard F. Fenno, Jr., *The Power of the Purse: Appropriations Politics in Congress* (Boston, 1966); Hugh Heclo and Aaron Wildavsky, *The Private Government of Public Money: Community and Policy inside British Political Administration* (London and Berkeley, 1974); Stephen Horn, *Unused Power: The Work of the Senate Committee on Appropriations* (Washington, D.C., 1970); Guy Lord, *The French Budgetary Process* (Berkeley, 1973); Arnold Meltsner, *The Politics of City Revenue* (Berkeley, 1971); Leonard Merewitz and Stephen H. Sosnick, *The Budget's New Clothes: A Critique of Planning-Programming-Budgeting and Benefit-Cost Analysis* (Chicago, 1971); Jeanne Nienaber and Aaron Wildavsky, *The Budgeting and Evaluation of Federal Recreation Programs, or, Money Doesn't Grow on Trees* (New York, 1973); Allen Schick, *Budget Innovation in the States* (Washington, D.C., 1971); Ira Sharkansky, *The Politics of Taxing and Spending* (Indianapolis, Ind., 1969).

Is there, then, nothing I would change in this new edition? Of course, but the changes are fewer than the additions. I would certainly rescue Senator Mundt from an undeserved demise and avoid confusing Frankenstein with his monster. I would also be less cautious about defense budgeting. In the first edition I warned that I had not studied military budgets thoroughly and that nothing I said would necessarily apply to them. Apparently, this precaution was unnecessary. Numerous participants in budgeting for defense have assured me that this book, with reasonable allowances, may also be taken to apply to defense budgeting. According to Admiral John K. Leydon, who was Chief of Naval Research in 1966, my "disclaimer has no validity. Every aspect of budgeting of which he writes has its counterpart in the military budgetary spectrum from formulation to execution." [2] Further reinforcement comes from research by John P. Crecine and Gregory Fischer on budgeting in defense, which shows that nothing much changed even after the introduction of PPBS.[3] Now I would also be more severe in my judgments about PPBS. The few pages on program budgeting that appeared in the first edition, written when the system had barely begun in the Defense Department, are not so much wrong as insufficient. The new chapter on the subject added to this edition should serve to put it in its proper perspective.

Only in one critical area — the relation between budgetary incrementalism and organizational learning — would I make a decided change in emphasis. I would no longer assume, in

[2] Rear Admiral John K. Leydon, "Review of *The Politics of the Budgetary Process*," *U.S. Naval Institute Proceedings* (February 1966) p. 115.

[3] John P. Crecine, "Defense Budgeting: Constraints and Organizational Adaptation," Discussion Paper, University of Michigan, Institute of Public Policy Studies (July 1969); and John P. Crecine and Gregory Fischer, "On Resource Allocation Processes in the U.S. Department of Defense," Discussion Paper, University of Michigan, Institute of Public Policy Studies (October 1971).

the absence of direct evidence, that organizations, as distinct from individuals, actually make use of the method of successive limited approximation to move away from the worse and toward the better. Not that I doubt the essentially incremental nature of budgeting; nothing is to be gained by ignoring overwhelming evidence or the observation of everyday life. The last decade's experience with social policy, however, is enough to make anyone doubt whether agencies do, in fact, use the undoubtedly incremental moves they make to observe what happens, evaluate the consequences, and adjust their activities accordingly. Perhaps, after all, there is no getting away from theory of cause and effect that relates actions to consequences. Without such theory (what economists call a production function connecting inputs to outputs), there may be no practical way either to separate the consequences of one small act from those of countless others or, amidst the confusing welter of events, to trace them back to their origins as intentional actions.

The "who" as well as the "what" of organizational learning may also be in question. Not all organizations necessarily learn the same thing, or communicate it in the same way, or receive a similar message. Nor, given their different institutional positions and motivations,[4] need they be inclined or able to act in the same way to make use of the latest findings — if, indeed, we may so term what must often seem random sounds and ambiguous happenings. What is encapsulated in the organizational memory in the form of standard operating procedures, as distinguished from actual events, then, may be a product not only of compromise within the agency and among available instruments for securing the desired results but also of an inability to grasp collectively either what has occurred or what might be done about it. Hopefully we will become wiser as well as sadder.

[4] See Aaron Wildavsky, "The Self-Evaluating Organization," XXXII *Public Administration Review* (September/October 1972) pp. 509–520.

The steps by which complex problems are broken into simpler ones, so that smaller aspects can be handled in sequence rather than all at once, need to be more explicitly identified. Learning has to be demonstrated, not assumed.

There are certain limitations to the present volume, often stemming from a lack of appropriate research data, that should be pointed out to the reader. The "inarticulate major premise" of this book, as of all studies in this field, is that there is close connection between Congressional appropriations and actual expenditures. If (or, more likely, where) there is not, we are obviously watching the wrong ball. True, the reader is warned that the formal budget should be considered a hypothesis which can be invalidated, but he is not given much idea of how to separate the real from the imaginary. Nor can I offer much help now, for the simple reason that no one has done any work on the subject in America.[5] For what it is worth, my general impression is that most appropriations, most of the time, are generally reliable indicators of the object upon which most of the money in them will be spent. Federal budgets do have predictive value. The question is how much in regard to what programs under which conditions.

A clue to one type of discrepancy between appropriation and expenditure is the phenomenon of "underspending." While agencies normally attempt to spend their yearly al-

[5] An unanticipated, though welcome, consequence of the furor over Presidential impounding of Congressional appropriations, however, has been increased interest in the final act of expenditure in relation to the preliminary act of authorization. Louis Fisher's pioneering studies of impoundment have fortunately been expanded to include transfer of funds from one program to another, as well as the timing of fund releases by the Office of Management and Budget. See the following articles by Fisher: "Impoundment of Funds: Uses and Abuses," XXIII *University of Buffalo Law Review* (Fall 1973) pp. 141–200; "Presidential Spending Discretion and Congressional Controls," XXXVII *Law and Contemporary Problems* (Winter 1972) pp. 135–172; "Reprogramming of Funds by the Defense Department," XXXVI *Journal of Politics* (February 1974) pp. 77–102.

lotment, thus leading to the well-known practice of buying everything and anything toward the end of the fiscal year, they often do not succeed; they cannot figure everything out exactly. Underspending of 1 to 3 per cent would be standard. When Naomi Caiden and I studied budgeting in poor countries, we discovered that being poor meant not only lack of money but also inability to spend what one had. Underspending went as high as 75 per cent. The syndrome of poverty — lack of trained personnel, lack of knowledge, and lack of unity, as well as lack of money — meant that the poor did not have the capacity to absorb expenditures. Testing these hypotheses on the most comparable American experience, Robert Paulson found that underspending among local participants in Model Cities programs varied from 5 per cent to 80 per cent, and that the average city spent just under 50 per cent of the funds made available to it by the program.[6] No matter how much Congress voted or the President directed be spent on Model Cities, spending could not easily go above limits imposed by local capacities, such as ability to agree on what should be done, who should do it, and how it was to be accomplished. Self-evident? There's nothing wrong with rediscovering the obvious, especially when the cautions suggested by recent experience have been (and are being) almost universally ignored. Implementation is rarely easy,[7] and the problems of going from policy design to program execution are just as relevant for the budgetary process as they are for the rest of administration.

Had we not neglected the growing practice of annual authorizations, indicating a deterioration in relationships between legislative and appropriations committees, we should

[6] Robert I. Paulson, "Poverty, Uncertainty, and Goal Dissensus: The Causes of Underspending in the Model Cities Program," (Paper submitted to my seminar, "Budgets as Political Instruments," Political Science Department, University of California, Berkeley, Spring 1973).

[7] Jeffrey Pressman and Aaron Wildavsky, *Implementation* (Berkeley and Los Angeles, 1973).

not have been so surprised at the existence of a Congressional crisis of confidence in its own processes of budgeting. A Congressional malady must have a Congressional cure. If my own recommendations in the last chapter lack a certain persuasiveness, and I think they do, this is largely because I was unable to increase my understanding of inter-committee relationships. With some $60 billion in tax subsidies — money allowed to remain in private hands because of special tax provisions — funneled through the House Ways and Means Committee, and with still more mandated through the "back door" of the Treasury under the aegis of legislative committees, it does not take a genius to figure out that if these committees are not part of the solution, they are surely most of the problem.

Another major omission in this study is treatment of tax policy as a process of strategic interaction, in much the same way as budgeting is handled here. Corresponding presentation of the tax process would no doubt require more than a single treatise.[8] But, if the necessary research were done, understanding of *The Politics of the Budgetary Process* would be enhanced by knowledge of how expenditure totals were influenced by (or emerged as by-products of) efforts to manage the economy. Hugh Heclo and I have attempted to do this sort of thing for British central government, and it could also be done for the United States.[9]

A major study of what is now the Office of Management and Budget would also be useful. Its early struggles through

---

[8] The first study of taxation as a political process in recent times is Arnold Meltsner's *The Politics of City Revenue* (Berkeley and Los Angeles, 1971). Tom Reese, a graduate student in the Department of Political Science at Berkeley, is now beginning a dissertation on the federal tax process, and Alex Radian is doing the same in regard to several poor countries.

[9] The best book on the general subject of fiscal policy, from this point of view, is Lawrence Pierce's *The Politics of Fiscal Policy Formation* (Englewood Cliffs, N.J., 1971), but it does not quite reach the relationship between taxing and spending.

the 1950's have been chronicled with characteristic incisiveness by Richard Neustadt,[10] but its last decade has been relatively neglected.[11] Studies from other analytic perspectives — behavioral, sociological, and micro- and macro-economic — would add a great deal to Neustadt's original political analysis. What are the habits of these men and how is their behavior to be explained? Who are they? Where do they come from and where are they going? What functions do they serve for others? Are they worth their cost? Has spending become an appendage of efforts to manage the economy by varying expenditure totals?

The last query should have come first. Understanding the OMB depends on the role it plays within the Executive, and that is clearly in flux. Although President Nixon's effort to divide governmental activities into three parts — foreign and defense, economic management, and domestic welfare — have been shot down by the flak aimed at Watergate, the needs that impelled him to simplify his life by appointing super-secretaries may well reassert themselves. If the thrust of policy is such that future Presidents will also want to tri-chotimize their lives in this way, the implications for the OMB, and hence for the budgetary process, would be considerable. Bargaining for relative shares would proceed with Mr. Economy trying to make expenditure limits stick and Messrs. Foreign and Domestic alternatively trying to in-

[10] See Richard Neustadt, "Presidency and Legislation: The Growth of Central Clearance," XLVIII *The American Political Science Review* (September 1954) pp. 641–671; and "Presidency and Legislation: Planning the President's Program," XLIX *The American Political Science Review* (December 1955) pp. 980–1021.

[11] The best works are Robert Gilmour's perceptive review of developments in the central clearance of legislation, "Central Legislative Clearance: A Revised Perspective," XXXI *Public Administration Review* (March/April 1971) pp. 150–158; and Allen Schick's fine study of the OMB's decline as a Presidential agency, "The Budget Bureau that Was: Thoughts on the Rise, Decline and Future of a Presidential Agency," XXXV *Law and Contemporary Problems* (Summer 1970) pp. 519–539.

crease the total or their share within it. Effective jurisdictions of super-secretaries would be so large that detailed scrutiny of expenditures along the lines of the old Bureau of the Budget would be out of the question. Something would have to give. The OMB would no longer be able to perform as it has in the past. Following a current tendency, the OMB might become a technical management agency devoted to small efficiencies and divorced from top leadership (except during the inevitable ritualistic economy drives). Or the OMB might split up into staff units for each super-secretary, a tendency that briefly manifested itself and then drowned during its baptism. Who could have guessed that President Nixon (via the Watergate affair) would play Ten Little Indians with the White House Staff, thus leaving the OMB as the major channel of advice on domestic policy? The Office of Management and Budget regained power because it survived. Après moi the OMB! This move may just signify a renewed commitment to the kind of messy Presidential politics we have in the United States, where the press tells the President off, Congressmen insist that their provinciality is just as legitimate as his nationality, bureaucrats have (as the Constitution presupposes) divided loyalty, Cabinet members quarrel in public because they are so situated as to need, differ with, and frustrate one another — and all these conflicts are what he is paid to preside over, work through, and get around. Then, perhaps, a President would want the services of a budget office as a listening post, control station, and pressure point. Then the new OMB would look more like the old BOB,[12] except that it would be dealing with vastly greater sums.

The huge increase in the size of the budget — from around $112 billion in 1963, when the first edition was completed,

[12] There is not much to choose from between the instructions issued by any Director of the BOB and the latest (1973) version from their successor in the OMB:

to \$256 billion in 1973,[13] to an estimated \$290 billion in 1974 — should end the vacuous debate over the importance of making decisions in small increments as opposed to large proportions of the total. For one of the secrets of incrementalism is that the base is as important as the rate of increase. A mere one-tenth of 1 per cent, an increment of an increment, turns out to be \$300 million if the base is \$300 billion, which is where the United States Federal Budget will shortly be. An OMB examiner who handles as little as a billion dollars will be looked down at by his richer relations. So OMB will have to get out of the retail business and learn how to make budgets wholesale. Budgets will have to be considered in terms of blocks. Formulas will have to be found for disposing of large sums without always going through the experience of seeing how they come out, because experience will have become expensive. The term for what one does to cope with complex interactions involving large aggregates when one lacks experience (and can't afford to acquire it) is policy analysis. The old suspicion of analysis will persist, as it should, but the technique will be relied upon increasingly because there will be no other way. When the three famous wise men can no longer feel any but the

---

The continuing sharp growth in relatively uncontrollable programs is a special problem in the year ahead. A larger and larger proportion of total outlays is for programs that are not susceptible to much discretionary control in the short run. This condition puts heavy pressure on the relatively controllable programs in 1974 and requires that ways be found to restrain the growth of uncontrollable programs in the future.

To hold to the dollar levels that the President has set, we must continue to search for offsetting reductions to any proposals involving new or additional programs. . . .

The enclosed ceiling figures for budget authority and outlays for your agency should not be exceeded. Each agency must adhere strictly to the totals provided, both in the initial submission and throughout the budget process. . . .

[13] Charles L. Schultze, Edward L. Fried, Alice M. Rivlin, and Nancy H. Teeters, *Setting National Priorities: The 1973 Budget* (Washington, D.C., 1972) p. 11.

smallest and least interesting parts of the elephant, they will have to use their imaginations in a disciplined way. The analytic imagination may be better or worse, but it will be used.

Another secret of incrementalism is that one can get a long way by rapid movements, if they continue long enough. With spending at all levels of government rising above one-third of the Gross National Product,[14] interest in limiting or making better use of expenditures is bound to increase. Adaptability and flexibility will be key words as efforts are made to switch resources from less to more productive uses. Evaluation of programs, therefore, not only before they are begun but during their operation as well, will become standard procedure. Thus the General Accounting Office, in response to social needs, is moving from auditing after the fact to evaluation while the first sums are being spent. And evaluation, as everyone knows, is just analysis spelled sideways, or at least brought forward.[15]

Early drafts of *The Politics of the Budgetary Process* received an unusually negative response. Readers found it too critical of government (if they were in it) or too tolerant of bad practices (if they suffered from them). There were stern admonitions to abjure frivolity from those who felt that treating budgeting like a game made little of their earnest efforts. The large number of anecdotes (a derogatory term among some classes of social scientists) should be aban-

[14] See Charles L. Schultze, Edward L. Fried, Alice M. Rivlin, and Nancy H. Teeters, *Setting National Priorities: The 1974 Budget* (Washington, D.C., 1973) p. 8. This invaluable series should be part of every serious person's effort to gain understanding of the policy choices inherent in the budget.

[15] The final secret of incrementalism, revealed here for the first time, is that it is really a subject of the occult. Try this: Say "marginal" (with conviction!) three times (as in marginal cost, marginal revenue, or just at the margins) as economists do, and no one will ask how come or say what for but only nod approval, though a "margin" for present purposes is in no way different from an "increment."

doned, they said, in favor of more rigor. Apparently they meant I should use more numbers, though when I later turned to mathematical formulations [16] I was told with equal conviction that these arid formulations would not help determine what would happen the following week in any number of vital bureaus. At first the reaction in the old BOB was that none of it was true. After about two years the word was that some of it might be true. By the time four years had elapsed, the line was that most of it was true, but wasn't it a shame. Now everyone has relaxed and can use the book to show how the process works and might be improved, and that is where the trouble begins.

For the book has now received almost too good a rating. It first appeared as a counter to existing ways of thinking about budgeting. Now it is standard fare, the conventional wisdom. I am not sure exactly what principle of mine that contravenes, but there must be one. To render this state of affairs less likely, I have assumed the function of critic so that no one will miss the major sins of omission and commission. And I have gone further to suggest research that, if undertaken, would rapidly outdate what is said here.

In a decade the book has begun to assume a life of its own, as if it were a house of historic interest in which nothing could be moved without committing an impropriety. Who am I to argue with public opinion? But I will anyway. As usual, there are two choices: "leave well enough alone," or "there is only one way to go, and that is down." I have made my choice in presenting this second edition, and I hope the reader won't regret his.

[16] See Otto A. Davis, M. A. H. Dempster, and Aaron Wildavsky, "A Theory of the Budgetary Process," LX *The American Political Science Review* (September 1966) pp. 529–547. See also our "On the Process of Budgeting II: An Empirical Study of Congressional Appropriations," in Byrne, Charnes, Cooper, Davis, and Gilford, editors, *Studies in Budgeting* (Amsterdam and London, 1971) pp. 292–375; and our latest piece, "Toward a Predictive Theory of the Federal Budgetary Process," *The British Journal of Political Science* (forthcoming, 1974).

To the many public officials who have written and called to express their views, I owe a continuing vote of thanks. They buoyed me up when others claimed the book was unreal, and they kept me down to earth by reminding me of what I had missed. I hope they will continue to set me straight. Paul Wilson, formerly of the House Appropriations Committee Staff, deserves special thanks for pointing out to me earlier than anyone else the significance of the moves toward annual authorization and "back door" spending.

The chapter on program budgeting relies heavily on two articles — "The Political Economy of Efficiency" and "Rescuing Policy Analysis from PPBS" — previously published in *Public Administration Review*. Alex Radian and Brian Tannenbaum assisted me in reviewing the federal experience with program budgeting. The last chapter — first published under the title "The Annual Expenditure Increment" — was prepared for the House Committee on Committees and the Senate Government Operations Committee and was originally published in *The Public Interest*. I have benefited from numerous discussions of budgetary reform with my colleague William Niskanen, [17] who was formerly Assistant Director for Evaluation, Office of Management and Budget.

[17] See William A. Niskanen, *Structural Reform of the Federal Budget Process* (Washington, D.C., 1973).

CONTENTS

1 BUDGETS   1

2 CALCULATIONS   6

Complexity 8
Aids to Calculation 11
Fair Share and Base 16
The Agency: Roles and Perspectives 18
Deciding How Much to Ask For 21
Deciding How Much to Spend 31
Department Versus Bureau 32
The Bureau of the Budget: Roles and Perspectives 35
Deciding How Much to Recommend 42
*The Appropriations Committees: Roles and
    Perspectives* 47
*Deciding How Much to Give: The Appropriations
    Committees* 56
Summary 62

3 STRATEGIES   63

Ubiquitous and Contingent Strategies 64
Clientele 65

Confidence 74
Congressional Committee Hearings 84
Results 90
*Strategies Designed to Capitalize on the
      Fragmentation of Power in National Politics* 98
Contingency and Calculation 101
*Defending the Base: Guarding Against Cuts in the
      Old Programs* 102
*Increasing the Base: Inching Ahead with Existing
      Programs* 108
Expanding the Base: Adding New Programs 111
Outcomes 123

4 REFORMS   127

A Normative Theory of Budgeting? 128
The Politics in Budget Reform 131
A Typical Reform 133
Program Budgeting Versus Traditional Budgeting 135
The Program Budget in the Department of Defense 138
Efficiency 142
Knowledge and Reform 143

5 APPRAISALS   145

Comprehensiveness 146
Coordination 152
Neglect 156
Roles 160
PVPI Versus TVPI 165
Strategies 167
The Best Case 168

Support   171
Deceit?   174
Merit   176
Conclusion   178

6 PPB AND ZBB   181

Management by Objectives   184
PPB   186
Centralization   188
Politics   191
Practice   193
Policy   196
Why PPB is Irrational   198
Zero Base Budgeting   202
Practice   207
Information   214
Motivation   215
Organization   216
Theory   218
Learning   219

7 CONGRESS   222

Reasons for Reform   222
Congressional Realities   224
The New Rules of the Game   226
The New Timetable   229
The Process Outlined   230
The Control of Impoundment   233
Whose Budgetary Base?   233
Whose Budget?   238

Whose Information? 242
Whose CBO? 246
What Accomplishments? 249
Whose Total? 254
How Many Years? 262
External Forces 267

Appendix   271
A Guide to Budget Terms
   and Concepts   281
Bibliography   287
Index   301

THE POLITICS OF THE
BUDGETARY PROCESS

"Oh, it's great here, all right, but I sort of feel uncomfortable in a place with no budget at _all_."

Drawing by D. Reilly; © 1976 The New Yorker Magazine, Inc.

BUDGETS

1

IN THE MOST LITERAL SENSE a budget is a document, containing words and figures, which proposes expenditures for certain items and purposes. The words describe items of expenditure (salaries, equipment, travel) or purposes (preventing war, improving mental health, providing low-income housing), and the figures are attached to each item or purpose. Presumably, those who make a budget intend that there will be a direct connection between what is written in it and future events. Hence we might conceive of a budget as intended behavior, as a prediction. If the requests for funds are granted, and if they are spent in accordance with instructions, and if the actions involved lead to the desired consequences, then the purposes stated in the document will be achieved. The budget thus becomes a link between financial resources and human behavior to accomplish policy objectives. Only through observation, however, is it possible to determine the degree to which the predictions postulated in the budget document turn out to be correct.

In the most general definition, budgeting is concerned with the translation of financial resources into human purposes. A budget, therefore, may be characterized as a series of goals with price tags attached. Since funds are limited and have to be divided in one way or another, the budget becomes a mechanism for making choices among alternative expenditures. When the choices are coordinated so as to achieve desired goals, a budget may be called a plan. Should it include a detailed specification of how its objectives are to be achieved, a budget may serve as a plan of work for those who assume the task of implementing it. If emphasis is placed on achieving the most policy returns for a given sum of money, or on obtaining the desired objectives at the lowest cost, a budget may become an instrument for ensuring efficiency. Yet there may be a wide gap between the intentions of those who make up a budget and their real accomplishments. Although the language of a budget calls for the achievement of certain goals through planned expenditures, investigation may reveal that no funds have been spent for these purposes, that the money has been used for other purposes, that quite different goals have been achieved, or that the same goals have been gained in different ways.

Viewed in another light, a budget may be regarded as a contract. Congress and the President promise to supply funds under specified conditions, and the agencies agree to spend them in ways that have been agreed upon. (When an agency apportions funds to its subunits, it may be said to be making an internal contract.) Whether or not the contract is enforceable, or whether or not the parties actually agree about what the contract purportedly stipulates, is a matter for inquiry. To the extent that a budget is carried out, however, it imposes a set of mutual obligations and controls upon the contracting parties. The word "mutual" should be stressed because it is so easy to assume that control is exercised in a unilateral direction by superiors (Congressmen, department heads, and so on) over those formally subordinate to them. But when an appropriations committee approves some expenditures and not others, when it sets down conditions for the expenditure of funds, the committee is also obligating itself to keep its part of the bargain. A department head (to choose another example) who hopes to control the actions of his subordinates must ordinarily follow through on a promise to support some of their requests or else find them trying to undermine him. A budget thus becomes a web of social as well as of legal relationships in which commitments are made by all the parties, and where sanctions may be invoked (though not necessarily equally) by all.

The proposed budgets that administrative agencies (departments, bureaus, commissions) submit to the Bureau of the Budget may represent their expectations. These are the amounts they expect to see enacted into law and actually spent. It is also possible that agency requests may represent their aspirations. These are the figures they hope to receive and spend for various programs if circumstances are especially favorable, so that they can generate the necessary political support. Since the amounts requested often have an effect on the amounts received, however, budget proposals are often strategies. The total sum of money and its allocation among various activities is designed to have a favorable effect in support of the agencies' budgetary goals. As each participant acts on the budget he receives information on the preferences of others and communicates his own desires through the choices he makes. Here the budget emerges as a network of communications in which information is continuously being generated and fed back to the participants. Once enacted, a budget becomes a precedent; the fact that something has been done once vastly increases the chances that it will be done again. Since only substantial departures from the previous year's budget are normally given intensive scrutiny, an item that remains unchanged will probably be carried along the following year as a matter of course. One cannot, therefore, state unequivocally that an agency budget is an expectation, an aspiration, a strategy, a communications network, or a precedent.

It should now be apparent that the purposes of budgets are as varied as the purposes of men. One budget may be designed to coordinate diverse activities so that they complement one another in the achievement of common goals. Another budget may be put together primarily to discipline subordinate officials within a governmental agency by reducing amounts for their salaries and their pet projects. And a third budget may be directed essentially to mobilizing the support of the clientele groups who benefit by the services that the agency provides. Nothing is gained, therefore, by insisting that a budget is only one of these things when it may be all of them or many other kinds of things as well.[1] One may, however, adopt a particular view of the budget as most useful for the purposes he has in mind. Without claiming to have found the only right perspective, or to have exhausted the subject in any way, I would like to propose a conception that seems useful in talking about the budgetary process as a phenomenon of human behavior in a governmental setting.

Throughout this volume we shall be concerned with budgets as political things. Taken as a whole the federal budget is a representation in monetary terms of governmental activity. If politics is regarded in part as conflict over whose preferences shall prevail in the determination of national policy, then the budget records the outcomes of this struggle. If one asks, "Who gets what the government has to give?" then the answers for a moment in time are recorded in the budget. If one looks at politics as a process by which the government mobilizes resources to meet pressing problems, then the budget is a focus of these efforts.

The size and shape of the budget is a matter of serious

[1] A good discussion of the nature and variety of budgets may be found throughout Jesse Burkhead's *Government Budgeting* (New York, 1956). See also the illuminating comments in Frederick C. Mosher, *Program Budgeting: Theory and Practice, with Particular Reference to the U.S. Department of the Army* (Chicago, 1954) pp. 1-18.

contention in our political life. Presidents, political parties, administrators, Congressmen, interest groups, and interested citizens vie with one another to have their preferences recorded in the budget. The victories and defeats, the compromises and the bargains, the realms of agreement and the spheres of conflict in regard to the role of national government in our society all appear in the budget. In the most integral sense the budget lies at the heart of the political process.

CALCULATIONS

2

PARTICIPANTS IN BUDGETING operate in an environment that imposes severe constraints on what they can do. Neither the opportunities they seize upon nor the disabilities they suffer are wholly, perhaps largely, within their control. Though their perceptions of reality differ somewhat, they are all cognizant of certain elementary facts of life to which they must adjust. Everyone is aware of the structural conditions of political life such as the separation of powers, the division of labor within the appropriations committees, and the customary separation between appropriations and substantive legislative committees. All participants face the usual overt political factors involving group pressures, relationships between Congressmen and their constituents, political party conflicts, executive-legislative cooperation and rivalry, inter-agency disputes, and the like. Sooner or later the participants go through a process of socialization in the kinds of roles they are expected to play. They come to know the rules of the budgetary game, which specify the kinds of moves that it is and is not permissible for them to make. It would be difficult for them to remain unaware of the contemporary climate of opinion, of the pressing and recognized needs of the times, as when a rise in defense expenditures becomes obvious to all after an enemy provocation, or growing unemployment requires measures to put people to work. Secular trends in the growth of national welfare programs and increasing federal responsibility for a host of services are unlikely to be reversed. The participants take these environmental conditions as "given" to a considerable extent and so must we if we expect to understand why they act as they do.[1]

In this and the following chapter, budgeting is approached from the standpoint of the participants as they perceive their environment and make the calculations upon which their decisions depend. By "calculation" I mean the series of related factors (manifestly including perceptions of influence relationships) which the participants take into account in determining the choice of competing alternatives. Calculation involves a study of how problems arise, how they are identified as such, how they are broken down into manageable dimensions, how they are related to one another, how determinations are made of what is relevant, and how the actions of others are given consideration. Special attention is paid to the much neglected problem of complexity. For if there is one thing that participants in budgeting share, it is a concern with the extraordinary complexity of the programs and processes with which they deal.

We begin with a statement of the problem of complexity and its "solution" through the use (some would say abuse) of various aids to calculation. Then we deal with problems of calculation as they bear upon three major institutional decisions: deciding how much to ask for (the agencies); deciding

---

[1] For other approaches see Anthony Downs, "Why the Government Budget Is Too Small in a Democracy," XII *World Politics* (July 1960) pp. 541-563; Fred Riggs, "Prismatic Society and Financial Administration," V *Administrative Science Quarterly* (June 1960) pp. 1-46; Louis R. Pondy, "A Mathematical Model of Budgeting," (Mimeo.) Carnegie Institute of Technology, January 24, 1962.

how much to recommend (the Budget Bureau); and deciding
how much to give (the appropriations committee). Discussion of these decisions is prefaced by a description of the roles
and perspectives available to the major institutional participants. In this way we are able to reach the goals of the participants. We see how their calculations (and later their strategies) are affected by the roles they adopt and their perceptions
of the roles and capacities of others.

COMPLEXITY

The mind of man is an elusive substance. It cannot be directly
observed for most purposes and inferences about it are notoriously tricky. No wonder our attention is more readily caught
by the clash of wills in the exercise of influence and the confrontation of rival strategies in the pursuit of funds. Yet the
ways in which the human mind goes about making calculations in the process of arriving at decisions have a fascination
for anyone concerned with how men attempt to solve problems. More important, perhaps, for our purposes, one cannot
hope to understand why men behave as they do unless one
has some idea about how they make their calculations. And,
most important, methods of calculation are not neutral; the
ways in which calculations are made affect the outcomes of
the political system: the distribution of shares in policy among
the participants, the "who gets what and how much" of politics. Different methods of calculation often result in different
decisions. Otherwise, it would make no difference what kinds
of calculations were made and there would be much less reason to pursue the topic.

Budgeting is complex, largely because of the complexity of
modern life. Suppose that you were a Congressman or a
Budget Bureau official interested in the leukemia research
program and you wondered how the money was being spent.
By looking at the National Cancer Institute's budgetary pre-

sentation you would discover that $42,012 is being spent on a project studying "factors and mechanisms concerned in hemopoiesis," and that $5,095 is being spent for "a study of the relationship of neutralizing antibodies for the Rous sarcoma virus to resistance and susceptibility for visceral lymphomatosis." Could you tell whether too much money is being spent on hemopoiesis in comparison to lymphomatosis or whether either project is relevant for any useful purpose? You might sympathize with Congressman Laird's plaintive cry, "A lot of things go on in this subcommittee that I cannot understand." It is not surprising, therefore, that one runs across expressions of dismay at the difficulties of understanding technical subjects. Representative Jensen has a granddaughter who is mentioned in hearings more often than most people, and who is reputed by him to have read "all the stuff she can get on nuclear science. She never reads a story book. . . . And she will ask me questions and she just stumps me. I say, 'Jennifer, for Heaven's sake. I can't answer that.' 'Well,' she says, 'You are on the Atomic Energy Commission Committee, Grandpa.' 'Yes,' he replies, 'But I am not schooled in the art.'" A cry goes up for simplification. "I just want this presentation made more simple and easy to grasp," a Representative says to an administrative official. Even those nominally "in the know" may be nonplussed. "That is a budget device," said an agency budget officer, "which is difficult for me to understand, and I have been in this business for over 20 years."

In our personal lives we are used to discovering that things rarely turn out quite as we had expected. Somehow when it comes to political activities we seem to expect a much greater degree of foresight. Yet life is incredibly complicated and there is very little theory that would enable people to predict how programs will turn out if they are at all new. When Representative Preston says "I cannot recall any project of any size that has ever been presented to this committee—that came out in the end like the witnesses testified it would be at the outset," the problem is less one of always estimating on the low side than of not having sufficient knowledge to do better.

There are cases in which one might do better if one had endless time, and unlimited ability to calculate. But time is in terribly short supply, the human mind is drastically limited in what it can encompass, and the number of budgetary items may be huge, so that the trite phrase "A man can only do so much" takes on real meaning. "We might as well be frank," Representative Mahan stated, "that no human being regardless of his position and . . . capacity could possibly be completely familiar with all the items of appropriations contained in this defense bill. . . ." But decisions have to be made. "There is a saying around the Pentagon," McNeil informs us, "that . . . there is only one person in the United States who can force a decision, and that is the Government Printer [when the budget must go to the press]."[2]

Aside from the complexity of individual budgetary programs, there remains the imposing problem of making comparisons among different programs that have different values for different people. This involves deciding such questions as how much highways are worth as compared to recreation facilities, national defense, schools, and so on down the range of governmental functions. No common denominator among these functions has been developed. No matter how hard they try, therefore, officials in places like the Bureau of the Budget discover that they cannot find any objective method of judging priorities among programs. How, then, do budget officials go about meeting their staggering burden of calculation?

[2] Subcommittee on National Policy Machinery, Committee on Government Operations, *The Budget and the Policy Process*, U.S. Senate, 87th Congress, First Session, 1961 (hereafter cited as *Jackson Committee Hearings*) p. 1061.

AIDS TO CALCULATION

Some officials do not deal with complexity at all; they are just overwhelmed and never quite recover. Others work terribly hard at mastering their subjects. "This [House Appropriations] Committee is no place for a man who doesn't work," a member said. "They have to be hardworking. It isn't just a job; it's a way of life."[3] But sheer effort is not enough. It has become necessary to develop mechanisms, however imperfect, for helping men make decisions that are in some sense meaningful in a complicated world.

Budgeting is experiential. One way of dealing with a problem of huge magnitude is to make only the roughest guesses while letting experience accumulate. Then, when the consequences of the various actions become apparent, it is possible to make modifications to avoid the difficulties. This is the rationale implicit in former defense comptroller McNeil's statement justifying the absence of a ceiling on expenditures at the beginning of the Korean War.

> There was no long background in the United States, with 150 years of peak and valley experience, as to what carrying on a high level of defense year in and year out for a long period would cost, or what was involved. I think a very good start was made in listing everything that anyone could think they needed . . . knowing full well, however . . . that if you overbought certain engines or trucks, it could be balanced out the following year. That method was used for a year or two and then sufficient experience had been gained . . . to know that . . . defense would cost in the neighborhood of $35 to $40 billion.[4]

Budgeting is simplified. Another way of handling complexity is to use actions on simpler items as indices of more

[3] Richard F. Fenno, Jr., "The House Appropriations Committee as a Political System: The Problem of Integration," LVI *The American Political Science Review* (June 1962) p. 314.

[4] *Jackson Committee Hearings*, p. 1075.

complicated ones. Instead of dealing directly with the cost of a huge atomic installation, for example, Congressmen may seek to discover how personnel and administrative costs or real estate transactions with which they have some familiarity are handled. If these items are handled properly then they may feel better able to trust the administrators with the larger ones. The reader has probably heard of this practice under some such title as "straining at gnats." And no doubt this is just what it is in many cases; unable to handle the more complex problems the Congressmen abdicate by retreating to the simpler ones. Here I am concerned to point out that this practice may at times have greater validity than appears on the surface if it is used as a testing device, and if there is a reasonable connection between the competence shown in handling simple and complex items.

A related method calls for directing one's observations to the responsible administrative officials rather than to the subject matter, if one is aware that the subject is so difficult and the operations so huge that the people in charge have to be trusted. They are questioned on a point here and there, a difficulty in this and that, in an effort to see whether or not they are competent and reliable. A senior Congressman reported that he followed an administrator's testimony looking for "strain in voice or manner," "covert glances" and other such indications and later followed them up probing for weaknesses.[5]

Budgeting officials "satisfice." Calculations may be simplified by lowering one's sights. Although they do not use Herbert Simon's vocabulary, budget officials do not try to maximize but, instead, they "satisfice" (satisfy and suffice).[6]

[5] L. Dwaine Marvick, *Congressional Appropriation Politics* (Ph.D. Dissertation, Columbia University, 1952) p. 297.

[6] Herbert Simon, *Models of Man* (New York, 1957); see also Bruner, Goodnow, and Austin, *A Study of Thinking* (New York, 1956), for a fascinating discussion of strategies of concept attainment useful for dealing with the problem of complexity.

Which is to say that they do not try for the best of all possible worlds, whatever that might be, but, in their words, they try to "get by," to "come out all right," to "avoid trouble," to "avoid the worst," and so on. If he can get others to go along, if too many others do not complain too long and too loud, then the official may take the fact of agreement on something as the measure of success. And since the budget comes up every year, and deals largely with piecemeal adjustment, it is possible to correct glaring weaknesses as they arise.

It is against a background of the enormous burden of calculation that the ensuing description of the major aid for calculating budgets—the incremental method—should be understood.

Budgeting is incremental. The largest determining factor of the size and content of this year's budget is last year's budget. Most of the budget is a product of previous decisions. As former Budget Director Stans put it, "There is very little flexibility in the budget because of the tremendous number of commitments that are made years ahead."[7] The budget may be conceived of as an iceberg with by far the largest part below the surface, outside the control of anyone. Many items in the budget are standard and are simply reenacted every year unless there is a special reason to challenge them. Long-range commitments have been made and this year's share is scooped out of the total and included as part of the annual budget. There are mandatory programs such as price supports or veterans' pensions whose expenses must be met. The defense budget accounts for about half of the total and it is rarely decreased. There are programs which appear to be satisfactory and which no one challenges any more. Powerful political support makes the inclusion of other activities inevitable. The convergence of expectations on what must be included is indicated in Representative Flood's comments on the census of

[7] *Jackson Committee Hearings*, p. 1118.

business, which had been in trouble in previous years. "I guess this is a sacred cow, is it not . . . ?" Flood said. "This has been generated by . . . the manufacturing industry community of the nation, for its particular benefit and the general welfare. . . . There is no longer any doubt that this is built right into our system any more. . . ." Agencies are going concerns and a minimum must be spent on housekeeping (though this item is particularly vulnerable to attack because it does not appear to involve program issues). At any one time, after past policies are paid for, a rather small percentage —seldom larger than 30 per cent, often smaller than 5—is within the realm of anybody's (including Congressional and Budget Bureau) discretion as a practical matter.

In order to be more precise, it is desirable to discover the range of variation of the percentage of increase or decrease of appropriations as compared to the previous year. Table 2-1 shows the results for 37 domestic agencies over a 12 year period. Almost exactly one-third of the cases (149 out of 444) fall within the 5 per cent range. A little more than half the cases (233) are in the 10 per cent bracket. Just under three-quarters of the cases (326) occur within 30 per cent. Less than 10 per cent (31) are in the extreme range of 50 per cent or more. And many of these are accounted for by agencies with extreme, built-in cyclical fluctuations, such as those of the Census Bureau.

TABLE 2-1*

Budgeting is incremental.**

0-5%	6-10%	11-20%	21-30%	31-40%	41-50%	51-100%	101+%
149	84	93	51	21	15	24	7

* Figures recalculated from those supplied by Richard Fenno.
** Table shows the number of cases of 37 domestic bureaus over a 12 year period that fall into various percentages of increase over the past year (444 cases in all).

Budgeting is incremental, not comprehensive. The beginning of wisdom about an agency budget is that it is almost never actively reviewed as a whole every year in the sense of reconsidering the value of all existing programs as compared to all possible alternatives. Instead, it is based on last year's budget with special attention given to a narrow range of increases or decreases. Thus the men who make the budget are concerned with relatively small increments to an existing base. Their attention is focused on a small number of items over which the budgetary battle is fought. As Representative Norrel declared in testifying before the House Rules Committee, "If you will read the hearings of the subcommittees you will find that most of our time is spent in talking about the changes in the bill which we will have next year from the one we had this year, the reductions made, and the increases made. That which is not changed has very little, if anything, said about it."[8] Most appropriations committee members, like Senator Hayden in dismissing an item brought up by the Bureau of Indian Affairs, "do not think it is necessary to go into details of the estimate, as the committee has had this appropriation before it for many years." Asked to defend this procedure, a budget officer (or his counterparts in the Budget Bureau and Congress) will say that it is a waste of time to go back to the beginning as if every year was a blank slate. "No need to build the car over again." No one was born yesterday; past experience with these programs is so great that total reconsideration would be superfluous unless there is a special demand in regard to a specific activity on the part of one or more strategically placed Congressmen, a new Administration, interest groups, or the agency itself. Programs are reconsidered but not all together and generally in regard to small

[8] The Committee on Rules, U.S. House of Representatives, *To Create a Joint Committee on the Budget*, 82nd Congress, 2nd Session, 1952, p. 61.

changes. The political realities, budget officials[9] say, restrict their attention to items they can do something about—a few new programs and possible cuts in a few old ones.[10]

Senate practice is undoubtedly incremental. "It has been the policy of our [appropriations] committee," Senator Thomas reported, "to consider only items that are in controversy. When the House has included an item, and no question has been raised about it, the Senate Committee passes it over on the theory that it is satisfactory, and for that reason the hearings as a rule do not include testimony for or against items contained in the House bill."

FAIR SHARE AND BASE

Time and again participants in the budgetary process speak of having arrived at an estimate of what was the "fair share" of the total budget for an agency. "None of this happened suddenly," a man who helps make the budget informed me. "We

[9] This term includes all those in government who deal regularly with federal budgetary matters.

[10] Professor James D. Barber of Yale University has conducted a valuable small-group experiment, which suggests that the kinds of aids to calculation described here have general application. Barber arranged for 13 Connecticut Boards of Finance to meet under controlled conditions and (among other things) to solve two hypothetical problems dealing with allocating a reduction in their most recent set of budgetary recommendations. In summarizing this part of his preliminary findings, Barber states that the Boards sought to simplify their tasks by several characteristic ways of thinking. "First, the BF tends to exclude from its consideration items over which it has little or no control. . . . Second, the Board repeatedly refers to the previous level and the magnitude of expenditure. . . . But the primary base line for budget decision-making appears to be the last appropriation. . . . Using the above criteria to isolate categories for special attention . . . the predominant consideration is the effect of a cut on actual services rendered by the department. . . . Very few comments compared expenditures in one department with those in another department: the Board considers the budget 'horizontally' (last year vs. this year) rather than 'vertically' (Department A vs. Department B). Comparisons almost never reached as far as another town."

never go from $500 to $800 million or anything like that. This [the agency's] total is a product of many years of negotiations in order to work out a fair share of the budget for the agency."

At this point it is necessary to distinguish "fair share" from another concept, "the base." The base is the general expectation among the participants that programs will be carried on at close to the going level of expenditures but it does not necessarily include all activities. Having a project included in the agency's base thus means more than just getting it in the budget for a particular year. It means establishing the expectation that the expenditure will continue, that it is accepted as part of what will be done, and, therefore, that it will not normally be subjected to intensive scrutiny. (The word "base," incidentally, is part of the common parlance of officials engaged in budgeting and it would make no sense if their experience led them to expect wide fluctuations from year to year rather than additions to or subtractions from some relatively steady point.) "Fair share" means not only the base an agency has established but also the expectation that it will receive some proportion of funds, if any, which are to be increased over or decreased below the base of the various governmental agencies. "Fair share," then, reflects a convergence of expectations on roughly how much the agency is to receive in comparison to others.

The absence of a base or an agreement upon fair shares makes the calculation of what the agency or program should get much more difficult. That happens when an agency or program is new or when rapid shifts of sentiment toward it take place. A Senate Appropriations Committee report on the United States Information Agency demonstrates the problem. "Unlike the State Department," the report reads, "the USIA does not have a fixed, historic structure which sets a floor or ceiling on the amount of money which should be expended. Furthermore, its role must necessarily vary with the times.

Therefore the issue of how much should be spent is not a matter of fixed obligations but a matter of judgment. . . ."

Agency people are expected to be advocates of increased appropriations. "You may blame the War Department for a great many things," General Douglas MacArthur said in 1935, ". . . but you cannot blame us for not asking for money. That is one fault to which we plead not guilty." A classic statement of this role was made in 1939 by William A. Jump, a celebrated budget officer for the Department of Agriculture, who wrote that in budgeting

> . . . there inevitably are severe differences of judgment as to whether funds should be provided for a given purpose and, if so, in what amount. . . . This simply means that two sets of individuals, starting from opposite angles, even though their final objective may be the same, will find themselves miles—or I should say, "millions"—apart.
>
> It is at this stage that the departmental budget officer becomes an advocate or special pleader of the cause he represents. His position in representing the department then is analogous to that of an attorney for his client. In such circumstances, departmental budget officers put up the strongest and most effective fight of which they are capable, to obtain . . . funds. . . . On these occasions no apologies are offered for a vigorous position, or even an occasional showing of teeth, if circumstances seem to require it. The [national political] system is one of checks and balances, and the Federal machinery for combatting and deflating departmental concepts of what is necessary is so extensive and at times so difficult of persuasion that unless departmental representatives proceed to present their viewpoint in a vigorous and tenacious manner, objectives which are essential . . . to the public welfare might, for the time being at least, be submerged by some purely budgetary objective, or by the budgetary power, rather than served thereby. At this point the departmental budget officer proceeds on the principle that

the government exists to serve the needs of a great people and not primarily for the purpose of creating a model budget system. . . .[11]

It is instructive to note that Jump justifies adoption of the advocate's role partly on the grounds that other participants have counter-roles that necessitate a strong push from the departmental side.

Appropriations committee members tend to view budget officials as people with vested interests in raising appropriations. This position is generally accepted as natural and inevitable for administrators. As Assistant Chief Thayer of the Forest Service put it, "Mr. Chairman, you would not think that it would be proper for me to be in charge of this work and not be enthusiastic about it and not think that I ought to have a lot more money, would you? I have been in it for thirty years, and I believe in it." At times this attitude may lead to cynicism and perhaps annoyance on the part of House Appropriations Committee members: "When you have sat on the Committee, you see that these bureaus are always asking for more money—always up, never down. They want to build up their organization. You reach the point—I have—where it sickens you, where you rebel against it."[12]

It is usually correct to assume that department officials are devoted to increasing their appropriations. Yet this assumption alone will not prove too powerful unless we also consider their perspectives toward other goals, toward time, and toward innovation. If a department head or budget officer is concerned only with maximizing appropriations, that is one thing. But if he also has other goals—strong policy preferences, gain-

[11] W. A. Jump, "Budgetary and Financial Administration in an Operating Department of the Federal Government." (Mimeo.) Paper delivered at the conference of the Governmental Research Association, September 8, 1939, p. 5. See also the psychological portrait in Robert Walker, "William A. Jump: The Staff Officer As a Personality," XIV *Public Administration Review* (Autumn 1954) pp. 233-246.

[12] Fenno, *op. cit.*, p. 320.

ing control of his organization, commendation from various reference groups—then a simple maximizing position will not be appropriate. He may decide to try to cut out a program or slap down a bureau chief even though these actions result in a loss of appropriations income. "Sometimes getting more funds increases your troubles," an official declared, in a reference to strengthening certain organizational tendencies to which he was opposed. This same individual pointed out that he could never quite get himself to act in a way that would decrease his total appropriations and that he would seek to offset decreases in some areas with increases in others. Perhaps the most useful axiom would be that agency people seek to secure their other goals so long as this effort does not result in an over-all decrease in income.

Time perspectives are important because the participant who wishes to raise or lower appropriations may not act quite the same way if he wants to secure this goal immediately than if he has a long-run view. The kinds of actions that appear likely to improve one's present position (claiming great things for a program) may have just the opposite effect (disenchanting Congressmen) when the claims prove specious over a period of time. Some agency people try to maintain an "even-keel" approach that will eventually lead to a greater total through gentle increases even though the prospects of a sharp rise at first might seem tempting.

Finally, we want to examine the orientation of the participant who considers the factors affecting his present position as given and seeks to adjust his actions accordingly, versus the participant who perceives at least part of his environment as subject to change. The opportunities that these hypothetical individuals find and create may be radically different. One person acts as if he were hemmed in on all sides and another, referring to much the same conditions, tries to alter the conditions.

Hence two administrators looking at the same circumstances may decide upon different strategies because of differences in perspectives. An agency felt it had a good case for a supplemental appropriation to meet an emergency situation. The agency head was told that it would be unwise to ask for too much and that a small request of $25,000 would stand a better chance than one that would really be sufficient to do the job. He later discovered that the President liked the idea but felt that the sum was too small to justify asking for a "supplemental." The following year the top official (an "innovator") overrode objections from a more cautious colleague (an "adjustor") and came in with a supplemental for $2 million, which was granted.

DECIDING HOW MUCH TO ASK FOR

Agencies do not usually request all the money they feel they could profitably use. Most agencies find that they cannot get funds for all the projects authorized by Congress. They also have projects not yet authorized but which they believe desirable. With appropriations always falling short of authorizations and apparent needs, how much of what they would like to get do agencies ask for from the Budget Bureau and Congress? The simplest approach would be to add up the costs of all worthwhile projects and submit the total. This simple addition is not done very often, partly because everyone knows there would not be enough resources to go around. Largely, however, the reason is strategic. If an agency continually submits requests far above what it actually gets, the Budget Bureau and the appropriations committee lose confidence in it and automatically cut large chunks before looking at the budget in detail. It becomes much more difficult to justify even the items with highest priority because no one will trust an agency that repeatedly comes in too high.

But how high is too high? The difficulties an agency encounters when it guesses wrong come through clearly in the following exchange.

> Rep. Rooney: How much did you [the Census Bureau] ask of the Department . . . ?
> Moore [of the Census Bureau]: We asked the Department of Commerce for $89,923,564.
> Rooney: How much did they cut you?
> Moore: $2,735,564.
> Rooney: How much did you ask of the Bureau of the Budget?
> Moore: $86,500,000.
> Rooney: How much did they cut you?
> Moore: $16,500,000.
> Rooney: So that there are other folks who do not depend as much as you ask us to depend on your estimates?

Yet it might be unrealistic for an administrator not to make some allowance for the cuts others will make.[13]

The word "pad" may be too crass to describe what goes on; administrators realize that in predicting needs there is a reasonable range within which a decision can fall and they just follow ordinary prudence in coming out with an estimate near the top. "If you do not do this," an official told me rather vehemently, "you get cut and you'll soon find that you are up to your ass in alligators." Another way of looking at it is to say

---

[13] Under different conditions, however, when a Congressman takes on the unusual role of advocate, the same sequence of events is given quite a different interpretation. What follows is the first exchange between the Director of the NIH and Representative John Fogarty:

Fogarty: What did you ask the Department for?
Shannon: $885,314,000.
Fogarty: What did you get from the Bureau of the Budget?
Shannon: $780,000,000.
Fogarty: Between the two, they only cut you $100 million. Did you ask for too much?
Shannon: No, sir.
Fogarty: Do you think you could use that $100 million if Congress voted it . . . ?
Shannon: I think we could use the bulk of it; yes, sir.

that in many cases "padding" consists of programs the agency wants badly but can do without, a matter of priorities.

Budgeting proceeds in an environment of reciprocal expectations that lead to self-fulfilling prophecies as the actions of each participant generate the reactions that fulfill the original expectations. Agencies are expected to pad their requests to guard against cuts. As Representative Jamie Whitten put it, ". . . If you deal with the Department [of Agriculture] long enough and learn that they scale down each time, the bureau or agency can take that into consideration and build up the original figures." The Budget Bureau is expected to cut partly because it has an interest in protecting the President's program and partly because it believes that the agency is likely to pad. The appropriations committees are expected to cut to fulfill their roles and because they believe that the agency has already made allowances for this action. Cuts may be made in the House in the expectation that the Senate will replace them. Congressmen get headlines for suggesting large cuts but they often do not follow through for they know that the amounts will have to be restored by supplemental appropriations. Things may get to the point where members of the appropriations committees talk to agency officials off the record and ask where they can make a cut that will have to be restored later. Whether it was disposed to pad or not, the agency finds that it must take into account the prospect of cuts and the cycle begins again as these prophecies confirm themselves.

William A. Jump, who spoke with the authority of great experience, believed that the internal life of agencies acted to prevent most padding. He observed to a Congressional committee:

> That there is what amounts to a natural law that is working all the time . . . that is more of a guaranty against overstaffing and similar offenses than anything that budget ex-

perts or anybody else might do, and that is that . . . our program leaders . . . have got so many things that they see that ought to be done within the range of authorized activity in their respective fields . . . and that are needed in the public interest but that they are unable to do at any given period. . . . People who have this kind of interest in their program simply do not use 25 employees where 20 would suffice. . . . To do so makes it impossible to utilize men and money for another part of the job they have been authorized to do.

Jump believed that there was greater danger of understaffing as program leaders tried to get in as many projects as possible without always considering whether adequate personnel was available.[14] Against this opinion we can place the private statement of a veteran budget officer: "It can be said without contradiction that seldom does the Bureau underestimate anything which it can reasonably see for the future."

We have seen that most of an agency's budget is a product of past decisions. Beyond this area is one of discretion in which budget people cannot get all they want but want to get all they can. Moreover, asking for too much may prejudice their chances of realizing a lesser amount. It soon becomes apparent that (to use a phrase of budget officials) ability to estimate "what will go" is a crucial aspect of budgeting.

Participants seek out and receive signals (indicators) from the Executive Branch, Congress, clientele groups, and their own organizations in order to arrive at a composite estimate of what to ask for in the light of what they can expect to get. After an Administration has been in office for a while, agency personnel have scores of actions and informal contacts to tell them how its various programs are regarded, especially for the last year. They also pay attention to public announcements

[14] House Appropriations Committee, *Hearings on Agriculture Dept. Appropriation Bill,* 79th Congress, 2nd Session, January 14, 1946, pp. 78-80.

and private reports on how tough the President is going to be in regard to new expenditures. Formal word comes in the shape of a policy letter from the Budget Bureau, which usually has some statement on how closely this year's budget should resemble the previous year's. This impression may be strengthened or weakened by reports of remarks made in Cabinet meetings or by statements from men high up in the Administration. Such a remark might be akin to one Maurice Stans, Budget Director for three years under President Eisenhower, reported that he made to the Secretary of Defense, "I hope that you can come up with a budget that will not exceed a given amount of money."[15] If the President's Science Advisor speaks favorably of a particular program, his comments may offset tough remarks by the Director of the Budget. And all these impressions are affected by the agency's experience in day-to-day dealings with the Budget Bureau staff. Their attitudes, nuances of behavior, may speak more eloquently than any public statements as to the Administration's intentions.

A major factor that agencies take into consideration is the interest of specialized publics in particular programs. Periodic reports from the field on the demand for services may serve as a general indicator. Top officials may travel and see at first hand just how enthusiastic the field personnel are about new programs. How detailed and concrete are the examples they give of public reaction? Advisory committees provide a source of information on the intentions of the interests concerned. Newspaper clipping services may also be used. The affected interests ordinarily lose no time in beating a path to the agency's door and presenting data about public support. Equally likely, the agency or its supporters in Congress generate this response. When the agency begins to notice connections between the activities of supporting interests and calls from Congressmen, it has a pretty good idea of the effectiveness of the program.

[15] *Jackson Committee Hearings*, p. 1119.

Agency officials are continuously engaged in "feeling the pulse" of Congress. What kind of action they take, however, depends on their attitudes toward Congress. Some feel comfortable in dealing with Congressmen, develop close personal relationships, and ask direct questions about future prospects. Others are fearful of Congressional contacts (though they cannot avoid them) and rely largely on the public record. The usual thing is for agency personnel to avoid blatant inquiries and to rely on other indicators. Since there is much continuity of personnel in agencies and their committees and staffs in Congress, there is a rich history on which to base predictions. The likes and dislikes of influential Congressmen are well charted. Hearings on the preceding year's budget are carefully perused for indications of attitudes on specific programs and particularly on items that may get the agency into trouble. The degree to which a Congressman goes into detail on an item and his expression at the hearings provide clues about the intensity of his feelings. First-hand information is necessary, however, because a detailed grilling may represent a Congressman's attempt to get information to take to the floor in support of the agency as well as possibly indicating hostility or concern. If the committee chairman makes a speech or lets a comment drop to the effect that not enough is being done in a certain area, the agency knows that a program in that area will meet with sympathetic consideration. Should a Congressman inform an agency, in case it did not know, that "We have heard Sam Rayburn and some of the other most distinguished members of Congress, urging us to bring up these 11 authorized watersheds more rapidly . . . ," the agency might well take the hint and ask for more. Over-all Congressional support may be indicated by debates on votes or amendments or new legislation. Finally, continuous contacts with appropriations committee staff may leave agency people with definite feelings about what is likely to go over with the committee.

Literature is now beginning to appear[16] that suggests that there is a great deal of stability with the passage of time in committee attitudes toward agencies, partly as a result of the socializing processes by which members are indoctrinated in committee norms, and partly as a result of years of contact. This finding fits in well with the point just made about agency attempts to take actions on the basis of stability in these attitudes and makes plausible the development of notions like base and fair share.

It would take a real dullard to disregard the indicators in the remarks that follow, taken from the House Appropriations hearings.

Representative O'Brien (1947, Census Bureau): I have just come back from Chicago and . . . the people of this nation are complaining about the spending of the Government's money, and they want to know when we are going to quit. . . . I do not know why you ask for these additional employees. . . . I have never been against anything you wanted. . . . It is now time to stop it. That is all I have to say.

Representative Thomas (1952, Housing and Home Finance Agency): Keep up your research. We want to admonish you to do that. We are not going to give you all of the money you think you ought to have. We are going to keep you going over a period of years because we know that you are going to come up with something that will save John Q. Public many millions of dollars.

Representative Flood (1957, Weather Bureau): Do you need dollars? . . . Can you "crash" weather observation? . . . You told Mr. Thomas that you do not have [the necessary equipment]. . . . The mood of the House is that they do not want to quibble about that [cost of equipment].

[16] See Fenno, *op. cit.*, and Charles O. Jones, "Representation in Congress: The Case of the House Agriculture Committee," LV *The American Political Science Review* (June 1961) pp. 358-367.

O'Brien's comments might be interpreted to signal a "go slow, be careful approach"; Thomas' statements might indicate "be sure to include this in moderately rising amounts"; and Flood's strongly suggests "you can get virtually anything you ask for that is remotely reasonable."

Bureaus seek information on the Department head's policy preferences. His speeches, press releases, and private comments are collected and evaluated. After an initial period of sounding him out the Bureau generally knows where it stands. One important indicator in some Departments is a letter on its budget sent out by the Secretary. Of course, a bureau may decide to disregard an unfavorable position by the Department if other signals are favorable.

The national political situation is also taken into account by agencies in deciding how much to try to get. Are there apparent political reasons for increasing or decreasing spending? Is control over the national government split between the parties with resulting competition for credit for support of particular programs or for holding the line? Do certain elements in Congress want to force Presidential vetoes or will the threat of veto result in program changes more favorable to the President? Has the concept of the balanced budget become a symbol in the political wars so that drastic efforts will be made to achieve it?

From time to time agencies are affected by emergent problems, current events which no one is in a position to predict but which radically alter budgetary prospects for particular programs. A change in missile technology, a drought, a new plant disease, advances in Soviet military capability, developments in the cold war, and similar events may drastically improve the prospects for some programs and possibly lead to restrictions on others. The agency that is able to exploit the recognized needs arising from these events is in an excellent position to expand its budgetary support and it is frequently expected to do so. When the rather sluggish Weather Bureau failed to respond immediately to the opportunities created by a series of climatic disasters in the middle 1950's, Representative Flood, who could not resist the obvious pun, was impelled to comment at an appropriations hearing: "Your Weather Bureau is looked upon by the people and has been for 100 years as a collection of old men on an island some place, and nobody ever heard of you until the last couple of years. Now you have become adults, and everybody is excited. If you do not take advantage of it you are not well advised. . . ."

The Weather Bureau did eventually respond to this prodding, but it is clear that the mental set of the listener plays an important part in the interpretation of signals. This is as good a time as any to say that although words like "signal" and "indicator" have their uses, we must not be led into an adding-machine approach to the budgetary process—looking at the process as a matter of adding up a number of signals in a neat total. The participants live in the world as real people and not as calculating machines. Just as Dexter has shown that Congressmen tend to select what they hear from their constituents,[17] so may administrators view their signals with preconceived notions or not view them at all. Nevertheless, one would expect that over the years reality would assert itself and strong and clear signals would be received with a minimum of static.

The indicators are not formally evaluated; rather, it appears that the results flow through the minds of the responsible officials and, through internal processes they are understandably hard put to describe, emerge as conclusions about what will and will not go. These conclusions may be modified or reinforced by conversations with other officials in the agency or with their counterparts in other agencies. The most that participants will claim is to have an informed judgment or an

[17] Lewis A. Dexter, "The Representative and His District," XVI *Human Organization* (Spring 1957) pp. 2-13.

educated guess. They claim to be right most of the time but are occasionally surprised at developments running contrary to their expectations.

One may ask whether the agencies simply add up the costs of the programs for which they can get support to arrive at their total or whether they arrive at the total amount by an independent estimate. The answer seems to be that both processes of calculation go on at the same time. Obviously, the total amount is dependent upon an evaluation of how much can be gotten to support individual projects. And after a certain level has been reached, estimates of whether or not funds can be secured to support individual items depend to some extent on whether or not the total is deemed too large. A bureau official pointed out that it was not difficult to conclude that the most his department could expect to get in additional funds was $100 million. At the outside, therefore, and considering the competition of many other bureaus in the same department, his bureau could get $5 million. This same official also gave a run-down on the individual increased appropriations his bureau could hope to get and the total just turned out to be between $4 and $5 million.

The kinds of conclusions that result from this process of determining expectations may be indicated by citing a few examples. One agency decided that the next year would be tough for its budget and that increases would be particularly hard to get. It decided to try to hold the line. Senator Smith noticed this approach once when she told an administrator, "you are telling us that you are asking for what you can get rather than for what you actually need." Another agency concluded that a new pet program simply would not be approved and decided to wait for a more propitious moment lest antipathy caused by inclusion of this item jeopardize the rest of its budget. Instead, the agency concentrated on a less-expensive new program for which it expected support. A third agency decided that prospects for one program were bleak but not hopeless and that it was worth fighting for as a means of mobilizing support for future attempts. A fourth agency saw events as uniquely favorable for several of its programs and decided to get as much as possible and then try to hold on to it as a base for future years. A fifth agency deliberately disregarded what it considered a favorable opportunity in order to create a record that would enable it to have a slightly rising and stable fund for administrative expenses. The most common conclusion resulted in some range of figures considered to be the most the agency could get; figures, however, which always bore some relationship to the agency's going base plus or minus increments involving a few programs expected to garner support or run into opposition.

DECIDING HOW MUCH TO SPEND

Not only is deciding how much to ask for a problem, it is sometimes difficult for an agency to figure out precisely how much to spend. If an agency has a substantial carryover, the Budget Bureau and especially the appropriations committees may take this as a sign that the agency does not need as much as it received the previous year and may cut off that amount in the future. This practice used to lead to a last-minute flurry of spending in the fourth quarter of the year but it has been somewhat reduced by Budget Bureau apportionment of quarterly allotments. On the other hand, if the agency comes out exactly even, the suspicion is raised that the agency has merely spent up to the limit without considering the need for economy. Coming out even seems just too neat to be true. "It just seems strange," a Representative told the Army, "that you are always able to consume everything you have purchased for that specific period." Should the agency run out of funds, however, it may be accused of using the tactic of the coercive deficiency, of trying to compel Congress to appropriate more funds on the grounds that a vital activity will suffer. (It is also true that deficiencies may serve a useful political function by allowing Congressmen to appear to cut the agency's request when attention is focused on appropriations and to restore the funds in the relatively less visible deficiency hearings.) Most agency budget people try to come out with a little amount in reserve for most programs with an occasional deficit permitted in programs to which they are quite certain the funds will have to be restored. They are acutely aware that the reputation they have built up can help or hinder them greatly in matters of this kind. The agency with a reputation for economy may be praised for turning funds back and not get cut the following year, whereas the agency deemed to be prodigal may get slashed.

One outside limitation on the funds that even an affluent agency finds it useful to spend is the number of competent personnel available, the time it takes to train people for special jobs, and the material resources at hand at a point in time. It may take several years to train expert personnel or to accumulate agricultural products or hospital space without which certain projects are not feasible. An agency may discover that its field officials have put in requests that cannot be fulfilled because they do not realize that they are all competing for the same limited number of experts. The agency need not always be helpless in a situation of this kind. Like the Cancer Institute, it may seek funds for training programs that, in the words of a spokesman, "are designed to increase the supply of manpower in the disciplines needed for cancer research."

DEPARTMENT VERSUS BUREAU

We have used the term "agency" thus far because the considerations apply for the most part with equal force to departments and bureaus. Now it will be useful to make this elementary distinction in discussing the special problems that departments face in deciding how much to try to get for the bureaus under their jurisdiction. Let us assume that the Department Secretary and his staff have managed to work out some notion of what his policy preferences are and would like to implement them. Problems of influence immediately arise.[18] The most obvious is that some bureaus may have considerable support in Congress and override the department in that way. Still, the Secretary and his staff might well decide to just push their preferences if that were all that had to be considered. One difficulty is that a record of recommending far less than Congress appropriates may lead to a general disregard of what the Secretary proposes. Why pay attention if he is obviously a loser? Another difficulty is that the department officials may be in need of bureau support in other matters and may find that hostility over deep cuts interferes with the necessary good relations. After all, the bureaus are administering the programs and have the day-to-day experience and information the Secretary needs. The need for cooperation also appears in balancing requests among the bureaus. For the feeling that one or another bureau has been unfairly treated may lead to serious internal dissension, foot-dragging, and other evils. So the department often finds it wise to temper its preferences with a strong dose of calculations as to what would be acceptable to the other participants.

Just allowing each bureau to ask the Budget Bureau for what it wants has obvious disadvantages. The Secretary may lose a position of leadership and the request may be turned down severely by the Budget Bureau and Congress. There are times, however, when this approach may appear to be necessary. One Secretary of Health, Education and Welfare (HEW) found that Congress was vastly increasing departmental, not to say Budget Bureau, requests for the National Institutes of Health (NIH). Submitting low estimates had obviously failed.

[18] See Simon, et al., "The Struggle for Existence," in *Public Administration* (New York, 1950) pp. 381-422.

So the Secretary decided that it might be better to come in much higher in the hopes of assuming at least part of the leadership for health research and thus having some say in determining the program. Adopting the notion of joining them if you cannot beat them may have been the lesser evil.

Considerations such as these involve the various departments (whether they know it or not) in resolving a basic question of political theory. Shall each bureau ask for what it wants or shall it give priority to the total departmental situation in making requests? (Put in a different way the question might be phrased: Is it best for each interest to pursue its own advantage or shall each seek a solution it believes is in the interest of all?) "One of my most difficult tasks," a budget official asserted, "is finding out what these bureau people really want so I will know how to deal and bargain and oppose them if I have to. Many [bureaus] won't speak up. I don't want them to tell me what's good for the department. That's the Secretary's job and my job and his staff's too. But it is difficult to divide the pie if you don't know for sure how much of a piece each one really wants." Of course, if every bureau just shoots for the moon, the total reaches astronomical figures and that is not much help. Except in years when there are exceedingly powerful reasons for keeping budget totals down, the approach preferred by most department officials is a modified version of "tell us what you really want." Fortunately, we have an acute statement by William Jump expressing this view:

> . . . By and large in normal times we start out on the theory that while every bureau and program head . . . is expected . . . to have fully in mind probable over-all budgetary limitations . . . nevertheless the Department ought to give each bureau a chance to express its ideas of what is necessary or desirable. . . . That is one way you can be sure . . . of determining the extent to which the various bureaus have a constructive approach . . . and a carefully planned program. . . . If . . . you get the original estimates . . . too

> strictly inhibited to start with . . . you will never see . . .
> the plans which the head of program may have in mind.
> . . . [T]hen the Department . . . [may] make such revi-
> sions as may be necessary, in the light of many over-all con-
> siderations. . . .[19]

The usual practice is for a high department official to lay
the whole budget down in front of the bureau heads in an
effort to explain why they cannot get any more than their
share despite the fact that their programs are eminently deserving. Some budget officials are extremely talented at cutting
without getting the blame.

THE BUREAU OF THE BUDGET: ROLES AND PERSPECTIVES

The dominant role of the Bureau of the Budget, in form and
in fact, is to help the President carry out his purposes.[20] The
orientation of the Bureau depends, therefore, on that of the
President. His concerns about the relative priorities of domestic and foreign policy programs, his beliefs about the desirability of a balanced budget, his preferences, in the areas
where he has them, determine a good deal of what the Bureau
tries to do. Thus the Bureau finds itself trying to get appropriations from Congress for Presidential programs and, at times,
prodding agencies to come in with new or enlarged programs
to meet the President's desires. Yet the Budget Bureau ordinarily does not give as much weight to advocating Presiden-

[19] Jump, House Agriculture Appropriations Committee, *op. cit.*
[20] See Fritz Morstein Marx, "The Bureau of the Budget: Its Evolution
and Present Role, II," XXXIX *American Political Science Review* (October 1945) pp. 869-898; Richard Neustadt, "Presidency and Legislation:
The Growth of Central Clearance," XLVIII *American Political Science
Review* (September 1954) pp. 641-671; Arthur Maas, "In Accord with
the Program of the President?" in Carl Friedrich and Kenneth Galbraith,
editors, IV *Public Policy* (Cambridge, Mass., 1954) pp. 77-93; Frederick
J. Lawton, "Legislative-Executive Relationships in Budgeting as Viewed
by the Executive," XIII *Public Administration Review* (Summer 1953)
pp. 169-176; Aaron Wildavsky, *Dixon-Yates: A Study in Power Politics*
(New Haven, 1962) p. 64.

tial programs as to seeing that they do not go beyond bounds, because everyone expects the agencies to perform the functions of advocacy. That can be seen in the responses of Budget Director Maurice Stans to a question on the role of the Bureau:

> Mr. Tufts: Did you conceive it as part of your job as Director to advise the President, then, whether departmental programs were adequate for what you call great purposes?
> Mr. Stans: I considered it our responsibility to do that just as much as to indicate that programs were excessive or unnecessary.
> I might say that the occasions for us to make recommendations along that line were very much less frequent because the agencies themselves did a pretty good job in asking for all the things that they thought they could effectively carry out.[21]

After all, if the President could count on the agencies to express his preferences, he would have less need for the Budget Bureau.

There are, of course, always some people in the Budget Bureau who identify more closely with an agency or program than do others, or who develop policy preferences independent of the President. They have a creative urge. "I don't like to think of myself as a red-pencil man." They see themselves as doing the right thing by pursuing policies in the public interest and they may convince themselves that the President would support them if only he had the time and inclination to go into the matter as deeply as they had. They would rarely resist a direct Presidential command, but these are few at any one time and ordinarily leave much room for interpretation. The role adopted by its budget examiners is important to an agency even if the general orientation of the Budget Bureau is different.

Even within the same Administration, different budget di-

[21] *Jackson Committee Hearings*, pp. 1104-1111.

rectors can have an impact of their own on the Budget Bureau's decisions. Some Directors have much better relationships with the President than others; they get in to see him more often and without going through subordinates; he backs them up more frequently on appeals from the agencies. This kind of information is eagerly sought and circulates rapidly. Not only did the four Directors under President Eisenhower differ in these respects, but their policy preferences also varied within the wide meaning of conservatism, and they exhibited rather striking differences in qualities like judgment, tenacity, and initiative.

Should the President turn down an appeal, the agency and its supporting interests may seek to discover how much of an increase they can get from Congress without risking a Presidential veto or strong opposition from him. The President really cannot insist on precise and strict limitation of funds. If he says $500 million, he can hardly object to $503 or probably $510 million and the agency may seek the highest point in this game. This tactic may encourage setting a lower figure to compensate for the expected small increase.

In bargaining on recommendations a Budget Director who is close to the President has an important advantage since he knows how much leeway he has within the Chief Executive's desires. In the final instance the President, though he lacks an item veto, may halt the spending of appropriations by impounding the funds. He cannot go too far lest he raise a great outcry in Congress; he can only choose a few items.[22] But there is today far more acceptance of impounding than in previous years. Congressmen sometimes object to impounding because it diminishes their power over appropriations. Upon hearing that the Department of Agriculture had secured a Presidential directive freezing funds for the Soil Conservation Service that had been appropriated only three weeks before,

[22] See Inter-University Case Program, "The Impounding of Funds by the Bureau of the Budget," ICP Case Series No. 28, November 1955.

Representative Whitten remarked angrily that, "To freeze these funds means that the policy expressed by Congress was not controlling." Yet Congressmen are ready enough to use it, as Representative Thomas did when he said, "I do not think the money [expanding the Air Force] should be used. I think it should be impounded, and I have the impression that if the money is appropriated it may not be used."

Congressmen manifest ambivalent feelings about the Bureau of the Budget; they regard it essentially as a necessary evil. The ambivalence comes through when a member of the House Appropriations Committee speaks at one time with a trace of contempt of Bureau officials as a bunch of bureaucrats who think they are making the budget, and at another occasion reviles them for not having done enough. The Bureau may be regarded as a rival for control of appropriations. Representative Flood dramatized this feeling when he said, "Mr. Secretary [of Defense] . . . you are a very important man in the Government . . . but you are a minor deity, believe me, compared to the Director of the Budget. He is the Poo-Bah of this town. . . . I feel so strongly about it and many members of the committee and Congress, that we think the Bureau of the Budget as it is now set up should be ripped out altogether. . . ." But it does help set the agenda of the appropriations committees by establishing a starting point, and it does serve to reduce the crushing amount of work for even the most conscientious member.

Attitudes toward the Bureau shift according to the degree to which its actions are believed to promote or hinder the particular program in which a Congressman or agency official is interested. Congressmen sometimes find the Bureau insensitive to considerations of practical politics both in relation to their constituency demands and to their requirements as members of a legislative social system who have to get along with their colleagues. "Don't they know we have to live, too?" says a Congressman. People in the Budget Bureau return the favor by viewing many Congressmen as people overly concerned with local advantage to the detriment of national interest. "All they care about is taking care of their parochial little corner," says a Bureau man.

Every agency and its officials have to decide what kind of relationship to maintain with the Budget Bureau and particularly with the examiners it assigns. Since no examiner can know everything unless the information is volunteered, the agency may decide to provide only that information which is specifically requested. More and more, however, there is a tendency to actually push information at the examiners all the time and not merely when they ask. Why? First, abundant information helps the examiners to be competent defenders of the agency's viewpoint at Budget Bureau meetings when agency personnel is not represented. Second, the examiners may become converted into advocates of particular programs. Third, the examiners' knowledge can be turned to advantage by getting them to secure Administration assistance in clearing up some difficulty. The major disadvantage, of course, is that the examiners "get to know where the bodies are buried this way," as one budget officer put it. But, he continued in words echoed by many others, "you can't hide serious weaknesses for very long anyway, and so the advantages far outweigh the disadvantages."

Budget Bureau and agency personnel have certain beliefs about one another which both vehemently deny but which are widespread. One belief is that Budget Bureau people get promotions on the basis of how successful they are in coming up with a figure that is not changed much by Congress. "You won't believe it, and they will deny it, and I can't prove it, but I am not alone in my belief that Budget people get ahead by how close Congress comes to what they recommend." A corresponding belief is that budget officers get promoted by the degree of success they have in getting the Bureau and Congress to raise appropriations.[23] Whether these beliefs are correct or not, the fact that they are so readily accepted suggests much about the images they have of one another. Where agency personnel have formerly worked for the Bureau, or where the Bureau has managed to help secure difficult appropriations, its image is much more positive. In general, however, the Bureau is regarded as an essentially negative institution. "It can hurt you," a typical response goes, "but it can't and won't help you very much."

Agency people agree that Budget Bureau support is worth having if you can get it without sacrificing too much in Congress. Given Congressional propensity to cut, what the Budget Bureau proposes for an agency is likely to be the upper limit (see Table 2-2). In addition, there are multitudes of small items which Congress would not ordinarily investigate but which might get into trouble if the Bureau's approval were lacking. On occasion, Bureau backing may be helpful in gaining support, particularly if the President is known to approve. Yet agency men recognize two basic limitations on Budget Bureau influence.

A most serious handicap under which the Budget Bureau labors is not so much that Congress may raise its estimates (though this is obviously important) but that it cannot guarantee that a cooperating agency will receive the amount it has recommended. (See Table 2-2, number 3, which shows that Bureau estimates are reduced about three-fourths of the time.) If agencies could depend on receiving the Budget Bureau's figures, they would have much greater incentive to cooperate. The Bureau thus becomes another important road-

[23] On the basis of interviews, David S. Brown reports that ". . . Budget officers know the success of their programs. One reported '1,000 batting average,' based on the fact Congress had not cut a penny from his agency estimates in six years. . . ." "The Staff Man Looks in the Mirror," XXIII *Public Administration Review* (June 1963) p. 63.

block in the governmental process; after agencies surmount this hurdle they still have to get money from Congress.

TABLE 2-2*

Congress frequently cuts Budget Bureau estimates.**

	No difference	Estimates greater than recommended	Estimates less than recommended	Other
(1) Budget estimate as compared to House Committee recommendation	74 cases	342 cases	27 cases	1 case
(2) Budget estimate compared to House Bill	70	344	29	1
(3) Budget estimate compared to final appropriation	62	316	66	

* Figures supplied by Richard Fenno.
** Table shows summary of appropriations histories of 37 bureaus dealing with domestic policies for 12 years (1947-59) (444 cases in all).

The most serious obstacle to acceptance of Budget Bureau leadership is that Congress determines appropriations. Everyone knows that agencies make end-runs around the Bureau to gain support from Congress. If they do so too often, the Budget Bureau finds that its currency has depreciated. Hence the Bureau frequently accepts consistent Congressional action as a guide. A close eye is kept on Congressional action for the preceding year before an agency's total is set for the next one. Failure to do so might leave the Bureau with a record of defeat that jeopardizes its effectiveness in other areas.

The basic situation is immediately apparent to other participants in budgeting. The man whose requests are continually turned down in Congress finds that he tends to be rejected in the Budget Bureau and in his own department as well. Again, the Budget Bureau follows Congressional action.

This fact is of enormous significance because it leads to pivotal strategic moves. Suppose an agency must choose between alternatives, one favored by Congressmen, another by the Budget Bureau. The strategy indicated would be to side with Congress because one's record with Congress determines how one is viewed and treated by the Budget Bureau and the Department. These considerations weaken the Bureau of the Budget in the eyes of the agency.

A popularity poll would no doubt reveal a strong tendency for agencies that get much more than the Budget Bureau recommends to be unpopular in that institution. This attitude is understandable. No one likes to be overruled. The Budget Bureau may go so far as to scrutinize the requests of such agencies with special care. But the political realities take most of the pleasure out of this practice. What is the point of more careful scrutiny if you cannot implement your findings and, in any event, do not want your recommendation to be consistently too far off? The Bureau finds itself treating agencies it dislikes much better than those it may like better but who cannot help themselves nearly as much in Congress. The "popularity" of those who cannot help themselves is bound to wane in the Budget Bureau as annoyance at having to take over the job of pushing the agency's programs if they are to be pushed at all (when the President would rather use his resources elsewhere) triumphs over the agency's willingness to accord deference.

DECIDING HOW MUCH TO RECOMMEND

The Bureau of the Budget (BOB) faces in an extreme form the perplexing problem of deciding how much it believes should be spent on particular programs. An agency may solve the problem by getting as much as it can. But in the absence of specific Presidential guidance, the BOB is put in the position of trying to decide how desirable a program might be on its intrinsic merits.

Let us take an extreme case. How much should be devoted to medical research sponsored by the Federal Government? Most of us would say, "quite a lot." But how much is that? A million, a hundred million, a billion? BOB personnel do not have the technical competence in medical research to evaluate specific proposals and they are not certain they should spend their limited time in this way; they would rather set priorities. Technical criteria like cost-benefit ratios would be helpful if they existed, but even so the determination of what may qualify as a benefit would be crucial. (Having decided how much one wants to spend, standards may be devised that permit that much to be justified.) No one really knows how much medical research might be carried on profitably in some sense,[24] and the BOB people have discovered that there seems to be no end to the work qualified people believe it desirable to attempt. With painful awareness that they are violating deeply held notions of rationality, the responsible officials leave the area of intrinsic merits because it does not help them make decisions and turn instead to other criteria which may not be "rational" but which do help them.

They may try to give the question a political cast—how much is our society willing to spend?—and come up with what we have described as an expected level of appropriations, which narrows their burden of calculation considerably by giving them directions.[25] But in the case of the NIH

[24] A beginning in discussing some economic guide lines has been made by Burton A. Weisbrod in *The Economics of Public Health; Measuring the Economic Impact of Diseases* (Philadelphia, 1961), but the implications of using pure economic criteria are startling, if not inhuman.

[25] In addressing himself to the question of evaluating program effectiveness, Elmer B. Staats, an experienced, high-level official in the Bureau of the Budget, declared: "I think basically and foremost there is the political test—'Political' in the broad policy and program sense, but also in the more traditional sense of party labels and political campaigns.

(which I have chosen for this very reason) there is not yet (though the time may be approaching) agreement on a fair share. Nor is there another formula, however arbitrary—such as devoting 1 per cent of the Gross National Product or allowing a rise of 10 per cent a year—which justifies a course of action. So the BOB has the choice of cutting NIH arbitrarily and being drastically overridden by Congress, or of raising it arbitrarily and feeling that the situation has gotten out of hand.

Here is a story of one actual attempt to wrestle with this problem.

> Respondent: My day to day work was not very effective. It was a desperate attempt at wondering how to grasp ahold of this whole business. . . . We couldn't get a meaningful standard to judge as to how much medical research the Government should support.
>
> Interviewer: How did the BOB decide where and how much to cut the NIH request?
>
> Respondent: This is a very good question. I wonder how we did decide. I would say as a generalization that it was some kind of a mechanical factor like "let's hold it to last year's budget" or "last year's budget plus 10% of new grants" . . . or just "10% increase over last year."
>
> Interviewer: How did you arrive at this figure?
>
> Respondent: We do it on an ad hoc basis. 10% sounds right. . . . They [the NIH] may point out that it doesn't demonstrate a 10% growth due to certain factors, so we will give them say 12.5%. . . . We were playing around with graphs and figures. Curves . . . projecting growth to 1965

This is the real test of program effectiveness. Society is constantly applying this test to the party organizations, to the Congress, to the President who is the only person elected by all of us, to the pressure group that is concerned with a particular program—and the test is the measure of whatever it is that causes people to identify themselves with one party or candidate rather than another." From "Evaluating Program Effectiveness," in D. L. Bowen and L. K. Caldwell, editors, *Selected Papers on Public Administration*, Institute of Training for Public Service, Department of Government, Indiana University (Bloomington, Ind., 1960) p. 62.

and say the figure was 1.3 billion. The people in the BOB will say, let's reach 1.3 billion not by 1965 but by 1975. So we cut the figure by the percent to reach it [by 1975]. . . . There was an argument on what to start with as the base, the unobligated balance to be included or not. If we take the lower figure we could give them the same rate of growth but it would be say $60 million less than they asked. . . . I would get the [NIH] estimate and come up with my recommendation. This would have to be a little lower than the department request.

Interviewer: Why?

Respondent: Because I didn't think it was appropriate to give the same amount the department asked, so I cut a little. From here my recommendation went to the division review meeting. . . . I would say they [the NIH] asked for say a 32% increase and I allowed 23%. Comments might go like this. "We have to put a stop to this NIH." "Congress will up it anyway no matter what we do. . . ." Then somebody will say, "Let's hold it to last year's level." But somebody else would reply, "No, that is no good. That isn't realistic at all. There has to be some increase." Then another would say, "Can we raise them 10% and get a rationalization for this?" and we will try to figure one out." . . .

Interviewer: How about apportionment of appropriations?

Respondent: Usually what happened was the President's budget got shot to hell with major increases. The staff [of the BOB] would consider the possibility of a veto. But you can't veto a health bill politically. It makes the President in favor of cancer. But you can't just crawl under a rock. What can you do?

There are several alternatives and we can at least set down the type of calculations that go into each one. The most obvious is for the BOB to shoot from the hip and let the bodies fall where they may. The feeling here may be that if the BOB does what it believes is right and protests long enough something will be done. The opposite rationale holds that it is foolish to continually estimate under or over what Congress will probably give. (Similar cries like "they'll roll us on the floor," or "the Senate will put the item in and get the

credit," are also heard on the House Appropriations Committee.) Note the dialogue in which a Census Bureau official
explained why the BOB turned down a request. "Representative Stefan: Apparently they [the BOB] anticipated what this
committee might do. Mr. Hauser: That was exactly the language they used." Another possibility is for the BOB to come
in just a little low in the hopes that it can slowly apply a
brake to a program it believes is expanding too fast. Or the
BOB may on rare occasion seek to take leadership by proposing greatly increased expenditures itself and in this way hope
to exercise a larger voice in determining the content of the
program. Now the Bureau appears to have adopted an incremental approach whereby it uses various rules of thumb to
estimate the relative importance of the last proposed increases,
and it is apparently making progress.

The case of the NIH is an unusual one but like a medical
case history it does serve to highlight factors operating to a
lesser degree in more normal organisms. The extreme case is
especially valuable for our purposes because of the understandable reluctance of people to admit that their decisions
are sometimes based on something less than the epitome of
reasoned judgment. In many areas of budgeting, of course,
there are more explicit criteria of judgment. Experience has
been accumulated and it is possible to speak more securely
of consequences of doing this or that. A level of funds has
been reached through the political process. Work-load data
or cost-benefit analysis has been developed to some degree. A
close look at this kind of criterion, however, shows that most
of the standards are not directly based on intrinsic merit—as
an ideal cost-benefit analysis might be—but on "extrinsic"
criteria such as limits beyond which Congress will not go. Yet
the problems of calculation would be so vast without the extrinsic standards—where would one begin?—that it is difficult
to see how decisions could be made unless some person or
group dictated them. Hence the paradox that the extrinsic

factors most often criticized—historical development, self-evident meeting points, stress on agreement—provide essential means for limiting the range of calculation so that factors intrinsic to the worth of the program have an opportunity to be given some weight.

THE APPROPRIATIONS COMMITTEES:
ROLES AND PERSPECTIVES

When Representative Preston asked, "Is there anything fantastic about this 18th Decennial Census that . . . we should know about as guardians of the taxpayer's money?" he was describing the prevailing role played by members of the House Appropriations Committee. As guardians of the public purse, committee members are expected to cast a skeptical eye on the blandishments of a bureaucracy ever anxious to increase its dominion by raising its appropriations. After an administrator spoke of the wonderful things accomplished by research in forestry, Representative Clarence Cannon struck the proper note by replying, "All these Government researchers every year come in here and outline . . . great progress that has been made in the various industries and claim credit for them where it would have gone ahead if they had not been in existence, and you are no exception to that rule."

There is perhaps something here of the romantic conception of the sheriff warding off the mob, Horatio at the bridge, or of the unknown and unappreciated but faithful servant who guards his master's fortune against the pernicious schemes of wasteful relatives. Fenno quotes a veteran committee member to the effect that "No subcommittee of which I have been a member has ever reported out a bill without a cut in the budget. I'm proud of that record."[26] In typical comments John Rooney, who guards the State Department budget, says, "I am questioning you for the taxpayer. I ap-

[26] Fenno, *op. cit.*, pp. 311-312.

proach [the budget] with the idea that it can be cut. It's an asking price." Another committee member says, "Here we look at the bright side. We see a reduction." In order to provide an objective check on the effectiveness of this orientation, Fenno examined the appropriations histories of 37 bureaus concerned with domestic policies from 1947-1959 and discovered that the committee reduced the estimates it received 77.2 per cent of the time.[27]

It cannot be emphasized too often, however, that we are describing the most generally accepted role, and not the only one, which guides all committee members in all cases. There are members who identify completely with an agency or its programs. "To me forestry has become a religion . . ." said Representative Walter Horan. In a profound violation of House Committee norms, he took his protest against his own appropriations subcommittee to the Senate hearings, declaring that "The items are totally inadequate and I do not care particularly which way *we* get them, but *we* do need funds. . . ." (Emphasis supplied.) There are also subcommittees such as the one headed by Representative Fogarty on the National Institutes of Health, which obviously see their role as proponents of greater spending. And there are also Congressmen like Daniel Flood who switch roles from one subcommittee to the next, acting like the protector of national defense in one place and an economy advocate in another.

At times, then, the sense of having served a great cause expressed in terms of public interest may create a sense of identification with an agency or program that overwhelms other considerations. This feeling comes through in the poignant remarks Representative Anderson addressed to the Administrator of the Soil Conservation Service.

> You know every man serving in Congress hopes to leave his imprint in some small way upon work in which he is interested.

[27] *Ibid.*, p. 312.

The activities of our Government and the responsibilities are so vast that we are fortunate if we leave Congress even after twenty or thirty years and have our name attached even in a slight degree to something really worthwhile, and I am proud of the fact that sixteen years ago, gentlemen, I was fighting to increase in this very room the money set aside for soil conservation operations.

The desire to cut the budget may conflict with the desire not to damage programs vital to the nation. At such a time a Congressman may try to get the best of both worlds by asking the agency to assume the responsibility of reconciling the divergent roles. As Representative Jensen once put it to the Atomic Energy Commission:

The members of this committee certainly would not take it upon themselves to blindly make a cut in your appropriation because of the fact that it is such an important function. However, it may be that after this so-called post mortem of your budget request for this committee you might be able to find an item or two that you could reduce to a degree. . . . I would not like to have it on my conscience.

In the case of local constituency interests, the deviation from guardianship of the budget is exceedingly powerful because it touches on the most basic relationship a Congressman may have—that with the people who elect him and might conceivably defeat him—and because Congressmen are prone to take as an article of faith another of their roles as defender of constituency interests. Where their constituencies are affected, appropriations committee members use all the vast leverage over men and money which their positions give them to secure favorable outcomes. The battle-royal that Representative John Rooney engaged in to keep a Department of Commerce office in New York City so that his constituents would not lose their jobs would make a fascinating story in itself. An Assistant Secretary of Commerce had the temerity to suggest that this was not exactly an example of ideal administration, and Rooney lit into him. "Do you mean that employees of long standing, who, for instance, live right in my Congressional district . . . have no right to . . . raise their voices to prevent the loss of jobs . . . ? Were any of the employees who came to this committee from that New York office penalized . . . ?" "I can assure you that was not done, Mr. Congressman," said the Assistant Secretary. Then there was Representative Ivor Fenton's tenacious campaign to have an anthracite laboratory located in Schuylkill Haven instead of Hazleton, Pennsylvania. Fenton said that he got no action until he got on the Appropriations Committee. At that time he accused the Secretary of the Interior of "the cheapest kind of politics" and decided "that no funds now available for the laboratory be obligated until this matter is clarified to the satisfaction of the Appropriations Committee." The funds were denied. In the other chamber, Senator Meyers spoke of "exceptional energy on the part of one of the subcommittee members in seeking to establish some sort of political plot to locate the laboratory in a district other than his." The law that was passed specified that the laboratory had to be built in Schuylkill Haven. A little arm-twisting was applied by Senator Lyndon Johnson in order to make certain that a prison was built in the right place. "I sure would hate to put in this money to build a prison in Congressman Grey's district and Senator Dirksen's state in Illinois and find out that they got it in X, Y, Z, somewhere." It is not surprising to discover that the new space center is being constructed in the home city of Representative Thomas, the subcommittee chairman dealing with the space agency.

Tough as they may be in cutting the budgets of their agencies, appropriations committee members, once having made their decision, generally defend the agencies against further cuts on the floor.[28] This kind of action is in part self-

[28] In an exchange with a member of the Appropriations Committee, Representative Clarence Brown complained that when an amendment is

interest. The power of the appropriations subcommittees would be diminished if their recommendations were successfully challenged very often. Members believe that the House would "run wild" if "orderly procedure"—that is, acceptance of committee recommendations—were not followed. But the role of defender also has its roots in the respect for expertise and specialization in Congress, and the ensuing belief that members who have not studied the subject should not exercise a deciding voice without the presence of overriding considerations. An appeal to this norm is usually sufficient to block an attempt to reduce appropriations, as Senator Douglas has discovered many times. Appropriations Committee members, McKellar cried on one occasion, had "worked almost like slaves on the bill. . . . Here at the last moment comes an amendment offered by a Senator who has not taken part in any hearings." Douglas was squashed then as he has been ever since on the same grounds.

A member of the Senate Appropriations Committee is likely to conceive of his proper role as the responsible legislator who sees to it that the irrepressible lower House does not do too much damage either to constituency or to national interests. Though members of the House Appropriations Committee tend to view their opposite members in the Senate as frivolous dilettantes who swap favors and do not care what happens to the public purse, Senators tend to reverse the compliment by regarding their brethren in the other chamber as jealous and power-hungry types who do not care what happens to "essential" programs so long as they can show that they have made cuts. Senator Mundt expressed this feeling in 1957 when he said, in regard to a Bureau of Indian Affairs ap-

---

offered "to reduce an appropriations item, the Appropriations Committee stands like a stone wall most of the time, saying 'No, you mustn't touch this.' That is one of the things that has brought complaint against your committee, sir, and you know it. . . ." House Government Operations Subcommittee, *Improving Federal Budgeting and Appropriations*, 85th Congress, 1st Session, 1957, p. 139.

propriation, "I think it is important to have in the record
. . . that the House finds no fault with the program of construction. They just failed to provide the money. The need is
there and it is our responsibility to meet that need. . . ."
House members would say that there is also a need for restraint. The difference in perspective between the two committees was illustrated by Senator Dirksen, who used to glory
in his role as tough guardian of the purse. Referring to a
House action to reduce from ten to six the number of employees, Dirksen said, "It was great, good fun when I was on
the House Appropriations Committee to cut four [positions].
Too often you discover that the six positions depend in large
measure on the four. You just wasted the money for the six.
I would rather give you nothing or whatever it takes to do a
good job."

The Senators are rather painfully aware of the House Committee's pre-eminence in the field of appropriations and they
know that they cannot hope to match the time and thoroughness that the House body devotes to screening requests. For
this reason, the Senate Committee puts a high value on having agencies carry appeals to it. "We all know," said Senator
Richard Russell, "that almost since the inception of the Government, the Senate Appropriations Committee has served
as an appeal body and has heard requests . . . that deal principally with items that have been changed or reduced or
eliminated by the House of Representatives." The Senators
value their ability to disagree on items in dispute as a means
of maintaining their influence in crucial areas while putting
the least possible strain on their time and energy. The dominant Senate role of responsible appeals court is dependent
upon agency advocacy and House committee guardianship.

Although it is true the Senate frequently increases the
amount of appropriations voted by the House, this relationship varies with the agency, the issue area, and the particular
item. Given significant differences in the degree of success

with which various agencies secure their appropriation goals, it is not overly helpful to say that the Senate generally grants more than the House. For we must account for the differences between agencies and programs, occasions when this relationship does not hold at all, and the broad differences in the percentages of increase offered by the Senate.

In policy areas such as natural resources, in which the Senate increases the amount passed by the House, the result may be a product of two factors. First, the interests desiring the increased appropriation are better represented in the Senate. The fact, for example, that the Reclamation Bureau works in seventeen western states gives it a much greater influence in the Senate than in the House, where a much smaller percentage of representatives are directly concerned. Second, the House, knowing that the Senate will increase funds, lowers its amount for bargaining purposes and the Senate correspondingly increases its amount in a pattern of reciprocal expectations. House and Senate members claim that the others do more of this than they do.

The impact of gerrymandering and failure to reapportion on representation in the House may be a third factor affecting its desire to spend. State legislatures are commonly strongholds of conservatism that resist giving more equality of representation to voters from urban areas who would elect men with a more favorable view on certain kinds of spending. Senators give more representation to constituencies that wish to spend. The result is that the Senate today is more liberal than the House in several senses of that word.[29]

Keenly aware of the particular roles adopted by the members of the appropriations subcommittees who deal with their programs, the predominant view that agency officials have of these legislators is that they are very powerful people. "They

[29] See Lewis A. Froman, Jr., "Why the Senate Is More Liberal than the House" in *Congressmen and Their Constituencies* (Chicago, 1963), pp. 69-97.

can do you a world of good and they can cut your throat."
"These men, notably the Chairman, can murder you and also
make things easy." The figures in Table 2-3, which show that
Appropriations Committee recommendations in both houses
are accepted almost nine out of every ten times, bear elo-
quent testimony to the accuracy of these perceptions. Experienced, tough, coming from safe districts, recognized as
pre-eminent in their specialized domains by other legislators,
these men are in a position to control the financial life of the
agencies within fairly wide zones of tolerance. So long as they
do not violate widespread and intense preferences among fellow legislators, they can do much to reward or punish agencies
and their personnel without much fear of being contradicted.
Newsweek (April 7, 1958) quotes a State Department official
as saying, "Let's face it. When Rooney whistles, we've just
got to dance." Another investigator reports that "one otherwise articulate official was so unstrung after testifying that he
offered his resignation as soon as he returned to his office. Another was caught by his wife arguing with an imaginary
Rooney."[30] There is no getting away from it: a single individual in these key committee positions can wield great
power, as the careers of Representatives John Rooney and
John Fogarty and Senators Carl Hayden and Lister Hill,
among many others, demonstrate.

Staff members of the Appropriations Committees view
themselves as neutral servants of Congressmen. Of course,
they know that they have opinions and that personal preferences may influence their opinions. But they try to serve
members of their committee well regardless of whether or not
they agree with them. Unless their relationship is close, the
staff rarely proffers advice to a Congressman on their own;
they wait to be asked. Then the staff will answer in terms of
the question and say that if the Congressman wants X, then

[30] Peter Wyden, "The Man Who Frightens Bureaucrats," *Saturday
Evening Post* (January 31, 1959) p. 87.

he should do Y. Or a staff man may confine himself to specifying the likely consequences of policy moves proposed by Congressmen. At all times the staff shuns publicity as an invasion of the prerogative of Congressmen.

TABLE 2-3*

Recommendations of the appropriations committees are usually adopted.**

	No difference	Committee recommendation greater than bill	Committee recommmendation less than bill	Other
House Committee recommendations compared with final House bill	387 (87.4%)	30	26	1
Senate Committee recommendations compared with Senate bill	390 (88.0%)	14	40	
Summary of floor action on committee recommendations in both houses	777 (87.6%)	44	66	

* Figures supplied by Richard Fenno.
** Table is based on histories of 37 bureaus dealing with domestic policies for 12 years (1947-59) (888 cases in all).

When the subcommittee chairman is less competent than usual and not very industrious, committee staff may find themselves shaping more policy. They may mold the line of inquiry, order the consideration of alternatives, and take a larger part in writing recommendations about appropriations. Even under different circumstances, however, the staff has extensive influence over the disposition of small items which may have escaped the attention of Congressmen or which may or may not be lost in the shuffle at the end of a session, depending on how the staff acts.

Many agencies choose to keep subcommittee staff informed

months and sometimes years ahead on new developments. This expedient enables the staff to have ready explanations if and when Congressmen make inquiries. At times, the agency is placed in a position in which it would not like to reveal certain information to the staff but fears that failure to do so will be considered a breach of confidence. Career officials and political appointees who look forward to years of service are often willing to make some sacrifices by providing information in the hope that they will gain by the increase in confidence that may result. They also tend to believe that it is better to provide the information themselves than to have it turn up without their cooperation and without their being able to put the best possible interpretation on it.

Although it appears that agency personnel are more dependent on committee staff than vice versa, the relationship is by no means a one-way proposition. The staff man knows that he can do a more effective job if he has the cooperation of the budget officer. For much of the staff's work is dependent on securing information from the agency about current programs and the possible effects of various changes. The staff may be blamed for not informing Congressmen of changes in agency plans and expenditures. And when complex problems arise, the agency may actually do the work for the staff. Mutual dependence is the order of the day and both sides generally regard their contacts as prerequisites to doing their best work. Yet mutual dependence is, of necessity, tinged with the realization that committee staff and budget officers represent different organizations, whose roles are not completely compatible.

DECIDING HOW MUCH TO GIVE:
THE APPROPRIATIONS COMMITTEES

The ways in which the appropriations committees go about making budgetary calculations are profoundly affected by their central position in the Congressional system. Their power to make budgetary decisions is in a sense dependent upon their ability to help keep the system going by meeting the needs of other Congressmen. Appropriations must be voted each year if the government is to continue to function. (The experience of the Fourth French Republic, in which the practice of voting "twelfths" [one month's appropriations] because of inability to agree sapped the stability of the regime, is instructive on this point.) To put together budgets running into the billions of dollars and involving innumerable different activities is a huge task. In order to make the necessary decisions the committees must reduce the enormous burden of calculation involved in budgeting. Otherwise, the necessity for decision might propel them into making random or wholly capricious choices that would throw governmental operations out of kilter by sudden stops and headlong starts. Nor could Congress as a whole take on the burden. The bulk of Congressmen are busy with other things. They can hardly hope to become knowledgeable in more than a few areas of budgeting, if that. Some way of reducing their information costs must be found unless they are to abdicate their powers. And the way they have adopted of doing so is to accept the verdict of the appropriations committees most of the time, intervening just often enough to keep the committees roughly in line.

Budgeting is specialized. There are multiple levels of specialization within Congress—the House and Senate Appropriations Committees, their subcommittees, the subject areas within these subcommittees, the Senate Appropriations Committee appeals procedure, the Conference Committee, and the authorizations functions of the substantive committees and their specialized subcommittees. Most of the decisions in the House Appropriations Committee are taken in its specialized subcommittees. "Why, you'd be branded an impostor," a House subcommittee chairman said, "if you went into one of those other subcommittee meetings. The only time I go is by appointment, by arrangement with the chairman at a special time. I'm as much a stranger in another subcommittee as I would be in [a substantive committee]. Each one [subcommittee] does its work apart from all others."[31] The full committee rarely acts and even then only in regard to a few items. Members ordinarily take the position that each subcommittee accepts the results of the others in their respective jurisdictions and that the House and Senate follow the recommendations of the committees. "Had I been sitting on this [sub]committee," a House member said, "I undoubtedly would not have agreed with all the items. I am not on that [sub]committee. It is not my responsibility." And within their subcommittees members ordinarily concentrate on a particular area such as mental health or small watersheds. Statements such as, "I will leave the questioning to our great expert on . . ." abound in appropriations hearings. The situation in the Senate differs somewhat in that there is considerable overlap of membership between substantive and appropriations subcommittees and outsiders from the substantive subcommittees are welcome at hearings. The Senate does, however, add another level of specialization through its appeals procedure. Each level of specialization, then, is wrapped within the other with the applicable decision-rule in most cases being that the most specialized member or members carry the day. Coupled with the preferred political style of long hours and hard work, especially in the House, specialization confers considerable influence upon those who practice it.

Budgeting is historical. Since members usually serve in Congress for several years before getting on the appropriations committees, and they are expected to serve an apprenticeship before making themselves heard, the more influential among

[31] Fenno, *op. cit.*, p. 316.

them typically have years of experience in dealing with their specialties. They have absorbed a series of past moves and are prepared to apply the results of their previous calculations to present circumstances. In this way the magnitude of any one decision at any one time is reduced and with it the burden of calculation. An historical approach is facilitated by a line-item budgetary form. Instead of necessarily focusing attention on various programs as a whole, the committees usually concentrate on changes in the various items—personnel, equipment, maintenance, specific activities—which make up the program. ". . . we will take an awfully long look when we come to the part of your budget that adds 5 additional people to the agency," Representative Jensen assured the Fish and Wildlife Service in 1960. By keeping the categories constant over a number of years, and by requiring that the previous and present year's figures be placed in adjacent columns, the calculations made in the past need not be gone over again completely. And though the members know that the agency is involved in various programs, the line-item form enables them to concentrate on the less divisive issue of how much for each item.

Budgeting is fragmented. Budgets are made in fragments. Each subcommittee, and sometimes specialists within these bodies, operates as a largely autonomous unit concerned only with a limited area of the budget. Even the subcommittees do not attend to all the items in the budget but pay special attention to instances of increases or decreases over the previous year. In this way, it might be said, the subcommittees deal with a fragment of a fragment of the whole. Fragmentation is further increased by the Senate Appropriations Committee, which focuses its attention on items that are appealed from House decisions. The Senators, therefore, often deal with a fragment of what is already (through House action) a fragment of a fragment.

Budgeting is treated as if it were non-programmatic. This statement does not mean that appropriations committee people do not care about programs; they do. Nor does it mean that they do not fight for or against some programs; they do. What it does mean is that they view most of their work as marginal, monetary adjustments to existing programs so that the question of the ultimate desirability of most programs arises only once in a while. "A disagreement on money isn't like a legislative program . . ." one member said in a typical statement, "it's a matter of money rather than a difference in philosophy." An appropriations committee member explains how disagreements are handled in the mark-up session when members retire behind closed doors to work out their recommendations. "If there's agreement, we go right along. If there's a lot of controversy we put the item aside and go on. Then, after a day or two, we may have a list of ten controversial items. We give and take and pound them down till we get agreement."[32]

Budgeting is repetitive. Decision making in budgeting is carried on with the knowledge that few problems have to be "solved" once and for all. Everyone knows that a problem may be dealt with over and over again. Hence considerations that a Congressman neglects one year may be taken up by himself another year or in a supplementary action during the same year. Problems are not so much solved as they are worn down by repeated attacks until they are no longer pressing or have been superseded by other problems.

Budgeting is sequential. The appropriations committees do not try to solve every problem at once. On the contrary, they do not deal with many problems in a particular year, and those they do encounter are dealt with mostly in different places and at different times. They allow many decisions made in previous years to stand or to vary slightly without

[32] *Ibid.*

question. Then they divide up subjects for more intensive inquiry among subcommittees and their specialists. Over the years the subcommittees center now on one and then on another problem. When the budgetary decisions made by one subcommittee adversely affect those of another the difficulty is handled by "fire-truck tactics"; that is, by dealing with each problem in turn in whatever jurisdiction it appears. Difficulties are overcome not so much by central coordination or planning as by attacking each manifestation in the different centers of decision in sequence.[33]

The Conference Committee carries on the process of sequential calculation by concentrating on the items of difference between the Senate and House. The bargaining is carried on in great secrecy to facilitate give and take. For the Conference Committee to fail to reach agreement on many items would disrupt the entire legislative process, especially since their deliberations frequently take place at the tail end of the session. One way to secure agreement is to swap items in dispute. Referring to a Conference Committee session on the United States Information Agency, Representative Coudert reported that the House agreed to raise its figure and "in return the Senate yielded on these little things. . . . When you have different things in dispute the two [subcommittee] chairmen [Representative Rooney and Senator Kilgore] just trade them off, back and forth." Another way of reaching agreement has been described by T. C. Schelling[34] as the presence of a unique solution that is evident to everyone. Given the necessity for arriving at agreement, and inability to decide what it should be, the conferees may settle on a formula that appears to be intuitively satisfying. They may split

---

[33] The method of calculation described here independently bears a striking similarity to those attributed to social scientists by David Braybrooke and Charles E. Lindblom in their *A Strategy of Decision* (New York, 1963), and to private firms by Richard Cyert and James March in their *A Behavioral Theory of the Firm* (Englewood Cliffs, N. J., 1963).

[34] See his *The Strategy of Conflict* (Cambridge, 1962).

the difference, choose the highest amount for each item, or the lowest amount for each item. Inevitably, there is a premium on raising or lowering amounts voted in the House or Senate so as to leave room for "concessions" to the other side.

SUMMARY

Although much more remains to be discovered about budgetary calculations, we have now completed a broad survey of the subject. Aids to calculations commonly used in dealing with the problem of complexity have been described. Budgeting turns out to be an incremental process, proceeding from a historical base, guided by accepted notions of fair shares, in which decisions are fragmented, made in sequence by specialized bodies, and coordinated through repeated attacks on problems and through multiple feedback mechanisms. The role of the participants, and their perceptions of each other's powers and desires, fit together to provide a reasonably stable set of criteria on which to base calculations. A variety of rules for decision, depending on a reading of "the signs of the times," and on differing attitudes toward time, innovation, and other goals, have at least been sketched out. We have been made aware of the kind of calculations that go into such basic choices as deciding how much to ask for and how much to appropriate. Now I would like to extend the range of budgetary behavior under consideration by turning to a separate (though related) set of questions: how do the agencies—the advocates in the process of budgeting—go about trying to get what they want? Which strategies are used under which circumstances? What are some of the counter-strategies employed by the other participants? What are some of the primary conditions associated with the achievement of budgetary goals?

STRATEGIES
3

BUDGETARY STRATEGIES are actions by governmental agencies intended to maintain or increase the amount of money available to them. Not every move in the budgetary arena is necessarily aimed at getting funds in a conscious way. Yet administrators can hardly help being aware that nothing can be done without funds, and that they must normally do things to retain or increase rather than decrease their income.

Our major purpose in this chapter is to describe in an orderly manner the major budgetary strategies currently being employed and to relate them to the environment from which they spring. In this way we can, for the first time, describe the behavior of officials engaged in budgeting as they seek to relate their requirements and powers to the needs and powers of others. Strategies are the links between the intentions and perceptions of budget officials and the political system that imposes restraints and creates opportunities for them. When we know about strategies we are not only made aware of important kinds of behavior, we also learn about the political world in which they take place.

Strategic moves take place in a rapidly changing environment in which no one is quite certain how things will turn out and new goals constantly emerge in response to experience. In this context of uncertainty, choice among existing strategies must be based on intuition and hunch, on an "educated guess," as well as on firm knowledge. Assuming a normal capacity to learn, however, experience should eventually provide a more reliable guide than sheer guesswork. When we discover strategies that are practiced throughout the entire administrative apparatus, we suspect that officials have discovered paths to success which may not be wholly reliable but which have proved to be more advantageous than the available alternatives.

UBIQUITOUS AND CONTINGENT STRATEGIES

What really counts in helping an agency get the appropriations it desires? Long service in Washington has convinced high agency officials that some things count a great deal and others only a little. Although they are well aware of the desirability of having technical data to support their requests, budget officials commonly derogate the importance of the formal aspects of their work as a means of securing appropriations. Budget estimates that are well prepared may be useful for internal purposes—deciding among competing programs, maintaining control of the agency's operations, giving the participants the feeling they know what they are doing, finding the cost of complex items. The estimates also provide a respectable backstop for the agency's demands. But, as several informants put it in almost identical words, "It's not what's in your estimates but how good a politician you are that matters."

Being a good politician, these officials say, requires essentially three things: cultivation of an active clientele, the development of confidence among other governmental officials, and skill in following strategies that exploit one's opportunities to the maximum. Doing good work is viewed as part of being a good politician.

Strategies designed to gain confidence and clientele are ubiquitous; they are found everywhere and at all times in the budgetary system. The need for obtaining support is so firmly fixed a star in the budgetary firmament that it is perceived by everyone and uniformly taken into account in making the calculations upon which strategies depend.

"Contingent" strategies are particular; they depend upon conditions of time and place and circumstance; they are especially dependent upon an agency's attitude toward the opportunities the budgetary system provides for. Arising out of these attitudes, we may distinguish three basic orientations toward budgeting in increasing order of ambition. First, defending the agency's base by guarding against cuts in old programs. Second, increasing the size of the base by moving ahead with old programs. Third, expanding the base by adding new programs. These types of strategies differ considerably from one another. An agency might cut popular programs to promote a restoration of funds; it would be unlikely to follow this strategy in adding new programs. We shall take up ubiquitous and contingent strategies in turn.

CLIENTELE

Find a clientele. For most agencies locating a clientele is no problem at all; the groups interested in their activities are all too present. But for some agencies the problem is a difficult one and they have to take extraordinary measures to solve it. Men and women incarcerated in federal prisons, for instance, are hardly an ideal clientele. And the rest of society cares only to the extent of keeping these people locked up. So the Bureau of Prisons tries to create special interest in its activities on the part of Congressmen who are invited to see what is going on. "I wish, Mr. Bow, you would come and visit us at one of these prison places when you have the time. . . . I am sure you would enjoy it." The United States Information Agency faces a similar problem—partly explaining its mendicant status—because it serves people abroad rather than directly benefiting them at home. Things got so bad that the USIA sought to organize the country's ambassadors to foreign nations to vouch for the good job it said it was doing.

Serve your clientele. For an agency that has a large and strategically placed clientele, the most effective strategy is service to those who are in a position to help them. "If we deliver this kind of service," an administrator declared, "other things are secondary and automatic." His agency made a point of organizing clientele groups in various localities, priming them to engage in approved projects, serving them well, and encouraging them to inform their Congressmen of their reaction. Informing one's clientele of the full extent of the benefits they receive may increase the intensity with which they support the agency's request.

Expand your clientele.   In order to secure substantial funds from Congress for domestic purposes, it is ordinarily necessary to develop fairly wide interest in the program. This is what Representative Whitten did when he became a member of the Appropriations Committee and discovered that soil conservation in various watersheds had been authorized but little money had been forthcoming: "Living in the watersheds . . . I began to check . . . and I found that all these watersheds were in a particular region, which meant there was no general interest in the Congress in this type of program . . . . It led me to go before the Democratic platform committee in 1952 and urge them to write into the platform a plank on watershed protection. And they did." As a result, Whitten was able to call on more general support from Democrats and increase appropriations for the Soil Conservation Service watersheds.

Concentrate on individual constituencies. After the Census Bureau had made an unsuccessful bid to establish a national housing survey, Representative Yates gave it a useful hint. The proposed survey "is so general," Yates said, "as to be almost useless to the people of a particular community. . . . This would help someone like Armstrong Cork, who can sell its product anywhere in the country . . . but will it help the construction industry in a particular area to know whether or not it faces a shortage of customers?" Later, the Bureau submitted a new program that called for a detailed enumeration of metropolitan districts with a sample survey of other areas to get a national total. Endorsed by mortgage holding associations, the construction material industry, and Federal and state housing agencies, the new National Housing Inventory received enthusiastic support in Congress where Representative Preston exclaimed, "This certainly represents a lot of imaginative thinking on your part . . . ." In another case the National Science Foundation made headway with a program of summer mathematics institutes not only because the idea was excellent but also because the institutes were spread around the country, where they became part of a constituency interest Congressmen are supposed to protect.

Secure feedback. Almost everyone claims that his projects are immensely popular and benefit lots of people. But how do elected officials know? They can only be made aware by hearing from constituents. The agency can do a lot to ensure that its clientele responds by informing them that contacting Congressmen is necessary and by telling them how to go about it if they do not already know. In fact, the agency may organize the clientele in the first place. The agency may then offer to fulfill the demand it has helped to create. Indeed, Congressmen often urge administrators to make a show of their clientele.

Senator Wherry: Do you have letters or evidence from small operators . . . that need your service that you can introduce into the record . . . . Is that not the test on how much demand there is for your services?

Ralston [Bureau of Mines]: Yes. . . . If it is important, as a rule they come to talk.

When feedback is absent or limited, Congressmen tend to assume no one cares and they need not bother with the appropriation. ". . . A dozen or more complaints do not impress me very much. . . . We cut this out last spring and we did not hear any wild howls of distress . . . ." When feedback is present it can work wonders, as happened with the Soil Conservation Service's Small Watershed program. Representative Andersen waxed enthusiastic:

. . . Will you point again to Chippewa-Shakopee? I know that project well because it is in my district. I wish the members of this subcommittee could see that Shakopee Creek watershed as it is today. The farmers in that neighborhood were very doubtful when we started that project. Now many of them tell us, Mr. Williams, that the additional crops they have obtained . . . have more than repaid their entire assessment . . . .

Guarding the treasury may be all right but it becomes uncomfortable when cuts return to haunt a Congressman. This is made clear in Representative Clevenger's tale of woe.

Clevenger: I do not want to economize on the Weather Bureau. I never did. I do want an economical administration . . . . I have been blamed for hurricane Hazel. My neighbor, who lived across the road from me for 30 years, printed in his paper that I was to blame for $500 millions in damage and 200 lives . . . . His kids grew up on my porch and yet he prints that on the first page and it is not "maybe." I just "am." He goes back to stories that related to cuts that I made when I was chairman of the Committee.

Most agencies maintain publicity offices (under a variety of titles) whose job is to inform interested parties and the general public of the good things the agency is doing, creating a favorable climate of opinion. There may be objections to this practice on the part of Congressmen who do not like an agency and/or its programs, but those who favor the agency consider it desirable. House subcommittee Chairman Kirwan urged this course on the Bureau of Indian Affairs in connection with its Alaskan Native Service, a worthy but not overly popular program. "Why don't you make some arrangement to tell the Americans every year," Kirwan suggested, "instead of telling this committee what is going on? If you write a letter when you go back to Alaska . . . I will guarantee you the press will get it." The Weather Bureau was urged to put out some publicity of its own by Representative Flood, who observed that

> . . . forecasts . . . were obviously, literally and figuratively all wet. Somebody pointed out in this [New York Times] editorial where this . . . forecast has been "a little cold, a little wet, a little snow, but not bad." . . . But something took place which . . . dumped the whole wagonload of snow on Broadway and made them very unhappy. This happened repeatedly over a period of 30 days, which did not make you look very good, if I can understate it . . . . All right. Why do you not prepare a statement for the many newspaper readers in the area and point out to them that you know the problem is there, and that this is what you want to do about it. . . .

A final example comes from a student who wrote away for a summer job and received in reply a letter from an administrator refusing him on account of budgetary limitations. "Because of our inadequate funds at this critical time," the official wrote, "many students, like yourself, who would otherwise receive the professional training that this work provides, will be deprived of that opportunity . . . . Only prompt action by Congress in increasing these funds can make the success of our mission possible."

Divided we stand. The structure of administrative units may be so arranged as to obtain greater support from clientele. It may be advantageous for a department to create more bureaus or subunits so that there are more claimants for funds who can attract support. "We have had the rather disillusioning experience that too often when we create a new agency of Government or divide up an existing agency," a Representative concluded, "that we wind up with more people on the payroll than we ever had before . . . ." There can be little doubt the division of the NIH into separate institutes for heart research, cancer research, and so on has helped mobilize more support than lumping them together under a general title with which it would be more difficult for individuals to identify.

United we fall. The Weather Bureau is an example of an agency that did rather poorly until it took the many suggestions offered by its supporters in Congress and established a separate appropriation for research and development. The new category was the glamorous one and it was easier to attract support alone; being lumped in with the others hurt its appeal. Indeed, putting projects under the same category may be a way of holding down the expenditures for some so that others will not suffer. One of the imposing difficulties faced in building up the Polaris missile program was the fear that it would deprive traditional Navy activities of resources.

Advisory committees always ask for more. Get a group of people together who are professionally interested in a subject, no matter how conservative or frugal they might otherwise be, and they are certain to find additional ways in which money could be spent. This apparently invariable law was stated by Representative Thomas when he observed that "All architects [doctors, lawyers, scientists, Indian chiefs] are for more and bigger projects, regardless of type. I have not seen one yet that did not come into that classification."

Advisors may be used to gather support for a program or agency in various ways. They may directly lobby with Congress or the President. "I happened to have lunch with Dr. Farber [a member of the quasi-governmental advisory committee of the NIH] the other day," Congressman Fogarty reveals, "and I learned there is considerable sentiment for these [clinical research] centers." Congressman Cederberg did not know of "anyone who would in any way want to hamper these programs, because I had lunch with Dr. Farber . . . ." Advisors may provide a focus of respectability and apparent disinterest to take the onus of self-seeking from the proponents of greater spending. They may work with interest groups and, indeed, may actually represent them. They may direct their attempts to the public media of information as anyone can see by reading the many columns written by Howard Rusk, M.D., a writer on medical subjects for the *New York Times*, requesting greater funds for the NIH.

Do not admit giving in to "pressure."

Civil Aeronautics Board official: . . . One of the reasons there has been such substantial expansion in local airline service, believe it or not, is largely due to the members of Congress.

Representative Flood: I hope you are talking about Hazleton, Pa.

CAB official: I am talking about Pennsylvania as well as every other state. I do not want to leave the impression here that there has been undue pressure or that we have been unduly influenced by members of Congress, but we have tried to cooperate with them.

Representative Flood: I do not care what the distinction is.

But if they press make them pay.

CAB official: . . . Senator . . . if there are any members of Congress apprehensive about the increasing level of subsidy, this has not been evident to the Board . . . . I cannot think of any local service case in which we have not had at least 15, 20, or 25 members of Congress each one urging an extension of the local service to the communities in his constituency as being needed in the public interest . . . . We felt that they, if anyone, knew what the public interest required . . . as to local service . . . with full knowledge that this would require additional subsidy.

Avoid being captured. The danger always exists that the tail will wag the dog and the agency must exercise care to avoid being captured. Rival interests and Congressmen may be played against each other. New clientele may be recruited to replace the old. The President and influential Congressmen may be persuaded to help out. Or the agency may just decide to say "no" and take the consequences. Dependence upon the support of clientele, however, implies some degree of obligation and the agency may have to make some compromises. The interests involved may also have to compromise because they are dependent upon the administrators for access to decisions, and they may have many irons in the fire with the agency so that it is not worth jeopardizing all of them by an uncompromising stand on one.

Spending and cutting moods. Unfortunately, no studies have been made about how cutting and spending moods are generated. Yet changes in the climate of opinion do have an impact on appropriations. Possibly a great many groups and individuals, working without much direct coordination but with common purpose, seize upon events like reaction to World War II controls and spending to create a climate adverse to additional appropriations, or upon a recession to create an environment favorable for greater expenditures.

Budget balancing and end-runs. It is clear that the slogan of the balanced budget has become a weapon in the political wars as well as an article of belief. This is not the place to inquire whether the idea has merit; this is the place to observe that as a belief or slogan budget balancing is one determinant of strategies.

When the idea of a balanced budget becomes imbued with political significance, the Administration may seek appropriations policies that minimize the short-run impact on the budget although total expense may be greater over a period of years. In the Dixon-Yates case a proposed TVA power plant was rejected partly because it involved large immediate capital outlays. The private power plant that was accepted involved much larger expenditures over a 25 year period, but they would have had comparatively little impact during the Eisenhower Administration's term of office.[1]

When clientele are absent or weak there are some techniques for making expenditures that either do not appear in the budget or appear much later on. The International Monetary Fund may be given a Treasury note that it can use at some future date when it needs money. Public buildings may be constructed by private organizations so that the rent paid is much lower in the short run than an initial capital expenditure. The Federal Government may guarantee local bond flotations. An agency and its supporters who fear hostile committee action may also seek out ways to avoid direct encounter with the normal budgetary process. This action is bitterly opposed, especially in the House Appropriations Committee, as back-door spending.

I do not mean to suggest that getting constituency support is all that counts. On the contrary, many agencies lay down tough criteria that projects must meet before they are accepted. The point is that there are ordinarily so many programs that can be truly judged worthwhile by the agency's standards that its major task appears to be that of gaining political support. Priorities may then be assigned on the basis

[1] See the author's *Dixon-Yates: A Study in Power Politics* (New Haven, 1962).

of the ability of the program and its sponsors to garner the necessary support.

CONFIDENCE

The sheer complexity of budgetary matters means that some people need to trust others because they can check up on them only a fraction of the time. "It is impossible for any person to understand in detail the purposes for which $70 billion are requested," Senator Thomas declared in regard to the defense budget. "The committee must take some things on faith." If we add to this the idea of budgeting by increments, where large areas of the budget are not subject to serious questions each year, committee members will treat an agency much better if they feel that its officials will not deceive them. Thus the ways in which the participants in budgeting try to solve their staggering burden of calculation constrains and guides them in their choice of means to secure budgetary ends.

Administrative officials are unanimously agreed that they must, as a bare minimum, enjoy the confidence of the appropriations committee members and their staff. "If you have the confidence of your subcommittee your life is much easier and you can do your department good; if you don't have confidence you can't accomplish much and you are always in trouble over this or that." How do agency personnel seek to establish this confidence?

Be what they think they are. Confidence is achieved by gearing one's behavior to fit in with the expectations of committee people. Essentially, the desired qualities appear to be projections of the committee members' images of themselves. Bureaucrats are expected to be masters of detail, hard-working, concise, frank, self-effacing fellows who are devoted to their work, tight with the taxpayer's money, recognize a political necessity when they see one, and keep the Congressmen

informed. Where Representative Clevenger speaks dourly of
how "fewer trips to the coffee shop . . . help make money in
most of the departments . . . ," Rooney demonstrates the
other side of the coin by speaking favorably of calling the
Census Bureau late at night and finding its employees "on the
job far later than usual closing hours." An administrator is
highly praised because "he always knows his detail and his
work. He is short, concise, and to the point. He does not waste
any words. I hope when it comes to the economy in your
laundry soap it is as great as his economy in words."

To be considered aboveboard, a fair and square shooter, a
frank man is highly desirable. After an official admitted that
an item had been so far down on the priority list that it had
not been discussed with him, Senator Cordon remarked, "All
right, I can understand that. Your frankness is refreshing." An
administrator like Val Peterson, head of the Federal Civil
Defense Agency, will take pains to stress that "There is nothing introduced here that is in the field of legerdemain at all
. . . I want . . . to throw the cards on the table. . . ."

The budget official needs to show that he is also a guardian
of the treasury: sound, responsible, not a wastrel; he needs to
be able to defend his presentations with convincing evidence
and to at least appear to be concerned with protecting the taxpayer. Like the lady who gets a "bargain" and tells her hus-
band how much she has saved, so the administrator is expected to speak of economies. Not only is there no fat in his
budget, there is almost no lean. Witness Dewey Short, a former Congressman, speaking on behalf of the Army: "We
think we are almost down to the bone. It is a modest request
. . . a meager request. . . ." Agency people soon catch on to
the economy motif: "I have already been under attack . . .
for being too tight with this money . . ." Petersen said. "I
went through it [a field hospital] very carefully myself to be
sure there were no plush items in it, nothing goldplated or
fancy."

If and when a subcommittee drops the most prevalent role and becomes converted into an outright advocate of a program, as with the Polaris missile system, the budget official is expected to shoot for the moon and he will be criticised if he emphasizes petty economies instead of pushing his projects. Democratic Subcommittee Chairman Kirwan and ranking Republican Jensen complained that the Bureau of Land Management did not ask for enough money for soil conservation. "It is only a drop in the bucket," Kirwan said, "they are afraid to come in." "This committee has pounded for the seven years I know of," Jensen responded, "trying to get them to come in with greater amounts for soil conservation and they pay no attention to it." The norm against waste may even be invoked for spending, as when Kirwan proclaimed that "It is a big waste and loss of money for the U.S. Government when only 6 million is requested for the management of fish and wildlife." In 1948 the head of the Cancer Institute was told in no uncertain terms, "The sky is the limit . . . and you come in with a little amount of $5,500,000. . . ." It is not so much what administrators do but how they meet the particular subcommittee's or chairman's expectations that counts.

Play it straight!   Everyone agrees that the most important requirement of confidence, at least in a negative sense, is to be aboveboard. As Rooney once said, "There's only two things that get me mad. One is hare-brained schemes; the other is when they don't play it straight." A lie, an attempt to blatantly cover up some misdeed, a tricky move of any kind, can lead to an irreparable loss of confidence. A typical comment by an administrator states, "It doesn't pay to try to put something over on them [committee members] because if you get caught, you might as well pack your bags and leave Washington." And the chances of getting caught (as the examples that follow illustrate) are considerable because interested committeemen and their staffs have much experience and many sources of information.

Administrators invariably mention first things that should not be done. They believe that there are more people who can harm them than can help and that punishments for failure to establish confidence are greater than the rewards for achieving it. But at times they slip up and then the roof falls in. When Congress limited the amount of funds that could be spent on personnel, a bureau apparently evaded this limitation in 1952 by subcontracting out a plan to private investors. The House Subcommittee was furious:

> Representative Jensen: It certainly is going to take a house-cleaning . . . of . . . all people who are responsible for this kind of business.
> Official: We are going to do it, Mr. Chairman.
> Representative Jensen: I do not mean "maybe." That is the most disgraceful showing that I have seen of any department.
> Official: I am awfully sorry.

If a committee feels that it has been misled, there is no end to the punitory actions it can take. Senator Hayden spoke of the time when a bureau was given a lump-sum appropriation as an experiment. "Next year . . . the committee felt outraged that certain actions had been taken, not indicated in the hearings before them. Then we proceeded to earmark the bill from one end to the other. We just tied it up in knots to show that it was the Congress, after all, that dictated policy."

Four months after a House subcommittee had recommended funds for a new prison, a supplemental appropriation request appeared for the purchase of an institution on the west coast that the Army was willing to sell. Rooney went up in smoke. "Never mentioned it at all, did you?" "Well," the Director replied, "negotiations were very nebulous at that time, Mr. Rooney." "Was that," Rooney asked, "because of the fact that this is a first-rate penal institution . . . and would accommodate almost 1,500 prisoners?" It developed that Rooney, catching sight of the proposed supplemental, had sent a man out to investigate the institution. The supplemental did not go through.

Integrity. The positive side of the confidence relationship is to develop the opinion that the agency official is a man of high integrity who can be trusted. He must not only give but must also appear to give reliable information. He must keep confidences and not get a Congressman into trouble by what he says or does. He must be willing to take blame but never credit. Like a brand name, a budget official's reputation comes to be worth a good deal in negotiation. (This is called "ivory soap value," that is, 99 and 44/100% pure.) The crucial test may come when an official chooses to act contrary to his presumed immediate interests by accepting a cutback or taking the blame in order to maintain his integrity with his appropriations subcommittee. It must not be forgotten that the budget official often has a long-term perspective and may be correct in trying to maximize his appropriations over the years rather than on every single item.

If you are believed to have integrity, then you can get by more easily.

> Rooney: Mr. Andretta [Justice Department], this is strictly a crystal ball operation; is it?
> Andretta: That is right.
> Rooney: Matter of an expert guess?
> Andretta: An expert guess. . . .
> Rooney: We have come to depend upon your guesswork and it is better than some other guesswork I have seen.

A good index of confidence is ability to secure emergency funds on short notice with skimpy hearings. No doubt Andretta's achievement was related to his frequent informal contact with Rooney.

Rooney: I am one who believes we should keep in close contact with one another so we understand one another's problems.

Andretta: I agree.

Rooney: You very often get in touch with us during the course of the year when you do not have a budget pending, to keep us acquainted with what is going on.

Andretta: Exactly. . . .

Make friends: The visit. Parallel in importance to the need for maintaining integrity is developing close personal relationships with members of the agency's appropriations subcommittee, particularly the Chairman. The most obvious way is to seek them out and get to know them. One official reports that he visited every member of his subcommittee asking merely that they call on him if they wanted assistance. Later, as relationships developed, he was able to bring up budgetary matters. Appropriations hearings reveal numerous instances of personal visitation. A few examples should suggest how these matters work: Representative Jensen: "Mr. Clawson [head of the Bureau of Land Management] came in my office the other day to visit with me. I don't know whether he came in purposely or whether he was just going by and dropped in, and he told me that he was asking for considerably more money for . . . administrative expenses and we had quite a visit. . . ." A subordinate employee of that bureau showed that he had caught the proper spirit when he told Representative Stockman, "If you would like some up-to-date information from the firing line, I shall be glad to call at your office and discuss the matter; will you like for me to do that?"

When columnist Peter Edson editorially asked why the Peace Corps did so well in appropriations compared to the difficult times had by the State Department and the Agency for International Development, he concluded that Sargeant Shriver, head of the Corps, "has tried to establish congressional confidence in him and his agency. Of the 537 members of Congress, he has called on at least 450 in their offices."

The pay-off.   Wherever possible, the administrators seek to accommodate the Congressman and impress him with their interest and friendliness. This attitude comes through in an exchange between a man in the Fish and Wildlife Service and Senator Mundt.

> Official: Last year at the hearings . . . you were quite interested in the aquarium there [the Senator's state], particularly in view of the centennial coming up in 1961.
> Mundt: That is right.
> Official: Rest assured we will try our best to have everything in order for the opening of that centennial.

The administrator recognizes and tries to avoid certain disagreeable consequences of establishing relationships with Congressmen. The Congressman who talks too much and quotes you is to be avoided. The administrator who receives a favor may get caught unable to return one the following year and may find that he is dealing with an enemy, not just a neutral.

I'd love to help you but . . . .   Where the administrator's notion of what is proper conflicts with that of a Congressman with whom it is desirable to maintain friendly relations, there is no perfect way out of the difficulty. Most officials try to turn the Congressman down by suggesting that their hands are tied, that something may be done in the future, or by stressing some other project on which they are agreed. After Representative Natcher spoke for the second time of his desire for a project in his district, Don Williams of the Soil Conservation Service complimented him for his interest in watershed activity in Kentucky but was "sorry that some of the projects that were proposed would not qualify under the . . . law . . . but . . . they are highly desirable."

The "it can't be done" line was also taken by the Weather Bureau in an altercation with Representative Yates.

> Weather Bureau official: We cannot serve the public by telephone . . . because we cannot put enough telephone lines or the operators to do the job. . . . We expect them [the public] to get it through the medium of newspapers, radio, television. If you have six telephones you have to have six people to deal with them. You have no idea. . . .
>
> Yates: Yes; I do have an idea, because I have been getting calls from them. What I want to do is have such calls transferred to you. . . . But as long as you have only one phone, I shall get the calls and you will not. . . .
>
> Weather Bureau official: We find we must do it on the basis of mass distribution.

Sometimes, action may be delayed to see if the committee member will protest. The Weather Bureau tried for a while to cut off weather reports from Savannah to the northern communities that constitute its major source of tourists despite the fact that the Bureau's House subcommittee chairman represented that city.

> Representative Preston: I wrote you gentlemen . . . a polite letter about it thinking that maybe you would [restore it] . . . and no action was taken on it. Now, Savannah may be unimportant to the Weather Bureau but it is important to me. . . .
>
> Weather Bureau official: I can almost commit ourselves to seeing to it that the Savannah weather report gets distribution in the northeastern United States.

Give and take. At other times some compromise may be sought. Secretary of Commerce Averell Harriman was faced with the unpalatable task of deciding which field offices to eliminate. He first used internal Department criteria to find the lower one-third of offices in point of usefulness. Then he decided which to drop or curtail by checking with the affected Congressmen, trying to determine the intensity of their reactions, making his own estimate of whom he could and could not afford to hurt. Harriman's solution was a nice mixture of internal and political criteria designed to meet as many goals as possible or at least to hold the Department's losses down.[2]

Truth and consequences. In the end, the administrator may just have to face the consequences of opposing Congressmen whose support he needs. Even if he were disposed to accommodate himself to their desires at times, he may find that other influential members are in disagreement. He may play them off against one another or he may find that nothing he can do will help. The best he may be able to do is to ride out the storm without compounding his difficulties by adding suspicions of his integrity to disagreements over his policies. He hopes, particularly if he is a career man, that the Congressmen will rest content to damn the deed without damning the man.

Emphasis. The administrator's perception of Congressional knowledge and motivation helps determine the kind of relationships he seeks to establish. The administrator who feels that the members of his appropriations subcommittees are not too well informed on specifics and that they evaluate the agency's program on the basis of feedback from constituents, stresses the role of supporting interests in maintaining good relations with Congressmen. He may not feel the need to be too careful with his estimates. The administrator who believes that the Congressmen are well informed and fairly autonomous is likely to stress personal relationships and demonstrations of good work as well as clientele support. Certain objective conditions may be important here. Some subcommittees deal with much smaller areas than others and their members are likely to be better informed than they otherwise would be. Practices of appointment to subcommittees differ between House and Senate and with passing time. Where

[2] Kathryn Smul Arnow, *The Department of Commerce Field Offices,* The Inter-University Case Program, ICP Case Series, No. 21, February 1954.

Congressmen are appointed who have direct and important constituency interests at stake, the information they get from back home becomes more important. If the composition of the committee changes and there are many members without substantial background in the agency's work, and if the staff does not take up the slack, the agency need not be so meticulous about the information it presents. This situation is reflected in the hearings in which much time is spent on presenting general background information and relatively little on specifics.

Subcommittee and other staff. Relationships of confidence between agency personnel and subcommittee staff are also vital and are eagerly sought after. Contacts between subcommittee staff and budget officers are often frequent, intensive, and close. Frequency of contacts runs to several times a day when hearings are in progress, once a day when the bill is before the committee, and several times a month during other seasons. This is the principal contact the committee staff has with the Executive Branch. Even when the staff seeks information directly from another official in the agency, the budget officer is generally apprised of the contact and it is channeled through him. Relationships between ordinary committee staff members and Budget Bureau personnel are infrequent, although the people involved know one another. The top-ranking staff members and the Budget Bureau liaison man, however, do get together frequently to discuss problems of coordination (such as scheduling of deficiency appropriations) and format of budget presentation. At times, the BOB uses this opportunity to sound out the senior staff on how the committee might react to changes in presentation and policy. The staff members respond without speaking for the committee in any way. There also may be extensive contact between committee staff and the staff attached to individual Congressmen, but there is not a stable pattern of consultations. House and Senate Appropriations Committee staff may check with one another; also, the staff attached to the substantive committees sometimes may go into the financial implications of new bills with appropriations staff.

When an agency has good relations with subcommittee staff it has an easier time in Congress than it might otherwise. The agency finds that more reliance is placed on its figures, more credence is given to its claims, and more opportunities are provided to secure its demands. Thus one budget officer received information that a million-dollar item had been casually dropped from a bill and was able to arrange with his source of information on the staff to have the item put back for reconsideration. On the other hand, a staff man can do great harm to an agency by expressing distrust of its competence or integrity. Asked if they would consider refusing to talk to committee staff, agency officials uniformly declared that this refusal would be tantamount to cutting their own throats.

CONGRESSIONAL COMMITTEE HEARINGS

The observer who knows that Congressmen and bureaucrats frequently engage in mutually profitable transactions during the year may make the mistake of discounting the hearings as mere ritual. In some cases it is true that the conclusions have been arrived at in advance and that the hearings serve only to create a record to convince others to support the committee's action.[3] But most of the time hearings do have an importance of their own so that what happens may have an effect on the committee's decision. Some agencies are rather wary of too close a relationship with Congressmen; their top officials may lack a gift for the personal touch; they prefer to make their

[3] It is worth noting that one of the functions that hearings may serve consists of getting administrators to make public commitments of private agreements. Once the administrator has committed himself in public, it is difficult for him to alter his position.

case in the open at the hearings. Even when personal relationships are close and continuous the pressure of time on the parties concerned may mean that prior consultation has been kept to a minimum. Not all items have previously been discussed and it may be necessary to muster support for them at the hearings. Not every Congressman on an appropriations subcommittee may have been included in personal visits and these votes may be needed when the subcommittees go into the mark-up session. Confidence may rapidly be dissipated by a poor performance. No one wants to trust incompetents.

The rehearsal. For all these reasons, administrators are aware that an effective presentation at hearings can help an agency whereas a poor one can nullify its efforts. It has become standard practice to hold mock hearings in which administrators can take turns in playing the roles of leading Congressmen. Based on past experience, tough questions are asked and answers prepared. "You'd be surprised," a budget officer commented, "how often we discover that something we thought was perfectly defensible turns out to lack a convincing rationale."

Avoid surprise. One of the basic rules of thumb arising out of hard experience is to avoid being surprised. A diligent search of hearings, a review of the agency's programs, are all useful. But there is nothing like some inside information on what is likely to come up.

The office of a budget official turns into a complex communication center in which the phone is always ringing and a constant flow of information is coming in and being sent out. Calls are received from the Executive Office, other agencies, Congressmen, interest groups, appropriations committee staff, the agency head, and many others. The budget official particularly conceives it to be his task to be a trouble shooter and head off difficult situations. This function requires him to keep informed and to inform others of what is going on, so he is continually engaged in coordination.

The plant.   What are the sources of the questions asked at committee appropriations hearings? The truly expert and hard-working subcommittee chairman who knows his subject may frame all his own questions without assistance from anyone. Men who know less or who find they cannot be fully informed may receive aid from committee staff, agency personnel, interest groups, experts, or other Congressmen. At one extreme there is the agency official who has strong personal connections with the committee member and may submit an entire list of questions and have all of them used. The men with seniority who do most of the questioning like to look alert and supplying them with perceptive but not dangerous questions is one way of satisfying this need. One official reported some embarrassment when he not only answered the first question he had planted but, inadvertently, the next one as well. On other occasions the agency may suggest just a few key questions or at least be informed by a friendly Congressman that it had better be prepared to answer some difficult ones.

The interchange between agency personnel and committee staff is often subtle. During the year, the staff and some Congressmen may ask questions about agency operations. If the question has an answer that will put the agency in a favorable light, the official may suggest that the hearings would be a good time to deal with it. If the answer might be difficult or damaging, the agency official may try to head it off by delay or partial answer or diversion of attention. Moreover, there are countless conversations during the year in which the budget officer may drop a hint as to a question, or the staff member may act so as to suggest that a certain question is likely to be asked. The staff member knows about planted questions, though he may not care much if they are useful. He is likely to take hints much more readily from officials in whom he has confidence.

The portrait. Hearings present an excellent opportunity for an agency to paint a self-portrait that not only reflects credit upon it but also helps create a favorable mood. The Bureau of Prisons, for example, portrays itself as a guardian of the country, protecting the populace against vicious criminals, doing a splendid job in spite of financial difficulties. Increases in the budget are always due to forces the Bureau cannot control, such as increasing prison population, and these increases are always necessary. Its personnel are dedicated career administrators who are selflessly serving the public without being overly concerned for material rewards and without ever receiving due recognition. The NIH and various science agencies, to choose another instance, play on the "dedicated-man-of-science" theme. Sincere, warm, devoted to suffering humanity, professional from head to toe, they work their wonders in ways mysterious to behold. Who would expect men who devote their careers to saving lives to know about material things like budgets? This portrait may be used to ward off deep probing as when a top official referred to "budget and fiscal considerations about which I am certainly not qualified to comment."

Know your budget. There is no substitute for knowing what you are talking about. The administrator who can answer questions, who can explain his agency's operations, is likely to have a much easier time. Department heads vary enormously in their interest in and knowledge of their budgets and this shows up at hearings if nowhere else.

Though they provide plenty of detail to back up their presentations, most budget officials find it advisable to make their presentations brief and to the point. Otherwise, busy Congressmen may lose patience and all the detailed work that goes

into justifications may be wasted. At the same time, it is inadvisable to give the Congressmen the impression that important items are being slighted. When in doubt, top officials
may ask Congressmen and staff for advice about which witnesses are likely to prove effective, how long the statements
should be, whether or not charts would be helpful, points of
special salience to individual members, and so on. When the
presentation has been done well, an administrator like Chairman Herzog of the National Labor Relations Board may receive a compliment. ". . . You rank very high . . . in . . .
being able to inform the committee of the operations of your
agency. . . . Unfortunately, all agency heads are not in that
position."

The kind of repartee that delights an administrator occurs
when his preparation pays off. When Representative Rooney
comments, "You always tell such a convincing story when you
come up here on the Hill that you always have enough fat to
absorb pretty nearly everything," Chief Administrator James
Bennett parries with a modest rejoinder: "You do me too
much credit." Rooney feels good when he can show that some
of his lower estimates of costs were more accurate than Bennett's. But there are times when Bennett puts up such an air-
tight case that Rooney can only say, "We are stymied. What
can we do with this to prevent giving you any of the taxpayer's
money?" "You cannot do very much, Congressman," Bennett
replies with evident satisfaction.

Play the game. The Bureau of the Budget, under Presidential direction, lays down the rule that members of the Executive Branch are not to challenge the Executive Budget. But
everyone knows that the administrative officials want more for
their agencies and are sometimes in a position to get it in
league with supporting Congressmen. The result on these occasions is a formalized game, which any reader of appropriations hearings will recognize. The agency official is asked

whether or not he supports the amounts in the President's Budget and he says "yes" in such a way that it sounds like yes but that everyone present knows that it means "no." His manner may communicate a marked lack of enthusiasm or he may be just too enthusiastic to be true. A committee member will then inquire as to how much the agency originally requested from the Budget Bureau. There follows an apparent refusal to answer in the form of a protestation of loyalty to the Chief Executive. Under duress, however, and amidst reminders of Congressional prerogatives, the agency man cites the figures. Could he usefully spend the money, he is asked. Of course, he could. The presumption that the agency would not have asked for more money if it did not need it is made explicit. Then comes another defense of the Administration's position by the agency, which, however, puts up feeble opposition to Congressional demands for increases.

When the game is played according to the rules, the administrator has a proper rejoinder available. Senator Ellender asked Admiral Burke how the House committee ever got the idea that the Navy wanted nine Polaris submarines when the Budget Bureau allowed only two. "Did you ever give [that number] to them?" The Admiral replied, "No, sir; however, let me amplify that. This number was brought out under specific questioning by the Defense Subcommittee of the House. We had recommended to the Secretary of Defense that there be nine."

The psychology of hearings is important. Some departmental budget officers believe that they can tell when a bureau man has "sold his goods" to a Congressman before the hearings and is merely responding to questions that have been set up before. If a man is too spontaneous, answers too readily, this reaction may give him away. When there is reason to believe that this is going on, the Department head may threaten and (more rarely) take disciplinary action. Word will go out warning others not to sell their goods on the Hill. At other times this technique works in reverse and word goes out that a bureau need not fight increases too hard.

It is often difficult to tell whether the game is played by pre-arrangement or not. Congressmen know all about it and often do not have to be prompted to ask the questions that the game calls for if they favor a particular program. Interest groups may spur a Congressman on to this kind of behavior. Demonstrating a violation of the Presidential directive may not be easy and it is difficult to decide when an offense gets so bad as to fire someone. The game is sufficiently widespread that if all suspected violators over a period of years were punished, there would be few top agency officials left.

RESULTS

Confidence rests to some extent on showing the Budget Bureau and Congress that the programs are worthwhile because they lead to useful results. The word "results" in this context has at least two meanings, which must be disentangled. In one sense it means that some people feel they are being served. In a second sense it means that the activity accomplishes its intended purposes. This sense of "result" itself involves a basic distinction. There are programs that involve a product or a service that is concrete, such as an airplane, and others that involve activities that resist measurement, such as propaganda abroad. The demonstration of results differs in both cases, as do the strategies employed.

Serve an appreciative clientele.   The best kind of result is one that provides services to a large and strategically placed clientele, which brings its satisfaction to the attention of decision makers. (The clientele may be producers of services, as in the case of defense contractors.) The kinds of strategies involved have been discussed under "clientele," and we shall go on to others in which the second sense of "result" is implicated.

It works: the problem of criteria. Outside of overwhelming public support, there is nothing that demonstrates results better than tangible accomplishment. The Polaris does fire and hit a target with reasonable accuracy; a nuclear submarine actually operates; a range-reseeding project makes the grass grow again. Interpretation of accomplishments as being worthwhile depends on finding criteria and on how tough these criteria are permitted to be. The Nike-Zeus missile may be fine if it is only supposed to knock down a few missiles or half of an enemy's missiles; it may be utterly inadequate if the criterion is raised to all missiles or most missiles or is changed to include avoidance of decoys. There is great temptation to devise a criterion that will enable a project's supporters to say that it works. At the same time, opponents of a project may unfairly propose criteria that cannot be met. And there are times when men reasonably disagree over criteria because no one knows what will happen. We hope and pray to avoid nuclear war. But if it comes, what criteria should a civil defense program have to meet? If one argues that it must save everyone, then no program can show results. Suppose, however, that one is willing to accept much less—say half or a third or a fifth of the population. Then everything depends on estimates which can surely be improved upon but which nobody can really claim to be reliable as to likely levels of attack, patterns of wind and radiation, and a multitude of other factors.

The invitation. Most governmental activity is conducted outside Washington and may seem somewhat remote to the Congressman or Budget Bureau official in the nation's capital. An impression of need, activity, heroic efforts by an overworked staff, may be much easier to substantiate on the spot than it would be through words on paper. A basic strategy, therefore, is to invite officials who pass on the budget to visit the agency and observe its work at first hand. The common belief is that the more these officials know, the more friendly they tend to be. True, it may work the other way and enable them to see some "soft spots" they might otherwise have missed, but the risk is usually thought to be worth taking.

When the "come up and see my installation" approach works well it can bring splendid results, as we can see from these comments:

> Representative Jensen: I can see the need up in Alaska for more help in the General Land Office. That is one place where I am going to be very liberal. . . . I was up there and saw with my own eyes what a big job it was.

> Senator Thye: I was out at the University of Minnesota last year during the time we were considering the appropriations, and they showed me a terrifically crowded laboratory. . . . That is one reason why I felt that we had to increase some of this research money, because I saw it with my own eyes.

But visits must be handled carefully lest they have unanticipated consequences.

Sometimes Congressmen must be "educated" so that they see things in the right way from the agency viewpoint. A Congressman may sweep through an office and draw negative conclusions because it is mostly empty, not realizing that the employees are legitimately out in the field. Despite all precautions, a favorable observation may have unfortunate implications for the agency concerned, as when Representative Laird was so impressed with the spirit shown by scientists at the University of Wisconsin that he inquired and was told that working together in a small group helped promote this wonderful spirit. "It seemed to me," Laird reported to his colleagues on the NIH subcommittee, "that maybe some of this spirit is destroyed if you put too much emphasis on large research installations . . ." like those sponsored by NIH. Sudden visits may show the agency at a disadvantage. Representative Engle said that his trip to the Air Transport Command had not been impressive. "You saw it, I am afraid, at a bad time," a General volunteered. Only ". . . in the sense that they did not know we were coming," Engle replied. There is also such a thing as overdoing it so that legislators, particularly on defense committees where junketing has reached epidemic proportions, complain that "there were so many public relations men running around to see what they could do for me that I was embarrassed."

Simplify or make complex. The difficulties in understanding budgetary subject matter, a major problem of calculation, creates strategic problems for budget officials. Items on which Budget Bureau people and especially Congressmen feel expert are much more difficult to justify than those which are technical and complex. One can see this problem in military construction, where Congressmen feel knowledgeable, as compared to complicated missile and observation systems. From the strategic point of view, the agency can adopt one of two general lines. If it feels that the Congressmen are likely to be sympathetic it may make special efforts to simplify presentations in order to enlist their informed support. If it feels that interested Congressmen would not appreciate the program, the agency may present the matter in its full complexity. The risk here is that Congressmen may be disposed to slash what they do not understand.

Avoid too good results. The danger of claiming superb accomplishments is that Congress and the Budget Bureau may reward the agency by ending the program. "Why would you need five more people in the supervisory unit?" John Rooney inquired of the Justice Department. "Since you are doing so well, as we have heard for fifteen minutes, you surely do not need any more supervision." However good it may be said that results are, it is advisable to put equal stress on what remains to be done. "Progress has been realized in the past," the Civil Defense agency asserted, "but we cannot permit these past accomplishments to lull us into a false sense of security."

Now we turn to strategies pursued by agencies that do not produce tangible items that are easy to measure.

Our program is priceless. If it is true that "In the final analysis the only thing in the world that can save the American people . . . is civil defense," then the conclusions drawn by Civil Defense Administrator Petersen—"Congress . . . should not exercise undue frugality"—would appear to be a huge understatement even if the agency could show little in the way of results. To agree with Dr. Sidney Farber—"one cannot put a dollar value on medical research if it pertains directly to the saving of human lives . . ."—is to say that there should be no monetary limits on medical research whatsoever regardless of the "state of the art" or other claims on the treasury.

It can't be measured. The USIA lacks confidence partly because it is particularly vulnerable to a line of attack based on the lack of results. "I have been on this committee now for twenty years," Senator Ellender told the agency, "and I have not seen any results from the money we have expended." A USIA official could only say that ". . . It would be very good to have a fine and exact measure of total results. We just don't have it. We will never get it. . . ." When an affluent agency that has confidence runs into this kind of difficulty the approach is quite different. "I wish," Representative Fogarty said, "that you would supply the committee with a list of things that the National Institutes of Health have accomplished . . . because we are being continually reminded that we are appropriating a lot of money for research and nothing ever comes of it." The best response is a scientific breakthrough, when a disease is brought under control.

Tomorrow and tomorrow. If there are no results today, they can always be promised for some remote future.

Representative Kirwan: Can you give us a few recent results of your research?

Bureau of Mines: [Reads a prepared statement.]

Representative Kirwan: . . . that is something that you are going to undertake, is it not?

Bureau of Mines: It is something that is under way.

Representative Kirwan: But there are no results. . . .

Bureau of Mines: That is correct. There have been no immediate results by industry at the present time but as the program proceeds, new findings are made continually which will lead to further research on the subject.

Representative Kirwan: . . . Were there any results. . . ?

This program's estimate was cut by $150,000 by the committee.

Statistics. Research of all kinds is a complicated subject because the results are difficult to measure and there is always hope that something good will turn up. Since significant results are not easily demonstrable, the advocates of a research program may resort to presenting a procession of figures that may or may not have any relevance. Take a look at a doctor's testimony:

To mention just a few of the research contributions . . . merely as being indicative of progress. There have been . . . 2,800 compounds tested which have some tumor-damaging properties. Four hundred of these have proved to be very interesting and, narrowing these down, twelve of them have been found to have very, very interesting possibilities in the future treatment of cancer.

Is this research valuable? No one can tell from this presentation.

Stretching things. Should results directly germane to the agency's program not be forthcoming, it is always possible to stretch things a little. A claim like the one by the Weather Bureau that follows is not only difficult to prove; it is virtually impossible to disprove.

Representative Rooney: [Do you take] editorial credit for the sentence near the top of page two: "Guidance to motorists regarding the use of antifreeze is estimated to be worth $50 million per year"? . . . How do you arrive at that figure?

Weather Bureau Official: Total value of motor vehicles is of the order of billions. . . . Some $3 billion is the estimated value of all automotive equipment in the United States. . . . It does not take a very high percentage of motor blocks in terms of the millions of motor vehicles that are to be protected, to roll up a total of $50 million a year preventable loss. That figure has been very carefully arrived at.

Avoid extreme claims that can be tested. There are times when a desire to show direct results boomerangs because of the very absurdity of the claim. Such is the unhappy tale of the State Department official who refused to admit that a Chinese language program would necessarily have a deferred pay off in view of the fact that we had no formal diplomatic relations with Communist China and the number of men we could send to Formosa was limited.

Representative Rooney: I find a gentleman here, an FSO-6. He got an A in Chinese and you assigned him to London.

Mr. X: Yes, sir. That officer will have opportunities in London—not as many as he would have in Hong Kong, for example—

Representative Rooney: What will he do? Spend his time in Chinatown?

Mr. X: No, sir. There will be opportunities in dealing with officers in the British Foreign Office who are concerned with Far Eastern affairs. . . .

Representative Rooney: So instead of speaking English to one another, they will sit in the London office and talk Chinese?

Mr. X: Yes, sir.

Representative Rooney: Is that not fantastic?

Mr. X: No, sir. They are anxious to keep up their practice. . . .

Representative Rooney: They go out to Chinese restaurants and have chop suey together?

Mr. X: Yes, sir.

Representative Rooney: And that is all at the expense of the American taxpayer?

Procedures, not predictions. As a result of the daily requirement that the Weather Bureau "stick its neck out" in its forecasts, and the frequent public humiliation of wrong predictions and consequent ridicule, the Bureau is reluctant to engage in any activity for which it can be called to strict account by an input-output formula. The best kind of activity from the Bureau's point of view is one that involves the passive, repetitive measurement or collection of some sort of meteorological data, which is then filed, analyzed, and tested —but from which no prediction need be issued. Funds are sought on the basis of the procedures involving the analysis of weather.

Weather Bureau official: This observer is extremely busy . . . He has certain scheduled observational functions he must perform. . . . Those have to go on the teletype circuit on the hour every hour. Then he has another scheduled report that has to go in between 15 and 20 minutes after the hour, and another between 35 and 40 minutes after the hour. During the rest of the hour he is busy posting the weather charts for pilots to look at and he is busy taking teletype reports that come in from roughly 250 stations in the area and posting those on clipboards. Some stations have 10 or 12 clipboards. Every 20 minutes or so he has . . ."

Representative Flood: He had better not have any trouble with his personal plumbing. What does this fellow do?

Weather Bureau official: He has to wait.

Faith. The foreign aid operation has a hard time showing results. Part of the difficulty lies in the presence of so many other variables—the strength of local subversive movements, the resources of the recipient nation, the cultural habits of a people—that it is difficult to single out any one factor as making a special contribution. But this difficulty is minor compared to that of measuring results when you are not clear about your goals. Is the program supposed to keep nations free, make them beholden to us, keep communists out, raise living standards even if it increases communist strength? If we adopt the goal of keeping a country out of communist hands, we have no theory to guide us in accomplishing this purpose. The basic idea behind foreign aid is that economic development will do the trick. Conceivably, an investment of $200 million would keep a nation outside this bloc, $400 million would bring it closer, $600 million even closer, $800 million would bring it back, and so on. And if any of these eventualities occur we cannot now be certain of the part played by foreign aid.

STRATEGIES DESIGNED TO CAPITALIZE
ON THE FRAGMENTATION OF POWER IN NATIONAL POLITICS

The separation of powers and the internal divisions of labor within Congress and the Executive Branch present numerous opportunities to play one center of power off against another.

Compensation. Supporters of a program who have superior access to one house of Congress may seek to raise the program's grant to allow for bargaining with the other branch. If they can get their way or arrange to split the difference in the Conference Committee, they are that much ahead. A Congressman may ask the agency for the lowest addition that would make a project possible so he will know how far he can go in Conference. Thus Senator McCarran told the Census Bureau that he "just wanted to see . . . how much we could lose in the conference, and still give you some assistance to be of value." Frequently, appeals are taken to the Senate in the hope of securing an increase. This procedure works both ways, however, and an agency that expects hostility in the

Senate may get its friends to prepare questions and answers in the House hearings and floor debates in anticipation of trouble with the other chamber.

Cross fire. Although the presence of differing interests and degrees of confidence in the House and Senate may provide the agency with room to maneuver, it may also subject it to a withering cross fire from which there is no immediate escape. In the controversy over grazing fees on public lands the House was for increases and the Senate was opposed. Representative Tarver asked the Forest Service whether anything could be done to expedite a study of the fee situation and the following exchange ensued:

> Forest Service official: I guess you really ought to try to get the Senate to go along with you. The Senate told us not to and you told us to do it; so that we are between two fires.
>
> Representative Tarver: I was wondering whether there was some place in this appropriation where we would make a substantial cut for the purpose of impressing upon you the desirability of making this study.

Both ends against the middle. The separation between appropriations and substantive committees creates another opportunity to exploit differences between dual authorities. Appropriations committees often refuse funds for projects authorized by substantive committees. And substantive committees, with or without agency backing, sometimes seek to exert influence over appropriations committees. A familiar tactic is the calling of hearings by substantive committees to dramatize the contention that an authorized program is being underfinanced or not financed at all. Knowing that the appropriations committees have the final say, the substantive committees can afford to authorize any project they deem good without too much concern for its financial implications. Appropriations committees sometimes seek to write legislation into appropriations bills; this effort may lead to a conflict with the substantive committee that spills over onto the floor of the houses of Congress. Participants believe that there is now greater awareness, particularly on the part of staff members, of the need to maintain contact between the two kinds of committees in regard to the financial implications of legislation and the legislative implications of appropriations.

Agencies stand to gain by exploiting these conflicts to their own advantage. They try to use an authorization as a club over the head of the appropriations committees by pointing to a substantive committee as a source of commitment to ask for funds. In seeking an increase for fishery research, the Fish and Wildlife Service declared that it "came about through direction of a Congressional Committee. . . . The [substantive] committee directed that hereafter the department should include this item for their appropriations." This strategy does not create much difficulty in the Senate, where some members of the substantive committees are likely to sit on the Appropriations Committee. But the House members do not like it at all—though a member may from time to time brag about how he got through a pet appropriation without a real authorization—and they are quick to remind administrators of their prerogatives.

> State Department official: I believe the legislation includes a specific amount of $8,000.
> Representative Rooney: We would not be discussing this at all if the legislation did not permit such a thing as entertainment, but never lose sight of the fact that the Appropriations Committees are the saucers that cool the legislative tea. Just because you have an authorization does not mean a thing to us. . . .
> State Department official: I understand, sir.

The conference committee adds another level of decision to an already fragmented power structure in Congress. Perhaps the most common device is to aim at resolution in Conference Committee by pushing an appropriations measure up in one of the houses of Congress. An item may be put in an appropriations measure for the sole purpose of providing the conferees with something to give in the bargaining sessions. A project may deliberately be given a low appropriation in one chamber so that its supporters on the Conference Committee will have to give something else.

The commitment. The Conference Committee is an ideal place in which to use the commitment strategy, whereby one side paradoxically increases its bargaining power by depriving itself of the ability to act.[4] A chamber may take an adamant position, thus giving notice that it will not back down so that the conferees from the other chamber will have to give in if Government activity is to continue. House conferees, for example, have been known to seek votes from their chamber in support of a motion insisting that they not give in. To get around this obstacle, no attempt may be made to secure an appropriation in the House where, once voted down, it could not be offered in conference. Instead, the appropriation is brought up in the Senate, where its chance of passage and inclusion in the Conference Committe bill are much better. It is difficult to overturn a Conference Committee decision.

CONTINGENCY AND CALCULATION

Because budgets are calculated incrementally from a base representing a widespread notion of fair shares, attention is focused on significant departures from what has gone before. "Naturally," says a Representative, "we are concerned about a project which shows an increase of 200 percent in cost to the Government and it is going to be very important that we have a full and detailed statement of the program." In the absence of attention-directing signals—a substantial increase or decrease in a going program or a new venture—the expecta-

[4] See T. C. Schelling, *The Strategy of Conflict* (Cambridge, Mass., 1960).

tion is that the base will remain undisturbed. Congressmen who specialize in appropriations lose no status if they continue the program base of an agency; they can serve as guardians of the public purse by resisting new programs or they can appear to play this role by admitting new ones in the guise of the old. In budgeting, as in other aspects of social life, appearances are tremendously important.

Under the historical frame of reference created by the incremental, base, fair-share types of calculation, agency officials are faced with a series of related problems. How can they keep their base intact so as to have an advantageous starting point next time around? How can they increase their appropriations income without giving the appearance of increasing them drastically? How can they make new programs look like old ones? How can they secure funds for new programs that are presented as just what they are? Another way of putting it is to ask how they can do what they believe is required in the public interest as they define it within the context of the budgetary system?

The answer to all these questions appears to be: by following strategies that take into account fundamental facts about human perception. It is not an event but its interpretation in comparison to other events that counts. Strategies involving calculations, therefore, revolve around the crucial question of what kind of frame of reference, inviting what kind of comparisons, will be used.

DEFENDING THE BASE:
GUARDING AGAINST CUTS IN THE OLD PROGRAMS

Cut the popular program. No one should assume that most agencies engage in perpetual feasting. There is always the specter of cuts. A major strategy in resisting cuts is to make them in such a way that they have to be put back.

Rather than cut the national office's administrative expenses, for instance, an agency might cut down on the handling of applications from citizens with full realization that the ensuing discontent would be bound to get back to Congressmen, who would have to restore the funds. When the National Institutes of Health wanted to get funds for a new, struggling institute such as one devoted to dental research, it would cut one or all of the popular institutes. The committee would be upset that heart, cancer, or mental health had been cut and would replace the funds. The same strategy was used in transferring funds from the popular research to the unpopular operating expenses category.

Cut the less-visible items.   Counter-strategies are available to legislators. Many Congressmen feel a need to cut an agency's requests somewhere. Yet the same Congressman may be sympathetic to the agency's program or feel obliged to support it because people in his constituency are thought to want it. Where, then, can the cuts be made? In those places which do not appear to directly involve program activities. The department office or general administrative expenses, for example, may be cut without appearing to affect any specific desirable program. And this fits in well with a general suspicion current in society that the bureaucrats are wasteful. Housekeeping activities may also suffer since it often appears that they can be put off for another year and they do not seem directly connected with programs. The result may be that deferred maintenance may turn out to be much more expensive in the end. But cutting here enables the Congressman to meet conflicting pressures for the time being.

Promotional activities, non-tangible items, are also difficult to support. Unless the appropriations committee members trust the agency officials more than it ordinarily happens, they will inevitably be suspicious of items that resist measurement and concrete demonstration of accomplishment. Here, again, is a place to cut where the bureaucracy can be chastised and where powerful interest group support is likely to be lacking.

All or nothing.   The tactic is to assert that if a cut is made the entire program will have to be scrapped. "Reducing the fund to $50,000 would reduce it too much for us to carry forward the work. We have to request the restoration . . ." said the Bureau of Mines. The danger is that Congress may take the hint and cut out the whole program. So this strategy must be employed with care in connection with a program that is most unlikely to be abolished.

Squeezed to the wall.   "It so happens," the Fish and Wild-life Service told the Senate Committee, that our budget is so tight that we have no provision at all for any leeway in this amount. This will simply result in a lower level of production at our fish hatcheries."

Alter the form.   We have seen that appearance counts for a great deal and that a program viewed and calculated in one light may be more attractive than when viewed in another. The form of the budget, therefore, may become crucial in determining the budgetary outcomes. Suppose that an agency has strong clientele backing for individual projects. It is likely to gain by presenting them separately so that any cut may be readily identified and support may be easily mobilized. Lumping a large number of items together may facilitate cuts on an across-the-board basis. Items lacking support, on the other hand, may do better by being placed in large categories. A program budget may help raise appropriations by focusing attention on favored aspects of an agency's activities while burying others. The opposite result is also possible and an agency may object to presenting its budget in categories that do not show it off to best advantage.

Shift the blame. A widespread strategy is to get the other party to make the difficult decisions of cutting down on requests, thus shifting the onus for the cuts. If he has to take the blame he may not be willing to make the cut. In many bureaus it is the practice to submit initial requests to the agency head or budget officer that are considerably above expectations for support either in the Executive Branch or Congress. By including many good projects the bureau hopes to compel the department head to make the difficult choice of which ones are to be excluded. As a counter-strategy, the agency head may set down a ceiling and insist that the subdivision decide which of its desired projects are to be included. Both the agency head and the subdivision may be restrained, however, by their desire not to come in so high or so low that they risk loss of confidence by others.

Everyone knows that many agencies raise their budgetary requests (among other reasons) in order to show their supporting interests that they are working hard but are being thwarted by the Administration. So the Budget Bureau is disposed to cut. The most frustrating aspect of this activity is that when an agency's budget is squeezed it is often not the "wasteful" things that come out; priorities within the agency and Congress vary greatly and the legendary obsolete munitions factory may survive long after more essential activities have disappeared. Thus the Budget Bureau may be caught between its desire to make the agency responsible for cuts and the need to insist that they be made in certain places rather than others.

After reviewing their program, agency officials often find that they have many programs in which they believe and which cost more than they think the Budget Bureau will allow. Rather than choose the priorities themselves, the officials may try to get the Bureau to do the paring on the very best items. In this way they maintain their reputation for submitting only first-class programs and let the Budget Bureau take the blame for denying some of them. When clientele groups complain, the agency can always say that it tried but the Budget Bureau turned it down.

The ceiling. This is the context in which setting a ceiling becomes highly attractive for the Budget Bureau. The agency is thereby compelled to establish priorities at the top and when complaints are made the Director can say that the agency chose certain projects in preference to others. In order to prevent an agency from excluding vital items that everyone knows Congress will support, instructions may be given to specifically include key items in the agency's budget.

We love them all. One device that Congressmen use is to get the agencies to set priorities among programs. Should anyone protest a cut later on, the legislator would be able to say that he was not to blame; the agency had a choice and made it. Agencies are reluctant to set priorities and counter with a strategy of their own. Representative Stefan wondered what Director Capt of the Census Bureau would do if he were a Congressman and had to consider the poor taxpayer. "What is your opinion of the most vital item among these ten items?" The administrator gallantly replied that "It is something like asking a parent which one of his five children he would hate most to give up."

It may not be so much a question of preference as of the relationships among things; such is another standard reply to a call for priorities. "In view of the inter-relationships of the three activities—mail-rate cases, route cases, and field audits—it would be extremely difficult to determine which one . . . should be accorded the highest priority . . ." a Civil Aeronautics Board witness said.

You choose. An agency may try to turn the tables by enticing a Congressman into choosing priorities so that he becomes committed to what has become his own choice. James Bennett of the Bureau of Prisons put the choice squarely up to his committee: "A question arises—which I think you are as well able to answer as I—as to whether it would be wise to put the $3.5 million . . . into reconstruction of Alcatraz, or whether to take the money and add a little more to it and locate the institution a little more centrally." Another time, when Bennett talked about a project in a what-do-you-think manner, Representative Rooney called him up on it: "Mr. Bennett, you have now repeated a couple of times certain language, from which I deduce you are trying to pass the ball to us."

They made me. Congressmen have developed strategies of their own for making cuts without taking full responsibility. Just as budget officials say that circumstances have compelled them to ask for increases, so do Congressmen assert that outside forces—a climate of opinion against spending, the strong views of influential colleagues, attempts by the other party to make spending an issue, the overriding need to balance the budget—leave them with little choice. Representative Mahon spoke in this vein about the Army's construction activities: "Day before yesterday one of the most influential members of the House of Representatives stopped me in the corridor and asked me how the hearings were progressing. He is a great friend of the military forces and the cause of national defense. He said to me, George, heretofore I have stayed with you on military appropriations, but this year I am going to vote to cut, and to cut deep, because the military people are wasting so much money." Senator Johnson told the Bureau of Prisons, "We are going to be accused of being spenders here if we are not careful. . . . Now, Mr. Bennett, I wonder if you would not give consideration to our postponing the new power-plant." The plant was postponed. The USIA was told that "The general feeling among the Senators that I have talked to is that they want to keep the budget not in excess of what you had last year . . . and they want to cut it if they can." A favorite tactic is hiding behind the Budget Bureau, as when Representative Sikes told the Bureau of Prisons, "Historically, the administration has generally refused to allow money to be spent that the Bureau of the Budget did not request. We are in a box, too, when it comes to meeting these problems."

When cuts mean increases.   There are times when an agency wishes to cut its own budget because it has lost faith in a program, for internal disciplinary reasons, or because it would like to use the money elsewhere. If the agency is particularly well endowed with effective clientele groups, however, it may not only fail in this purpose but may actually see the appropriation increased as this threat mobilizes the affected interests. One budget officer tried to convince the Budget Bureau to continue two projects which the agency did not want but which several influential Congressmen felt strongly about. Otherwise, the official argued, the Congressmen would secure their desires by offering additional projects to their colleagues. The Budget Bureau turned him down and the result was nine projects instead of two.

As a result of unhappy experiences in attempting to cut their own budgets, agencies may mobilize for this purpose in the same way that they do to get substantial increases. They may assemble a task force of program administrators, Congressional liaison men, executive office personnel, sympathetic interests, and others to explain the logic of their position and head off stiff resistance.

INCREASING THE BASE:
INCHING AHEAD WITH EXISTING PROGRAMS

Old stuff.   Since appropriations for new programs are particularly difficult to obtain, agencies are motivated to claim that what they want to do is just what they have been doing. The funds requested are said to be part of the agency's base, its continuing program, rather than some new way to spend money. "Our programs have grown a lot," an official confided, "but we have never begun anything we described as fundamentally new in the twenty years I have been here."[5]

Don't stand pat. Although agencies may at times find it advantageous to follow a strategy of asking or appearing to ask for what they received the previous year, they may run into difficulty if they forget to vary it a little so as to show that they are thinking. "You are not asking any change," a Congressman comments in defense hearings, "that always makes me suspicious." In a revealing statement, Representative Michael Kirwan, a power in the resource field, gave some homely advice to the Bureau of Mines when it came up with identical requests two years in a row. "It would look better," the experienced Congressman said, "if you just juggled around the numbers, for example, from 7 to 3 . . . so it will not look stereotyped."

The advantages of rounding. The rules for rounding off figures are not universally agreed upon, presenting opportunities for gaining a little. A neat case was found by John Rooney:

> Representative Rooney: . . . You suggest an increase in limitation to $1.8 million for administrative expenses. You actually need, you say, but $1,782,900. You have delightfully rounded this out so as to increase the amount of the limitation by $17,100. Did you know that this was done?

[5] In his book, *On Thermonuclear War* (Princeton, 1960) p. 339, Hermann Kahn describes the strategic situation: ". . . It is always easier to 'sell' something that can be presented as carrying out an existing program, or (a last resort) as a necessary modification of such a program. Barring a crisis or an exceptionally 'glamorous' idea, it is usually risky to phrase the recommendation as an expansion of an existing program and disastrous to let it look like the initiation of a new program."

State Department official: That it was rounded out?
. . . No, sir; I did not notice that figure.

Like most others, this game can be played in two ways and we find a house subcommittee proposing to round off a large sum for the military to $68 million, a reduction of some $155,000.

The transfer.   One way of moving ahead while appearing to stand still is to keep appropriations for particular categories constant so that no change seems to be made although various expenditures of the past are no longer being made and have been replaced with others. Items may be transferred from one category to another so that no particular one stands out as being too far out of line. Transfer may be made between agencies to effect the same purpose. Representative Rooney saw this tactic when he said, "The taxpayer cannot win with this kind of business. You are going to have the $50,000 covered in the Department of Commerce budget and now use the $50,000 that was in this budget for other purposes." If a committee or the Budget Bureau is concerned over increases in administrative expenses, ways may be found of transferring these expenditures to other items by including them as part of less suspect costs. Some agencies include administrative expenses under each program instead of under the administrative category.

Congressmen realize how dependent they are on a historical and comparative approach to budgeting and try to keep the categories constant from one year to the next so they will know what they are doing. Their dependence on consistency helps account for the insistence of appropriations committee members that budgetary forms not be changed too often.

The numbers game.   There are other ways of increasing income without making it obvious. Rather than pay attention to total appropriations, an agency may try to establish a right to a specific number of categories of appropriations and then increase the content while keeping the number constant. The NIH has done so by increasing the size of research grants and complaining that the total number—its preferred comparison —has gone down.

Herman Kahn has noted that for many years it was widely believed that the Air Force was entitled to a set number of wings. Costs soared as the planes had to meet higher standards of performance and as the Air Force used many more planes per wing. Given a choice between renovating 100 units of old equipment or keeping the old and buying 50 new ones, the former might be more expensive but it would be much preferred because the latter would look like an increase in the size of the force.[6] In the American belief system a high value is put on repair and making do; it seems so much more thrifty than buying something new. In response to this type of situation an agency may deliberately engage in irrational behavior, like spending more for maintenance than it would cost to buy a new item, in order to secure at least some of its budgetary requests. Kahn reports that:

> One of the most amusing and brazen examples of disguised procurement occurred in the early days of the Republic. It seemed that Congress was unwilling to retire old naval ships and replace them with new ones, so the Navy disguised its replacement program as a repair and maintenance program. They took old ships, tied them up at the docks and let them deteriorate. The money was saved, and as soon as it amounted to enough a new ship was bought and given the same name as the old ship.[7]

EXPANDING THE BASE: ADDING NEW PROGRAMS

The wedge or the camel's nose. A large program may be begun by an apparently insignificant sum. The agency then claims that (1) this has become part of its base and that (2)

[6] *Ibid.*, pp. 339-340.
[7] *Ibid.*

it would be terrible to lose the money already spent by not going ahead and finishing the job. As Representative Rooney observed, "This may be only $250 but this is the camel's nose. These things never get out of a budget. They manage to stay and grow." It was for a long time common practice for agencies to submit a request for a relatively small sum to begin a project without showing its full cost over a period of years. Congress has sought to counter this strategy by passing legislation requiring a total estimate for a project before any part can be authorized. But estimates are subject to change and a small sum one year rarely seems imposing even if a larger amount is postulated for the future.[8]

An agency may engage in wedging by requesting a small sum for research and using it to justify the feasibility of a big new project. The agency may borrow some personnel and equipment, use a few people part time in order to develop a program, and then tease Congress and the Budget Bureau with an established operation that has generated support for its continuance. A change in the wording of authorization legislation may then be sought so that the agency does not appear to be building empires.

The desire of budget officials to keep items in the budget,

[8] In arguing against a change in accounting procedures, Representative Mahon sketched the strategic implications:

"Now let me say that the accrued expenditure procedure is used now, as everyone knows, to some extent. I believe it was last year that we appropriated $1 million, just a little $1 million to start a public works project of the Army Engineers which is to cost $1 billion. Why, if I go to Congressmen Kilgore and say, 'Listen, Joe, we have been colleagues a long time, can't you vote for just this little $1 million for my area to help me and my people?

"Well, Joe, I am sure he would do whatever was right and proper, but it might be something tempting, particularly if I had voted for a million-dollar project for Joe on a former occasion to vote for my proposal. But if I go up to Joe and I say, 'Listen, Joe, I want you to vote for this project, it costs a billion dollars over a period of years, and if you start it, it is going to be completed." (*Improving Federal Budgeting and Appropriations*, House Subcommittee on Government Operations, 85th Congress, 1st Session, pp. 132-133.)

even if they are small and underfinanced, is readily explained once it is understood that they may one day serve to launch full-blown programs when conditions are more favorable. Research projects are often not terminated when they have proven successful or have failed; a small item concerning applicability of the research is kept in the budget so that if the agency wishes to resume it has a foot in the door, and if it wishes to begin a new project that may be connected with the old one.

Just for now. "Is there anything more permanent than a temporary agency of the Government?" Representative Phillips wanted to know. His colleague, Mr. Thomas, spoke with some asperity of a temporary activity that had begun four years ago. "Of course, [the agency] said it would take them about two years to clear it up and then they would be off the payroll. Since then I think you have added 30 to this group." A temporary adjustment to a passing situation results in an emergency appropriation for a fixed period, which turns out to be a permanent expenditure.

So small. When an increase is presented as one, a first line of defense is to say that it is so small as to be eminently justifiable or, if not, then certainly not worth bothering about. Here, as elsewhere, much depends on the basis of comparison. Administrator Petersen was fond of comparing the "negligible" costs of Civil Defense with the "outrageous" advertising costs of a certain beer. "The costs of the investigations that we make," the Fish and Wildlife Service asserted, "are tiny in relation to the total project costs of the engineering agencies. Normally they can be accomplished for a few thousand dollars on a project that cost millions. . . ." A more extreme example was furnished by Representative Siemanski who defended the Narcotics Bureau by asserting that it would cost $279 million to run for one hundred years. "Stack that against the two billion cargo that vanished in 1950 and the issue is clear. In 100 years, at 500 tons a year, opium runners at present prices would net 200 billion."

This strategy is also meant to suggest that a particular item or class of items is too insignificant to warrant study. A Justice Department Official spoke of "a net increase of $162,000 made up of a number of small items. I question seriously whether the committee wants to spend time on them, they are so small." He was wrong. But it is impossible to go into everything and the way in which the agency presents its budget, the kinds of emphasis it gives, the comparisons it suggests, may serve to direct attention to and from various objects. A miscellaneous category is unlikely to excite anyone's imagination. Every once in a while a Congressman will say, "Give us a breakdown here of 'other objects,' $2,264,000," as happened to the Weather Bureau in 1961.

Absorb it if it is so small. The tables may be turned in Congress or the Budget Bureau when agencies are told that if the increase they want is so terribly small they must surely be able to find some other money in their accounts. Representative Flood wanted to know why a mere $130,000 could not be absorbed by the Defense Department with their billions. "Why," he said, "it is hard to get a general you can discuss such a small sum with." Senator Hayden asks, "Can't you pinch out the $2,000?" An official of the Bureau of Mines knows defeat when he sees it—"Certainly it would be foolish for me to say we could not . . ."—but he takes a stab at suggesting some awful consequences. As Dr. Reichelderfer of the Weather Bureau so aptly expressed it, "Well, whenever there is a cut of a relatively small amount of that kind one is between the devil and the sea. . . . We felt that it could be taken as quibbling if we appealed for its restoration because, in an appropriation of $38 million, the point can always be made that certainly the Bureau can absorb a cut of $100,000."

The commitment or no choice. Although expenditures may rise and requests for money may increase, an agency can hardly be blamed if it had no choice. As one official put it, "The increases are in every case presented as either related to commitments . . . or other uncontrollable factors. . . ."

A favorite strategy is to lay down long-range goals for an existing program, which the agency can use to say that its requirements are not being met. The very statement that there are so many acres not yet under soil conservation practices or so many Indian children who need schooling may serve to create an implied commitment to meet the demand. The NIH and its Congressional allies go one step further by speaking of "moral obligations" for continuing projects mounting up to tens of millions of dollars.

If this, then that. If it can be shown that new projects are an integral part of old ones included in the agency's base, then the implied obligation to go on with the old passes on to the new. "This whole series of items . . . tie together very closely," a spokesman for the Bureau of Indian Affairs stated. "The question of supervision of forest and range land . . . tie in with the soil conservation practices in those areas . . . including some of the irrigation work that have to do with development . . . go together more or less in one bundle." One thing leads to another. The Congress was interested in bettering the education of American Indians. So the Bureau made a tie-in: ". . . As they become better educated, they are more apt to come and ask assistance to move to another area." If you appropriate more for education as you intend, then you must also do more for relocation.

The backlog. Nobody loves a backlog. The very use of the term suggests that there is an obligation to do something about it. Thomas tells the Federal Communications Commission that "It is well known that we do not like backlogs and we always try to get rid of them and cut them down."

The agency has to be careful, however, lest Congress or the Budget Bureau suggest that other employees be devoted to the task of catching up with the work. "There are 90 employees in the Office of Management," Thomas said. "Could you take 15 or 20 . . . and . . . cut down this backlog?"

Look, no hands. Strategies involving the use of work-load data fit nicely into those using the idea of an accepted base with a commitment to continue the program. Once acceptance of a particular kind of project has been gained, increases may be presented as an inevitable outgrowth of increases in the tasks to be performed. It is often easier to secure appropriations when the work can be broken down into easily quantifiable units and work-load data can be supplied to give an estimate of costs. There is something about categories like the number of applications processed, or number of operations performed, which appears to be reasonable. The Budget Bureau and Congress may be impressed with a computer program arranged so that the ultimate figure appears to pop out untouched by human hands.

In mandatory programs such as veterans' benefits or farm price supports, appropriations are largely dependent upon securing an agreement on workload data. Where the work is routine and history provides a fund of experience, the area of dispute may be reduced to small dimensions. The agency does well to establish a record of correct estimation or to choose those units for quantification which will permit it to do well. Chairman Herzog hoped that his statement did not sound boastful but he assumed "this [House] committee will want to take into consideration the fact that the [National Labor Relations Board] has not been inflating its estimates in order to look as though we are going to get a lot of work which we do not really expect to get."

Work loads and work loads. Yet there are many ways to skin a cat: a work load based on number of inquiries may disregard the differences in time and skill that inquiries take; there is room for disagreement on the appropriate unit of measurement. Observe the following colloquy:

> Representative Thomas: I note you have 60 people handling 268 loans; that represents about 4½ loans per person. Are they not a little overworked . . . ?
>
> Housing and Home Finance official: . . . This . . . is . . . the most difficult program . . . with which I ever had any experience. . . .

Yet it is not obvious that this work load is any less appropriate than the fourteen convictions per agent in the field used by the Narcotics Bureau. If quantification does not seem advantageous an agency may resist the implementation of a workload plan as a scheme to derogate the character of its operations by breaking them up into oversimplified units. Or it may devise a measure that results in a more favorable appearance. Agencies may use the concept of "man-years," which assumes that an employee will work 365 days a year, instead of "jobs," a practice that enables them to present a figure lower than the number of positions to be filled because it takes more than one person to work a man-year. This practice may create difficulties for the Congressmen who must interpret the concept. "For 1957, you want 34.5 man-years at a cost of $233,000 which is about 38 or 39 or 40 jobs against 28 man-years in 1956, or about 31 or 32 jobs." Finally, Congressman Thomas flared up saying, "We'd like to have it [the table] in jobs rather than man-years as we can understand what jobs mean."

It pays for itself; it makes a profit. An increase may not seem like an increase if it can be shown that it brings in revenue equal to or greater than the cost. Although government is presumably not conducted for profit, the delight Congressmen take in finding an activity that returns money to the Treasury is indicated by the frequency with which they use this fact to praise administrators and to support programs they prefer. Senator Dworshak told the Fish and Wildlife Service that "when you return money like that [$1 million from seal furs] back in, you should be proud of it and have the record show it." Not to be outdone, J. Edgar Hoover pointed out that the FBI had recovered $73 million more through its investigation activities over a ten-year period than it had received in appropriations.

Spend to save. Of certain activities it may be claimed that the more you spend the more the government earns. Properly conceived, this may seem more like a decrease than an increase in spending. The Soil Conservation Service, for example, declared that any money spent on soil erosion studies would soon be repaid by reduced costs in dredging channels and reservoirs. It made a study that demonstrated that "the extra income taxes paid by farmers as a result of their soil conservation work and by retailers, processors and distributors who profit by the extra business would total $69,-192,185. Thus it appears that in 1948 the Federal Government recovered, in increased income tax, the entire amount spent by the SCS (a total of $39,189,654) and made 76% profit on its investment." The slogan, "we are going to save billions," used in this case by Senator Thye to support cancer research, is also used as an inducement to loosen the public purse by advocates of slum clearance, accounting reforms, education, and other advocates of spending.

The crisis. There comes a time, however, when it is necessary to admit that a new program is in the offing or that substantial increases in existing ones are desired. This situation calls for a special campaign in which three techniques—the crisis, salesmanship, and advertising—are often called into play. Their purpose is to generate extraordinary support so that the agency or program does not merely inch ahead but secures sizable new appropriations.

Events do not have meaning in themselves; they are given meaning by observers. From time to time situations arise—war, drought, depression, plant disease, atomic energy—which virtually everyone recognizes as crises. The agency in a position to meet a crisis, as TVA was by supplying huge amounts of power to atomic-energy installations, can greatly increase its appropriations. Soon after a jet plane had crashed because of contact with a flock of starlings, the Fish and Wildlife Service was able to obtain funds for research into the habits of these birds. There is also a borderline area of discretion in which crises may be made to appear more real. A number of agency officials are famous in budgetary circles for their ability to embellish or make use of crises. By publicizing a situation, dramatizing it effectively, and perhaps asking for emergency appropriations, an agency may maneuver itself into a position of responsibility for large new programs.

Good examples of crises are the Bureau of Land Management's emergency program for controlling the noxious weed, halogeton, the Polaris system, and the reaction in many areas to the Soviet sputnik. But not every such appeal succeeds. The unpopular USIA was slapped down while others were successfully crying crisis: "What have you to say about this statement that you used the Suez crisis as an excuse for increasing the information efforts?" Arthur Larson, its hapless Director, was asked.

Salesmanship runs the gamut from a cops-and-robbers appeal—"agents of our [Narcotics Bureau] . . . engaged in a 45-minute gun battle with Mexican smugglers"—to the "agony sessions" at the NIH hearings. Who could resist Senator Hill's plea:

> As we begin today's hearings on appropriations . . . we take notice of the passing of . . . John Foster Dulles [who] fell victim to the most dread killer of our time, cancer.
> Cancer, that most ancient and accursed scourge of mankind, has . . . robbed the U.S. Senate of some of its greatest

leaders: Robert A. Taft, Arthur Vandenberg, Kenneth
Wherry, Brian McMahon, and Matthew Neely. What more
fitting . . . memorial . . . could there be than a high re-
solve . . . to re-double our research efforts against the mon-
strous killer which . . . will claim the lives of 250,000 more
Americans before this year has ended? . . . We are very
happy to have with us our colleague, Senator Neuber-
ger. . . .

The impact on a Congressman of many vivid descriptions
of disease is described by Representative Scrivner:

A week ago, Mr. Chairman, after this hearing about cancer,
I went home and checked all the little skin flecks and felt
for bumps and bruises. I lay awake that night and could
have convinced myself I had cancer. And then more recently I lay awake listening to my heart after hearing the
heart-trouble talk. I listened to see if it went too fast or if
it was too weak or if it was irregular or whether it was pump-
ing too hard. . . . And here I am listening to all this mental
health talk . . . and I wonder what I am going to dream
about tonight.

Who would vote against appropriations for medical research
after being subjected to this treatment?

The crisis strategy is well known to appropriations committee members. Rooney begins exclaiming, "That is the
magic word this year, Africa. That is the gimmick that is
really giving the taxpayer the business. . . ." His colleague
obligingly responds with, "It is taking the place of sputnik."
And Rooney comes back with, "Every year it is something
different." But this does not mean that Congressmen are immune. They recognize the signs of the times as a fact of life.

Advertising and salesmanship. Proponents of new programs or of greatly increased old ones, be they agency personnel, interest group leaders, or Congressmen, stress the need
for advertising and salesmanship to garner the necessary support. A program may be dressed up by giving it a dramatic
name such as Mission 66 (a ten-year program designed to

improve facilities in national parks by 1966) or by giving it a glamorous label like Polaris or Titan. These designations are supposed to make the programs easier to remember and to refer to in publicity releases. Much thought is given to the name. The B-70 bomber became the RS-70 (reconnaissance strike) overnight as soon as the Air Force discovered that it could not get funds by attempting to justify the plane as useful for its original mission and had to find a new one with more appeal. What some call "Peter Rabbit" presentations—fancy brochures, stirring pictures, simple graphs—are used to advertise the program in Congress and the public media of information. Congressmen are taken on grand guided tours and constituency response is encouraged. An astronaut is paraded before a committee to make a pitch. Releases are distributed to the press. Attempts are made to tie the program to heartfelt needs—a cure for cancer, protection against old age, the joys of outdoor living.

Let us look at "Operation Outdoors," the Forest Service's answer to Mission 66. For some time the Forest Service had a rather ordinary $3 million program with the uninspiring name of "Recreation-public use" in budgetary documents. In 1957, however, the Service made a special field survey, occasioned, it said, by increased public use of its facilities. It was determined that additional funds were urgently needed and a revitalized program, Operation Outdoors, carried a proposed $85 million price tag to be raised over the next five years. By 1960 the Forest Service had succeeded in more than tripling the usual appropriation for this activity. Thanks to hurricanes Carol, Edna, Hazel and others, for example, the Weather Bureau appropriations rose from $28 million to $42 million in 1956.

The defense motif. From the beginning of World War II national defense retained an aura of necessity and importance shared by few other activities. It is ideal for crisis strategies.

The temptation to say that almost anything one can think of has implications for national defense is overwhelming and few agencies have been able to resist it. The National Labor Relations Board in 1952 was no exception: "I recognize that every agency of the government will come before you and say, 'Well, we may not nominally be a defense agency, but what we do is essential to the . . . war effort.' In spite of that, I am going to make that statement." A list of all the projects said to be connected with national defense would fill up a good many pages. "I notice," Chairman Thomas wryly remarked to the House and Home Finance Agency, "in the summary statement . . . everything pointed at the national defense. . . . The author of the language is putting on a good act of walking the tight wire with two buckets of water on each shoulder . . . —national defense, national defense." Mental health is related to national defense by statements like "During World War II . . . more people were kept out of the service for mental illnesses than there were men and women under arms in the Pacific Theater of Operations." We also learn that "during the last war 32,000 were rejected for cancer and other neoplasms. This would have been sufficient to man at least two Army infantry divisions. . . ." Everyone knows, to be sure, that our national defense depends upon such things as a prosperous farm and urban population (that is, everybody), conservation of resources, utilization of resources, etc. A twist is performed by the military and civil defense agencies, which are prone to argue that their programs will have valuable secondary results for peacetime purposes. The Space Agency will not only get us to the moon but will also improve our existence on the way up through many new discoveries.

Overselling. Occasionally, a program may be oversold in the sense that it becomes so popular that the large sums appropriated to it threaten to deprive others of support. This has happened to Polaris. The result was that the Navy, knowing that Polaris would do well, concentrated on building up less popular projects such as new aircraft carriers. The possibility of creating a sort of budgetary Frankenstein exists but it does not seem to deter advertising and salesmanship.

OUTCOMES

Having described the major kinds of calculations and strategies used in federal budgeting, we are now in a position to develop (in Chapter 4) a critique of the usual proposals for budgetary reform and to appraise (in Chapter 5) the main features of the existing process. But at this early stage in the study of budgeting, descriptions of calculations and strategies, however helpful in improving our understanding, are not sufficient for the purpose of accounting precisely for the outcomes of the budgetary process. Although we have been able to elucidate basic strategic requirements such as confidence, clientele, and response to crises, we cannot now (in the absence of intensive studies of a wide range of strategies employed under specific historical circumstances)[9] explain precisely which strategies are most efficacious under which conditions. Nor is this difficulty surprising, since particular historical conditions were taken as given, and we dealt only with those parts of the budget within the control of the participants. It is possible, however, to suggest how the propositions in this volume might be connected with a general theory accounting for the pattern and level of public expenditures over an extended period of time. Fortunately, a recent attempt in this direction has been made.

In a pioneering work, Peacock and Wiseman propose an explanation accounting for the long-term trend—stability, sharp rise, plateau, stability at new level, and continuation of the cycle—in governmental expenditures.

[9] The author is in the midst of preparing such a study for Resources for the Future, Inc.

. . . In settled times [they write] notions about taxation are likely to be more influential than ideas about desirable increases in expenditure in deciding the size and rate of growth of the public sector. There may thus be a persistent divergence between ideas about desirable public spending and ideas about the limits of taxation.[10] This divergence may be narrowed by large-scale social disturbances, such as major wars. Such disturbances may create a displacement effect, shifting public revenues and expenditures to new levels. After the disturbance is over new ideas of tolerable tax levels emerge, and a new plateau of expenditure may be reached, with public expenditures again taking a broadly constant share of gross national product, though a different share from the former one.

This displacement effect has two aspects. People will accept, in times of crisis, methods of raising revenue formerly thought intolerable, and the acceptance of new tax levels remains when the disturbance has disappeared. It is harder to get the saddle on the horse than to keep it there. Expenditures which the government may have thought desirable before the disturbance, but which it did not then dare to implement, consequently become possible. At the same time, social upheavals impose new and continuing obligations on governments both as the aftermath of functions assumed in wartime (*e.g.*, payments of war pensions, debt interest, reparation payments) and as the result of changes in social ideas.[11]

[10] For validation of this proposition in the American context, see Eva Mueller, "Public Attitudes Toward Fiscal Programs," LXXVII *The Quarterly Journal of Economics* (May 1963), pp. 210-235. The article is based on a national survey conducted by the Survey Research Center of the University of Michigan.

[11] Alan T. Peacock and Jack Wiseman, *The Growth of Public Expenditures in the United Kingdom* (Princeton, 1961) p. xxiv. We assume here that the theory is also useful for the United States. See the following sources cited by the above authors: R. A. Musgrave and J. M. Culbertson, "The Growth of Public Expenditures in the United States, 1890-1948," VI *National Tax Journal* (June 1953) pp. 97-115; G. Colm and M. Helzner, "The Structure of Governmental Revenue and Expenditure in the United States," in *L'Importance et la Structure des Recettes et des Dépenses Publiques*, International Institute of Public Finance (Brussels, 1960).

A similar trend for the United States is described by Mosher and Poland:

> The upward trend in [governmental] expenditures . . . has conformed rather consistently to the following patterns:
>
> *Defense-related spending* rises sharply during war, then declines after hostilities but steadies at a plateau considerably higher than before the war. . . . *General domestic spending* moves in nearly opposite directions. During wars, it stays about the same or declines. . . . At the onset of major depressions . . . it increases greatly. During other peacetime periods, it tends to rise gradually.[12]

Peacock and Wiseman provide one kind of explanation for the periodic rise in expenditures and for the plateau and stability that follows until the next social disruption. We can add to their theory by answering questions appropriate to our level of exposition: why do expenditures (except those mandated by the disturbance) not sharply decrease to their former level? Why, in more ordinary times, do we observe steady (though comparatively) gentle increases in expenditures? Explanations based on the calculations and strategies used in budgeting are available to us.

Budgetary calculations are incremental, using a historical base as the point of departure. The existing level of expenditures is largely taken for granted and, for the most part, only small changes are seriously considered. The distribution of roles among the participants operates in such a way that most transactions involve reductions in the increased amounts proposed by agency advocates, thus helping account for the slightly rising trend of expenditures. The use of strategies by the affected administrative units and their supporters also helps account for the difficulty of sharp reductions as well as the likelihood that the new conditions created by a depression or war or other social disturbance will be seized upon

[12] Frederick C. Mosher and Orville F. Poland, *The Cost of Governments in the United States: Facts, Trends, Myths,* (Mimeo., August, 1963) p. II-9.

through crisis stategies. Disturbances are evidently more likely to affect some areas of expenditure more severely than others. The analysis in this volume makes a beginning in accounting for the distribution of funds by explaining why some agencies are in a better position to exploit their environment than others.

In devising models of budgeting it may be possible to build in "shocks" (that is, social disturbances) to the system and simulate the reaction of a budgetary process that operates much like the one described in these pages.[13] By creating an artificial but realistic approximation of the budgetary process, and subjecting it to shocks of various kinds, we may be able to emancipate ourselves from complete dependence on knowledge of individual cases and still be able to explain the general shape and trend of budgetary outcomes.

Perhaps the "study of budgeting" is just another expression for the "study of politics"; yet one cannot study everything at once, and the vantage point offered by concentration on budgetary decisions offers a useful and much-neglected perspective from which to analyze the making of public policy. The opportunities for comparison are ample, the outcomes are specific and quantifiable,[14] and a dynamic quality is assured by virtue of the comparative ease with which one can study the development of budgetary items and programs over a period of years.

[13] The close connection between the types of calculations described in Richard Cyert and James March, *A Behavioral Theory of the Firm* (Englewood Cliffs, N. J., 1963), and those found in the budgetary process suggests that elements of organization theory may be applicable to studies of budgeting. The participants who normally deal with budgets and programs of particular agencies might be considered as members of an organizational coalition whose goals, roles, aspiration levels, decision rules, search behavior, and feedback mechanisms might be studied to provide predictions of likely kinds of budgetary behavior under various conditions.

[14] The author and Otto Davis, an economist at the Carnegie Institute of Technology, are now engaged in a statistical analysis of federal appropriations since the end of World War II. They hope to test various propositions concerning relationships among participants in budgeting and to discover new relationships that demand explanation.

REFORMS

4

A LARGE PART OF THE LITERATURE on budgeting in the United
States is concerned with reform. The goals of the proposed
reforms are couched in similar language—economy, efficiency,
improvement, or just better budgeting. The President, the
Congress and its committees, administrative agencies, even
the interested citizenry are all to gain by some change in the
way the budget is formulated, presented, or evaluated. There
is little or no realization among the reformers, however, that
any effective change in budgetary relationships must necessarily alter the outcomes of the budgetary process. Otherwise,
why bother? Far from being a neutral matter of "better
budgeting," proposed reforms inevitably contain important
implications for the political system; that is, for the "who gets
what" of governmental decisions. What are some of the major
political implications of budgetary reform? We begin with
the noblest vision of reform: the development of a normative
theory of budgeting (stating what ought to be) that would
provide the basis for allocating funds among competing activities.

A NORMATIVE THEORY OF BUDGETING?

In 1940, in what is still the best discussion of the subject, V. O. Key lamented "The Lack of a Budgetary Theory." He called for a theory that would help answer the basic question of budgeting on the expenditure side: "On what basis shall it be decided to allocate X dollars to Activity A instead of Activity B?"[1] Although several attempts have been made to meet this challenge,[2] not one has come close to succeeding. No progress has been made for the excellent reason that the task, as posed, is impossible to fulfill.[3] The search for an unrealizable goal indicates serious weaknesses in prevailing conceptions of the budget.

If a normative theory of budgeting is to be more than an academic exercise, it must actually guide the making of governmental decisions. The items of expenditures that are passed by Congress, enacted into law, and spent must in large measure conform to the theory if it is to have any practical effect. This is tantamount to prescribing that virtually all the activities of government be carried on according to the theory. For whatever the government does must be paid for from public funds; it is difficult to think of any policy that can be carried out without money.

The budget is the lifeblood of the government, the financial reflection of what the government does or intends to do. A theory that contains criteria for determining what ought to be in the budget is nothing less than a theory stating what the

[1] V. O. Key, Jr., "The Lack of a Budgetary Theory," XXXIV *The American Political Science Review* (December 1940) pp. 1137-1144.

[2] Verne B. Lewis, "Toward a Theory of Budgeting," XII *Public Administration Review* (Winter 1952) pp. 42-54; "Symposium on Budget Theory," X *Public Administration Review* (Winter 1950) pp. 20-31; Arthur Smithies, *The Budgetary Process in the United States* (New York, 1955).

[3] Key, in fact, shies away from the implications of his question and indicates keen awareness of the political problems involved. But the question has been posed by subsequent authors largely as he framed it.

government ought to do. If we substitute the words "what the government ought to do" for the words "ought to be in the budget," it becomes clear that a normative theory of budgeting would be a comprehensive and specific political theory detailing what the government's activities ought to be at a particular time. A normative theory of budgeting, therefore, is utopian in the fullest sense of that word: its accomplishment and acceptance would mean the end of conflict over the government's role in society.

By suppressing dissent, totalitarian regimes enforce their normative theories of budgeting on others. Presumably, we reject this solution to the problem of conflict in society and insist on democratic procedures. How then arrive at a theory of budgeting that is something more than one man's preferences?

The crucial aspect of budgeting is whose preferences are to prevail in disputes about which activities are to be carried on and to what degree, in the light of limited resources. The problem is not only "how shall budgetary benefits be maximized?" as if it made no difference who received them, but also "who shall receive budgetary benefits and how much?" One may purport to solve the problem of budgeting by proposing a normative theory (or a welfare function or a hierarchy of values) which specifies a method for maximizing returns for budgetary expenditures. In the absence of ability to impose a set of preferred policies on others, however, this solution breaks down. It amounts to no more than saying that if you can persuade others to agree with you, then you will have achieved agreement. Or it begs the question of what kind of policies will be fed into the scheme by assuming that these are agreed upon. Yet we hardly need argue that a state of universal agreement has not yet arisen.

Another way of avoiding the problem of budgeting is to treat society as a single organism with a consistent set of desires and a life of its own, much as a single consumer might

be assumed to have a stable demand and indifference schedule. Instead of revenue being raised and the budget being
spent by and for many individuals who may have their own
preferences and feelings, as is surely the case, these processes
are treated, in effect, as if a single individual were the only
one concerned. This approach avoids the central problems of
social conflict, of somehow aggregating different preferences
so that a decision may emerge. How can we compare the
worth of expenditures for irrigation to certain farmers with
the worth of widening a highway to motorists and the desirability of aiding old people to pay medical bills as against the
degree of safety provided by an expanded defense program?

The process we have developed for dealing with interper-
sonal comparisons in government is not economic but political.
Conflicts are resolved (under agreed-upon rules) by translat-
ing different preferences through the political system into
units called votes or into types of authority like a veto power.
There need not be (and there is not) full agreement on goals
or the preferential weights to be accorded to different goals.
Congressmen directly threaten, compromise, and trade favors
in regard to policies in which values are implicitly weighted,
and then agree to register the results according to the rules
for tallying votes.

The burden of calculation is enormously reduced for three
primary reasons: first, only the small number of alternatives
politically feasible at any one time are considered; second,
these policies in a democracy typically differ only in small
increments from previous policies on which there is a store
of relevant information; and, third, each participant may ordinarily assume that he need consider only his preferences and
those of his powerful opponents since the American political
system works to assure that every significant interest has representation at some key point. Since only a relatively few interest groups contend on any given issue and no single item
is considered in conjunction with all others (because budgets

are made in bits and pieces), a huge and confusing array of interests is not activated all at once.

In the American context, a typical result is that bargaining takes place among many dispersed centers of influence and that favors are swapped as in the case of log-rolling public-works appropriations. Since there is no one group of men who can necessarily impose their preferences upon others within the American political system, special coalitions are formed to support or oppose specific policies. Support is sought in this system of fragmented power at numerous centers of influence —Congressional committees, the Congressional leadership, the President, the Budget Bureau, interdepartmental committees, departments, bureaus, private groups, and so on. Nowhere does a single authority have power to determine what is going to be in the budget.

THE POLITICS IN BUDGET REFORM

The seeming irrationalities of a political system that does not provide for even formal consideration of the budget as a whole[4] (except by the President, who cannot control the final result) has led to many attacks and proposals for reform. The tradition of reform in America is a noble one, not easily to be denied. But in this case it is doomed to failure because it is aimed at the wrong target. If the present budgetary process is rightly or wrongly deemed unsatisfactory, then one must alter in some respect the political system of which the budget is but an expression. It makes no sense to speak as if one could

[4] See Charles E. Lindblom, "The Science of 'Muddling Through,'" XIX *Public Administration Review* (Spring 1959) pp. 79-88, for a description and criticism of the comprehensive method. See also his "Decision-Making in Taxation and Expenditure," in National Bureau of Economic Research, *Public Finances: Needs, Sources, and Utilization* (Princeton, 1961) pp. 295-336, and his "Policy Analysis," XLVIII *American Economic Review* (June 1958) pp. 298-312. His recent book (with David Braybrooke), *A Strategy of Decision* (New York, 1963) contains the most extensive statement of his position.

make drastic changes in budgeting without also altering the distribution of influence. But this task is inevitably so formidable (though the reformers are not directly conscious of it) that most adversaries prefer to speak of changing the budg-etary process, as if by some subtle alchemy the intractable political element could be transformed into a more malleable substance.

The reader who objects to being taken thus far only to be told that the budget is inextricably linked to the political system would have a just complaint if the implications of this remark were recognized in the literature on budgeting. Since these implications have not been spelled out, it seems worth-while to do so now. One implication is that by far the most significant way of influencing the budget is to introduce basic political changes (or to wait for secular changes like the grow-ing industrialization of the South). Provide the President with more powers enabling him to control the votes of his party in Congress; enable a small group of Congressmen to command a majority of votes on all occasions so that they can push their program through. Then you will have exerted a profound influence on the content of the budget.

A second implication is that no significant change can be made in the budgetary process without affecting the political process. There would be no point in tinkering with the budg-etary machinery if, at the end, the pattern of budgetary deci-sions was precisely the same as before. On the contrary, re-form has little justification unless it results in different kinds of decisions and, when and if this has been accomplished, the play of political forces has necessarily been altered. Enabling some political forces to gain at the expense of others requires the explicit introduction and defense of value premises that are ordinarily missing from proposals for budgetary reform.

Since the budget represents conflicts over whose preferences shall prevail, the third implication is that one cannot speak of "better budgeting" without considering who benefits and who loses or demonstrating that no one loses. Just as the supposedly objective criterion of "efficiency" has been shown to have normative implications,[5] so a "better budget" may well be a cloak for hidden policy preferences. To propose that the President be given an item veto, for example, is to attempt to increase the influence of the particular interests that gain superior access to the Chief Executive rather than, say, to the Congress. Only if one eliminates the element of conflict over expenditures, can it be assumed that a reform that enables an official to do a better job from his point of view is simply "good" without considering the policy implications for others.

A TYPICAL REFORM

Arthur Smithies may stand as a typical proponent of a typical reform. Identifying rationality with a comprehensive overview of the budget by a single person or group, Smithies despairs of the fragmented approach taken by Congress and proposes a remedy. He suggests that a Joint (Congressional) Budget Policy committee be formed and empowered to consider all proposals for revenue and expenditure in a single package and that their decisions be made binding by a concurrent resolution. And he presents his reform as a moderate proposal to improve the rationality of the budget process.[6] If the proposed Joint Committee were unable to secure the passage of its recommendations, as it would surely be, it would have gone to enormous trouble without accomplishing anything but a public revelation of futility. The impotence of the Joint Commit-

[5] Dwight Waldo, *The Administrative State* (New York, 1948); Herbert A. Simon, "The Criterion of Efficiency," in *Administrative Behavior*, 2nd edition (New York, 1957) pp. 172-197.

[6] Smithies, *op. cit.*, pp. 192-193 ff. See also Jesse Burkhead, *Government Budgeting* (New York, 1956), for a useful historical account of proposals for reform.

tee on the Legislative Budget,[7] the breakdown of the single
Congressional attempt to develop a comprehensive legislative
budget,[8] and the failure of Congressional attempts to control
the Council of Economic Advisers[9] and the Budget Bureau,[10]
all stem from the same cause. There is no cohesive group in
Congress capable of using these devices to affect decision
making by imposing its preferences on a majority of Congressmen. Smithies' budgetary reform presupposes a completely
different political system from the one that exists in the
United States. To be sure, there is a name for a committee
that imposes its will on the legislature and tolerates no rival
committees—it is called a Cabinet on the British model. In
the guise of a procedural change in the preparation of the
budget by Congress, Smithies is actually proposing a revolutionary move that would mean the virtual introduction of the
British parliamentary system if it were successful.

Smithies (pp. 188-225) suggests that his proposals would
be helpful to the President. But the membership of the Joint

[7] Avery Leiserson, "Coordination of Federal Budgetary and Appropriations Procedures Under the Legislative Reorganization Act of 1946,"
I *National Tax Journal* (June 1948) pp. 118-126.

[8] Robert Ash Wallace, "Congressional Control of the Budget," III
Midwest Journal of Political Science (May 1959) pp. 151-167; Dalmas
H. Nelson, "The Omnibus Appropriations Act of 1950," XV *Journal of
Politics* (May 1953) pp. 274-288; Representative John Phillips, "The
Hadacol of the Budget Makers," IV *National Tax Journal* (September
1951) pp. 255-268.

[9] Roy Blough, "The Role of the Economist in Federal Policy-Making,"
LI *University of Illinois Bulletin* (November 1953); Lester Seligman,
"Presidential Leadership: The Inner Circle and Institutionalization,"
XVIII *Journal of Politics* (August 1956) pp. 410-426; Edwin G. Nourse,
*Economics in the Public Service; Administrative Aspects of the Employ-
ment Act* (New York, 1953); Ronald C. Hood, "Reorganizing the
Council of Economic Advisors," LXIX *Political Science Quarterly*
(September 1954) pp. 413-437.

[10] Fritz Morstein Marx, "The Bureau of the Budget: Its Evolution and
Present Role, II," XXXIX *The American Political Science Review* (October 1945) pp. 869-898; Richard Neustadt, "Presidency and Legislation: The Growth of Central Clearance," XLVIII *ibid.* (September
1954) pp. 641-671; Seligman, *op. cit.*

Committee would be made up largely of conservatives from safe districts, who are not dependent on the President, who come from a different constituency than he does, but with whom he must deal in order to get any money for his programs. Should the members of the Joint Committee ever be able to command a two-thirds vote of the Congress, they could virtually ignore the President in matters of domestic policy and run the executive branch so that it would be accountable only to them.

PROGRAM BUDGETING VERSUS TRADITIONAL BUDGETING

The basic idea behind program budgeting is that instead of presenting budgetary requests in the usual line-item form, which focuses on categories like supplies, maintenance, and personnel, the presentation is made in terms of the end-products, of program packages like public health or limited war or strategic retaliatory forces. The virtues of the program budget are said to be its usefulness in relating ends to means in a comprehensive fashion, the emphasis it puts upon the policy implications of budgeting, and the ease with which it permits consideration of the budget as a whole as each program competes with every other for funds.[11] Interestingly enough, the distinguishing characteristics of the program procedure are precisely the reverse of those of the traditional practice. Federal budgeting today is incremental rather than

[11] On program budgeting see A. E. Buck, *Municipal Finance* (New York, 1926) and *Public Budgeting* (New York, 1929); The (Hoover) Commission on the Organization of the Executive Branch of the Government, *Budgeting and Accounting* (Washington, D.C., 1949); Arthur Smithies, *op. cit.*; Jesse Burkhead, *op. cit.*; Gladys Kammerer, *Program Budgeting: An Aid to Understanding* (Gainesville, Fla., 1959); Symposium, "Performance Budgeting: Has the Theory Worked?" XX *Public Administration Review* (Spring 1960) pp. 63-85; Stanley T. Gabis, *Mental Health and Financial Management: Some Dilemmas of Program Budgeting*, Public Administration Program, Department of Political Science Research Report, No. 3 (East Lansing, Mich., 1960).

comprehensive, calculated in bits and pieces rather than as a whole, and veils policy implications rather than emphasizing them.

This brief account will focus on three major consequences resulting from the differences in budgetary procedure. First, the traditional procedure increases agreement among the participants whereas the program device decreases it. Second, the program budgeting procedure increases the burden of calculation on the participants; the traditional method decreases it. And, third, the specific outcomes in the form of decisions are likely to be different.

The incremental, fragmented, non-programmatic, and sequential procedures of the present budgetary process aid in securing agreement and reducing the burden of calculation. It is much easier to agree on an addition or reduction of a few thousand or a million than to agree on whether a program is good in the abstract. It is much easier to agree on a small addition or decrease than to compare the worth of one program to that of all others. Conflict is reduced by an incremental approach because the area open to dispute is reduced. In much the same way the burden of calculation is eased because no one has to make all the calculations that would be involved in a comprehensive evaluation of all expenditures. Calculations are made sequentially, in small segments, by subcommittees, and are accepted by the Congress as a whole. Were each subcommittee to challenge the results of the others, conflict would be greatly exacerbated. Were each Congressman to fail to accept the decisions of the subcommittees most of the time there would be (assuming that time was available to make the necessary calculations) continual disagreement over most items instead of only a few as at present. Finally, agreement comes much more readily when the items in dispute can be treated as differences in dollars instead of basic differences in policy. Calculating budgets in monetary increments facilitates bargaining and logrolling. It becomes possible to swap an increase here for a decrease there or for an increase elsewhere without always having to consider the ultimate desirability of programs blatantly in competition.

Procedures that de-emphasize overt conflicts among competing programs also encourage secret deliberations, non-partisanship, and the recruitment of personnel who feel comfortable in sidestepping policy decisions most of the time. The prospects for agreement within the House Appropriations Committee are enhanced by closed hearings and mark-up sessions, and by a tradition against publicity. Were deliberations to take place in public—"open covenants openly arrived at"—committee members might find themselves accused of "selling out" as they made concessions. Willingness to compromise, to be flexible, is a quality sought in choosing members to serve on the appropriations committees.

Party ties might be disruptive of agreement if they focused attention on the policy differences between the two political persuasions. Instead, party differences are submerged during committee deliberations. Thus the usual process of taking something from a program here, adding to a program there, swapping this for that, can go on at the committee stage without having to take the kind of "yes" or "no" party positions that may be required at the voting stage on the floor.

Consider by contrast some likely consequences of program budgeting. The practice of focusing attention on programs means that policy implications can hardly be avoided. The gains and the losses for the interests involved become far more evident to all concerned.[12] Conflict is heightened by the stress on policy differences and increased still further by an in-built tendency to an all-or-nothing, "yes" or "no" response to the policy in dispute. The very concept of program packages sug-

[12] Gabis, *op. cit.*, p. 46, writes that "under program budgeting the increase or decrease in the power and influence of each program would be spelled out in detail. It would be surprising if each addition or subtraction were not accompanied by a complicated process of maneuver and counter-maneuver among the affected program heads."

gests that the policy in dispute is indivisible, that the appropriate response is to be for or against rather than bargaining for a little more or a little less. Logrolling and bargaining are hindered because it is much easier to trade increments conceived in monetary terms than it is to give in on basic policy differences. Problems of calculation are vastly increased by the necessity, if program budgeting is to have meaning, of evaluating the desirability of every program as compared to all others, instead of the traditional practice of considering budgets in relatively independent segments. Conflict would become much more prevalent as the specialist whose verdict was usually accepted in his limited sphere gave way to the generalist whose decisions were fought over by all his fellow legislators who could claim as much or (considering the staggering burden of calculation) as little competence as he. The Hobbesian war of all against all, though no doubt an exaggeration, is suggestive on this score.

I wish to make it clear that I am not saying that the traditional method of budgeting is good because it tends to reduce the amount of conflict. Many of us may well want more conflict in specific areas rather than less. What I am saying is that mitigation of conflict is a widely shared value in our society, and that we ought to realize that program budgeting is likely to affect that value.

THE PROGRAM BUDGET IN THE DEPARTMENT OF DEFENSE

By 1960 it had become clear that the major decisions of the Department of Defense revolved around the choice of hugely expensive weapons systems designed to accomplish the military missions of the nuclear era. In order to produce the data most relevant to the choice of alternative weapons systems, including the full cost of development, procurement, and maintenance, the Defense Department, under the aegis of Comptroller Charles J. Hitch, undertook the installation of a program budget. The nation's defense effort was categorized into seven basic programs—strategic retaliatory forces, continental air and missile defense forces, general purpose forces, airlift and sealift forces, special research and development, reserve and national guard forces, and general support—each composed of a number of program elements, such as Polaris submarines and Minuteman missiles, which were devoted to the accomplishment of a common military mission.[13] As it happened, the new program budget was used mainly for internal purposes; it was deemed desirable to present the defense budget to Congress by converting the program categories into the more traditional rubrics such as procurement, construction, and personnel. Although it might be good practice to use different kinds of budgets for internal and external purposes—or even to devise several different budget formulations for use by department officials—the installation of the program budget under these circumstances does raise interesting political problems that have largely been ignored in the debate over the superior efficiency of the old or new budget formulations.

Hearings before Senator Henry Jackson's Subcommittee on National Policy machinery in 1961,[14] in which program budgeting was discussed by knowledgeable participants, gives us an opportunity to suggest some of its likely policy implications. The hearings were held to help determine whether the newly installed program budget in the Defense Department was likely to have desirable consequences for defense policy.

Committee consultant Robert Tufts kept hammering away at the question of why the new program budget in defense would lead to different results than prior practice if the participants remained the same as they had in the past. Ulti-

---

[13] See Charles J. Hitch and Roland N. McKean, *The Economics of Defense in the Nuclear Age* (Cambridge, 1960), and Hitch's "Management of the Defense Dollar," XI *The Federal Accountant* (June 1962) pp. 33-44.

[14] *Jackson Subcommittee Hearings.*

mately, Defense Department Comptroller Charles Hitch admitted that one difference would be that "Program decisions . . . are decisions of the sort which can only be made by the Secretary and, therefore, the role of the Secretary *and of the Secretary's advisers* will be greater" (italics supplied) (pp. 1031-32). The most significant result of the program budget may turn out to be the increased power it gives to the Secretary of Defense.

Former Comptroller Wilfred McNeil asserted that program packages

> would not be conducive to economy of force. . . . I would assume the number of destroyers in active service is probably around 225. I can assure you that if you broke that package up . . . budgetwise, and allocated and assigned . . . separate groups of destroyers to the carrier force, to a possible convoy force, to an antisubmarine force, and to the various odd jobs they do, that you will find requirements above 225. . . . By budgeting for the maintenance of 225 destroyers and then thinking flexibly about their use, . . . you will find you don't need quite as many as you would if you divided them up in neat packages (p. 1066).

The point is that the way a budget is arranged suggests ways of thinking and comparison and that if you change the form you change the kinds of calculations and the probable outcomes.[15]

---

[15] In *Governing New York City*, Wallace Sayre and Herbert Kaufman show that "an almost incredibly detailed 'line item' budget, which the Budget Director has in fact prepared and of which only he and his staff are masters" is a potent factor in increasing that official's influence over budgetary decisions. They also observe that "Some of the city's most articulate interest groups have within the last decade found a weapon . . . by seizing upon a demand (widely supported by new budget doctrine in national, state, and local governments elsewhere) for a change . . . to a 'program' or 'performance' budget. This change would open up the budget process to more critical public scrutiny, increase the discretion of the Mayor and agency heads to make budget decisions, and restrict the opportunities of the Board of Estimate and the Budget Director to make their traditional detailed expenditure decisions." (New York, 1960) pp. 368-369.

Senator Jackson chimed in with the observation that "What troubles me is that if . . . under the program package approach, the service finds that with the big increase occurring [say] . . . in the strategic striking force—other items are cut back, maybe they would be reluctant to push the newer and more costly programs that would tend to offset the so-called balance of forces within their own department." "All I can say," Hitch replied, "is that . . . under the program package procedures there is less chance of those cutbacks affecting the same service so that the tendency to hold back for this reason should be considerably less" (p. 1019). Perhaps. But if Hitch were correct, then inter-service rivalry would be increased and these severe conflicts might lead to similar difficulties. And if we take McNeil's hint and note that "almost the entire Army, with the exception of Air Defense, is in one grouping [program package]" (p. 1063), the Army would have to defend the strategic concept behind that program to the bitter end or else see the service disappear with a change in program.

Another kind of jurisdictional problem was brought up by Senator Jacob Javits. "If you [the Defense Department] are going to bring programs to the Appropriations Committee rather than the Armed Service Committees of the House and Senate," Javits asked, "do you think that we are going to have to do something about our congressional review of your programs . . . ? You are coming now with the basic program concept. When Congress approves your budget it approves the concept" (p. 1027). Speaking of program packages seems mild enough. But who is brave enough to tell the Armed Services Committees to abdicate their present responsibilities and powers?

The late Senator Mundt had his own worries. Although he was perfectly willing to accept the idea of program packages, he was disturbed by Budget Director David Bell's talk about country program packages in foreign aid budgeting.

To me [Mundt declared] that opens up a Pandora's box of undesirable possibilities. I think if the word gets out that the U.S. Government, in its annual budgeting, is providing a country program . . . in Africa, Asia, and Latin America . . . that we are not too far away from the day when, in addition to the Appropriations Committees . . . listening to delegations from every one of our 50 States who come in for public works projects, we can anticipate we will have delegations from every one of 100 different countries (pp. 1150-51).

Whether or not program budgeting will lead to "better budgeting" in some sense is a moot point. (McNeil felt that those in authority might want to consider all sorts of packages at different times rather than being stuck with one in the budget. They might want to consider the portion of the effort allocated to offense as compared to defense of the United States, to look at the effort allocated to the defense of the fighting forces themselves in forward areas, and to group expenditures by geographic area to be defended and by proportion of defense effort going into research and testing versus actual procurement of military hardware [p. 1062]). What is clear is that the kind of categories used and the procedures of program budgeting are likely to have important consequences for our defense policies.

EFFICIENCY

I do not mean to disparage in any way the important problem of efficiency, of finding ways to maximize budgetary benefits given a specified distribution of shares. In principle, there seems to be no reason why policy machinery could not be so arranged as to alter the ratio of inputs to outputs without changing the distribution of shares. One can imagine situations in which everyone benefits or where the losses suffered in one respect are made up by greater gains elsewhere. It may happen that such losses as do exist are not felt by the participants and they may be happy to make changes that increase their benefits. The inevitable lack of full information and the disinclination of participants to utilize their political resources to the fullest extent undoubtedly leave broad areas of inertia and inattention open for change. Thus, the "slack" in the system may leave considerable room for ingenuity and innovation in such areas as benefit cost analysis and the comparability and interrelatedness of public works without running into outstanding political difficulties or involving large changes in the system. Most practical budgeting may take place in a twilight zone between politics and efficiency. Without presenting a final opinion on this matter, it does seem to me that the problem of distributing shares has either been neglected entirely or has been confused with the problem of efficiency to the detriment of both concerns. The statements in this chapter should be understood to refer only to the question of determining shares in the budget.

KNOWLEDGE AND REFORM

The overriding concern of the literature on budgeting with normative theory and reform has tended to obscure the fact that we know very little about the budgetary process. Aside from the now classical articles on Congressional oversight of administration by Arthur McMahon,[16] a splendid article on internal relationships within the House Appropriations Committee by Richard Fenno,[17] and several excellent books on aspects of military budgeting,[18] there is virtually nothing of

[16] Arthur MacMahon, "Congressional Oversight of Administration," LVIII *Political Science Quarterly* (June and September, 1943) pp. 161-190 and 380-414.

[17] Richard F. Fenno, Jr., "The House Appropriations Committee as a Political System: The Problem of Integration," LVI *The American Political Science Review* (June 1962) pp. 310-324.

[18] Frederick C. Mosher, *Program Budgeting: Theory and Practice, with Particular Reference to the U.S. Department of the Army* (Public Administration Service, 1954); Samuel Huntington, *The Common Defense* (New York, 1961) pp. 197-283; Warner Schilling, Paul Hammond, and Glenn Snyder, *Strategy, Politics, and Defense Budgets* (New York,

substance about how or why budgetary decisions are actually made. Chapters 2 and 3 were devoted to filling in this gap in our knowledge of budgeting.

Our concentration in this volume on developing at least the rudiments of an adequate description of the national budgetary process is not meant to discourage concern with normative considerations or reform. On the contrary, budgeting is worth studying from both standpoints. Surely, it is not too much to suggest that a lot of reform be preceded by a little knowledge. Until we develop a more adequate description of budgeting, until we know something about the "existential situation" in which the participants find themselves under our political system, proposals for major reform must be based on woefully inadequate understanding. A proposal which alters established relationships, which does not permit an agency to show certain programs in the most favorable light, which does not tell influential Congressmen what they want to know, which changes prevailing expectations about the behavior of key participants, or which leads to different kinds of calculations, would have many consequences no one is even able to guess at today. Of course, small, incremental changes proceeding in a pragmatic fashion of trial and error could proceed as before without benefit of theory; but this is not the kind of change with which the literature on budgeting is generally concerned.

Suppose, however, that a fresh appraisal of the budgetary process were made taking as its point of departure the material that has been presented in Chapters 2 and 3 on the kinds of behavior that actually take place in budgeting. How well, then, would the existing process stand up under criticism, especially when compared to the alternative mechanisms that have been suggested to replace it? This is the question we shall examine in the final chapter.

1962). See also the earlier study by Elias Huzar, *The Purse and the Sword* (Ithaca, N. Y., 1950).

APPRAISALS
5

In DESCRIBING THE budgetary process we have identified a number of basic characteristics that have called forth a great deal of criticism. The aids to calculation have been decried as arbitrary and irrational. The specialized, incremental, fragmented, and sequential budgetary procedures have been faulted as leading to a lack of coordination and a neglect of consequences. The participants in budgeting have been attacked for concern with "special" rather than general interests. Their roles are considered to be excessively narrow rather than broad, and the strategies they follow are condemned as opportunistic if not immoral.

The alternative budgetary process envisaged by the critics is quite different from the one we now have. Instead of aids to calculation such as the incremental method, they prefer comprehensive and simultaneous evaluation of means and ends. Coordination should be made the explicit concern of a central hierarchy that should consider a wide range of alternative expenditures and investigate rather fully the consequences of each and the probability of their occurring. Furthermore, each participant should seek to protect the general interest rather than the particular interests directly within his jurisdiction. Strategies should be eschewed or, at least, based on the merits of the program rather than on making the best possible case.[1]

Our purpose in this chapter is to appraise the existing set of budgetary practices and the major suggested alternatives. I shall argue that the present budgetary process, though far from perfect, performs much better than has been thought, and is in many ways superior to the proposed alternatives. Far from doing away with budgetary reform, however, this conclusion opens the way for changes that are both more appropriate and more feasible.

COMPREHENSIVENESS

The inherent difficulty of many programs such as space exploration, the huge mass and magnitude of items encountered in such areas as defense, the technical knowledge required to understand such budgetary devices as work-load data, and the subtleties of comparing people's varied preferences in such areas as welfare programs, make complexity a central concern of the participants. Yet time is in short supply, man's ability to calculate is limited, and there are few theories and no a priori bases that would enable the participants to predict the consequences of alternative actions. For the men concerned with budgeting, finding some method of calculation that will

[1] The position of the critics is a composite judgment based on a reading of the literature, private conversations, and remarks made on several occasions when the author has lectured on the budgetary process. The literature referred to includes A. E. Buck, *Public Budgeting* (New York, 1929); (Hoover) Commission on the Organization of the Executive Branch of the Government, *Budget and Accounting* (Washington, D.C., 1949); Jesse Burkhead, *Government Budgeting* (New York, 1956); Arthur Smithies, *The Budgetary Process in the United States* (New York, 1955); and various articles. For a recent exposition of the comprehensive approach see Edward A. Kolodziej, "Congressional Responsibility for the Common Defense: The Money Problem," XVI *The Western Political Quarterly* (March 1963) pp. 149-160.

enable them to make decisions is no small task. So they take short cuts. They specialize. They use the past as a rough experimental guide to the present, and they use decisions made in increments to gather information on consequences. They make decisions repetitively and sequentially so that values neglected at one time and place may be considered at another. They fragment their areas of concern so they are not dealing with too much at any one time, and they rely on feedback for information on whether or not others have been hurt by their actions. And so on down the list of aids to calculation we have previously discussed. In addition, there are a great many personal work procedures which ordinarily are not written down but which involve drastic simplifications and short cuts.

Far from being unique, the kinds of apparently arbitrary aids to calculation employed in budgeting are universally followed in dealing with complex problems. Business organizations use "share of the market" as an operational guide to simplify their calculations.[2] Citizens use party preference, a favorite columnist, advice from a friend, to cut their information costs in making voting decisions.[3] We often take small steps (buying a suit at a time instead of all clothing at once) to see how things will turn out as a way of approximating in time a reasonable choice. Yet when these methods are brought out into the open in governmental decision making there is much muttering and shaking of heads. They are decried as being arbitrary, extraneous, foolish, irresponsible, and (worst of all) the epitome of irrationality.

One prescription for "rationally" solving problems of calculation is to engage in comprehensive and simultaneous means-ends analysis. But budget officials soon discover that ends are rarely agreed upon, that they keep changing, that possible con-

[2] See Richard Cyert and James March, *A Behavioral Theory of the Firm* (Englewood Cliffs, N. J., 1963).

[3] See Anthony Downs, *An Economic Theory of Democracy* (New York, 1957).

sequences of a single policy are too numerous to describe, and that knowledge of the chain of consequences for other policies is but dimly perceived for most conceivable alternatives. The result, as Charles Lindblom has demonstrated, is that although this comprehensive approach can be described it cannot be practiced because it puts too great a strain by far on man's limited ability to calculate.[4] What budget officials need are not injunctions to be rational but operational guides that will enable them to manage the requisite calculations. Commands like "decide according to the intrinsic merits," "consider everything relevant," "base your decision on complete understanding," are simply not helpful; they do not exclude anything; they do not point to operations that can be performed to arrive at a decision as do the aids to calculation.

In this context it can be seen that across-the-board cuts, the so-called meat-axe approach, have definite utilities for Congressmen and Budget Bureau people. If one supposes unlimited comprehension and knowledge, then across-the-board cuts have little to recommend them. But when no one really is in a position to predict the consequences of various alternatives or the probability of their occurring, or even to know what the facts are, this approach may enable the decision makers to test the accuracy of the agency's prognostications. A Congressman will tell you that he often finds that nothing terrible has happened; and when he does he can change things next year or permit the agency to change them as they come up. A percentage cut or increase, providing it is not too large, may be viewed as a marginal change enabling the participants to observe the consequences in a complex area and deal with them piecemeal as they emerge in the future. Obviously, a percentage cut may also enable a Congressman to gain credit for cuts without doing much work and without taking the

[4] "The Science of 'Muddling Through,'" XIX *Public Administration Review* (Spring 1959) pp. 79-88. See also Lindblom and Braybrooke, *A Strategy of Decision* (New York, 1963).

responsibility for making them in specific areas. Indeed, this practice is commonly regarded as uncraftsmanlike by other Congressmen because it suggests that recommendations are not based on very great understanding. But it does appear that the method may have a more persuasive justification as an aid to calculation than is usually credited to it.

All that is accomplished by injunctions to follow a comprehensive approach is the inculcation of guilt among good men who find that they can never come close to fulfilling this unreasonable expectation. Worse still, acceptance of an unreasonable goal inhibits discussion of the methods actually used. Thus responsible officials may feel compelled to maintain the acceptable fiction that they review (almost) everything, yet when they describe their actual behavior, it soon becomes apparent that they do not. As a case in point take former Budget Director Stans' injunction to follow the comprehensive approach: ". . . every item in a budget ought to be on trial for its life each year and matched against all the other claimants to our resources." But when Jackson questioned Stans about his practice in relation to the defense budget, he replied, ". . . We dealt with specific issues and specific programs. . . . When all of these specific issues and programs were resolved . . . one way or the other—the budget then was the result of all the considerations up to that point and there were no further issues to be resolved in respect to the total size of the budget."[5] It would be amazing if the President or the Budget Director had the time, let alone the capacity, to deal with more than six to ten major defense items at the outside. The vast gulf between the theories espoused by some budget officials and their practice stems, I believe, from their adherence to a norm deeply imbedded in our culture, which

[5] Committee on Government Operations, Subcommittee on National Policy Machinery, U.S. Senate, *Organizing for National Security; The Budget and the Policy Process*, 87th Congress, 1st Session, 1961, p. 1103.

holds that the very definition of rational decision is comprehensive and simultaneous examination of ends and means.

In a complaint typifying those made by advocates of comprehensive budgeting, Senator Mundt scores the existing process for its evident lack of simultaneous consideration of appropriations.

> I thought you [Stans] made a tremendously interesting point when you said that the Bureau of the Budget or congressional Appropriations Committees sometimes have a tendency to feel that they have done pretty well if they look at the budget for last year and use that as a floor. . . . There is some kind of Sir Galahad merit about not exceeding the previous year's budget, without examining whether there were previous expenses which did not have a right to recur.[6]

Failure to consider the contributions toward calculation of the existing budgetary process distorts the magnitude of the problem. We have seen that new programs and substantial increases and decreases in old programs do receive close attention. In addition, the political system brings subjects to public attention as interest groups, politicians, or bureaucrats, anxious to make an issue, demand an investigation. What escapes intensive scrutiny is not the whole but only certain parts, which carry on much as before. The fact that some activities do not receive intensive scrutiny is hardly sufficient reason to do everything over every year.

Insofar as a problem exists, it can be met by following an incremental approach making use of the division of labor in the government. Attention may be focused on those activities which do not change much from year to year, since these are the ones that are not thoroughly reviewed. Certainly, since they do not alter radically, a thorough going over approximately once in every four or five years ought to be sufficient.

[6] *Ibid.*, pp. 1106-1107. The author and a student, Arthur Hammond, are now engaged in a study of the attempt of the Department of Agriculture to carry out a zero-base budget.

Nor need any one organizaton do it all. Department Budget offices and the Budget Bureau may use a sampling technique so that together they review a few programs of this kind every year. The results could then be used to see if more activity was warranted the next year. The bureaus themselves, the House Appropriations Committee investigating staff, the General Accounting Office, might also select a small number of programs on a sampling basis. In this way one could meet a good part of the criticism while adding only a little to the burden of these governmental organizations.

The procedure advocated here should also help to reduce the temptation to engage in strategies capitalizing on the incremental nature of budgeting. These strategies are designed to show that a new program is really an extension of an old one or that large increases are not as great as they seem and, therefore, should avoid special scrutiny. (If the costs of programs are "hidden," Congress may be letting itself in for greater increases in appropriations than it realizes.) The Budget Bureau and the appropriations committee are on the lookout for these strategies and this has helped somewhat. Further progress has been made by requiring agencies to set out proposed expenditures over the life of the program. The expectation that a sampling procedure may bring to light these strategies should go further to reduce their incidence. Thus an incremental approach may be used to mitigate the evils arising out of its less desirable consequences.

Rather than turn everything upside down, it is often possible to modify or compensate for existing practices in a way that lessens the burden of calculation. One central budget office made a study of cost estimates and actual costs in field offices. It discovered that field personnel had excellent records in pointing out the work that would have to be done in order to meet program requirements and that they were reasonably accurate in estimating the amount and kinds of labor required. Where they fell down badly was in estimating the

total cost, taking into account "hidden" factors such as pro-
rated time of office personnel. The analysis of the central
budget office permitted an incremental approach to the problem. In the reform, the estimates of field personnel for work
required and labor costs were accepted as before by the budget
office. It instituted new procedures, however, enabling it to
estimate more accurately total costs by adding other factors
to the figures supplied from the field. The goal of more accurate estimation was achieved by letting existing procedures go
as far as they could and then correcting them.[7]

Improvements in methods of budgetary calculation are
more likely to occur if the stigma attached to using some aids
to calculation is removed. Then it may be possible to see
whether some rules of thumb are not better than others. Instead of prestige attaching to the spurious claim to have considered everything, men might vie with one another to see
whether they could not develop shorter cuts and better ap-
proximations to lessen the burden of calculation. As it is now,
there is virtually no discussion of the rules of thumb currently
in use because the practitioners know how rough their tools
are and rightly fear that the necessity for using some such
methods will not be appreciated.

COORDINATION

The fact that the budgetary process is not comprehensive has
given rise to charges that it is uncoordinated. Indeed, the very
terms that we have used to describe budgetary practices—specialized, incremental, fragmented, sequential, non-programmatic—imply that at any one time the budget is not effec-

---

[7] At times it is more efficient to work with the data at hand than to go
to the expense of collecting new and better information. One agency
discovered that by ordering a re-run of information already on IBM
cards it could arrive at cost estimates that were tolerably close. By collecting new information, the reporting system could be improved to the
point at which estimates would be more accurate. It was judged, however, that the additional accuracy would not be worth the added cost.

tively considered as a whole so as to systematically relate its component parts to one another. As long as the lack of coordination is the result of ignorance of other people's activities or the complexity of organization, there is a good chance of overcoming it by dedicated staff work or some formal mechanism to accomplish the intended result. But in many cases lack of coordination is a result of conflicting views about policy that are held by men and agencies that have independent bases of influence in society and in Congress. The only way to secure coordination in these cases is for one side to convince or coerce or bargain with the other. When it is understood that "coordination" is often just another word for "coercion," the full magnitude of the problem becomes apparent. For there is no one, the President and Congressional leaders included, who is charged with the task of dealing with the budget as a whole and who is capable of enforcing his preferences. (The question of whether it is possible to consider all or most of the relevant considerations is omitted here.) Vesting of formal power to effectively coordinate the budget would, as I have argued previously, be tantamount to a radical change in the national political system, requiring the abolition of the separation of powers and a federally controlled party system, among other things. What may be said about coordination, then, if we take the existing political system as not subject to drastic change?

By taking as our standard of coordination the establishment of a formal structure charged with the task and capable of executing it, we come up with an obvious answer: there is very little coordination excepting what the President can manage through the Budget Bureau. By accepting the possibility of informal coordination, of participants who take into account what others are doing, we can say there is a great deal of coordination that has escaped the notice of many observers.

Let us pose the following question: how does an appropriations subcommittee know when things are not working out in other areas affected by its actions? Are its decisions coordinated with budgetary decisions made by other subcommittees? Part of the answer is found in a comment by a committee member to the effect that "People can't be too badly off if they don't complain." The subcommittees do not consider themselves to be the only participants in budgeting. They expect, in accordance with sequential decision making, that subcommittees in the affected areas will take corrective action. When an agency shouts more loudly than usual, when an interest group mounts a campaign, when other Congressmen begin to complain, subcommittee members have a pretty good idea that something is wrong. If their perceptions of the array of political forces lead them astray, the appropriations subcommittees can be brought back into line by a rebellion within the full committee or by an adverse vote on the floor. For unless members have an exceedingly intense preference, they will try to come up with appropriations that will not be reversed on the floor. To do otherwise would be to risk losing the great prestige the committee enjoys. The subcommittee may be thought of as exercising discretion within a zone of indifference within which others are not aware or not sufficiently concerned to challenge them but beyond which others will begin to mobilize against them. In this way, a semblance of coordination is maintained. And as time passes the participants come to develop a tacit understanding as to the general level of most appropriations, a phenomenon we have previously designated by the notion of fair shares. No one has to check up on everyone; it is sufficient that occasional marked departures from commonly held notions of fair shares would generate opposition.

Widespread acceptance of this concept of fair shares may go a long way toward accounting for the degree of coordination (the extent to which participants take into account what others do) that does exist among expenditure totals. The total budget was rarely drastically out of line with expenditures before it was formalized in 1921, and even without control by a central authority today we do not usually get extraordinary increases or decreases in the absence of national emergencies. There has been much more subtle and informal coordination by tacit agreements and accepted limits than there has previously been thought to be.

To some the procedure by which the agencies (as well as the Appropriations Committees and the Budget Bureau to a lesser extent) try to gauge "what will go" may seem unfortunate. They feel that there must be a better justification for programs than the subjective interpretation of signals from the environment. Yet we live in a democracy in which a good part of the justification for programs is precisely that they are deemed desirable by others. What is overlooked is that these informal procedures are also powerful coordinating mechanisms. When one thinks of all the participants who are continuously engaged in interpreting the wishes of others, who try to feel the pulse of Congress, the President, interest groups, and special publics, it is clear that a great many adjustments are made in anticipation of what other participants are likely to do. This, it seems to me, is just another term for coordination.[8]

Instead of the enormous burden of calculating the consequences for others being placed on one man or organization, the fragmentation of influence assures that the task will be factored out to many participants. Those directly affected are expected to make their preferences felt so that they can be taken into account by others. The point is not that this system is perfect but rather that it does do some coordinating in a rough-and-ready way. One need not contemplate the

[8] If one insists that coordination be defined to include conscious control by a single individual or group, then the usage in this paragraph does not fit.

hopeless task of replacing the system; improvement is possible by an incremental approach, which asks where the system does not function well and seeks to remedy the worst difficulties.

NEGLECT

There can be no doubt that lack of comprehensiveness in budgeting means that in making a specific decision important values affected by that decision are neglected at that time. Hence the budgetary process is attacked for its apparent neglect of consequences. In countering this criticism, Charles Lindblom has put forth the proposition that consequences neglected by one participant may be considered by another or by the same participant working on another problem.[9] To the extent, therefore, that all significant interests tend to be represented in a fragmented political system, decision makers may reduce their information costs by neglecting many alternatives in the confidence that they will be picked up by others or by themselves at another time. Thus the budgetary process as a whole may be considered reasonable even though the actions of individual participants may not seem to be because they omit from their calculations consequences important for others. In response to this line of argument, the noted economist Abram Bergson has agreed that a realistic consideration of rationality should certainly include the costs of finding and using information on alternatives. But he "wonders . . . whether the official who neglected important aspects on the ground that they would be properly weighed in the decision-making process as a whole might not often be disappointed."[10]

We may begin to meet this objection by observing that many consequences are taken into account by someone in the

[9] See his "Decision-Making in Taxation and Expenditure," *Public Finances: Needs, Sources and Utilization,* National Bureau of Economic Research (Princeton, 1961) pp. 295-336.

[10] *Ibid.,* p. 333.

system. Moreover, the political process in a democracy has a built-in feature that assures that some presently neglected values will be considered. This mechanism exists because politicians and interest-group leaders are motivated, by their hope of retaining or winning office, to find needs that have not been met and proposing to fulfill them in return for votes. We need to concentrate, then, on those values which are likely to receive little or no consideration.

Some groups of people find that their preferences are neglected. Migrant laborers, for example, do not vote and are not organized. That the prizes in democratic politics go to the active and organized should come as no great surprise. The situation is not quite as bad as it might be, however, because the Department of Labor has to some extent constituted itself as a guardian of the interests of migrant laborers. By joining with private citizens who have some altruistic interest in this underprivileged group, the Labor Department has managed to do something for them. Thus one way of compensating for the defects of this system is to make a part of a bureaucracy the protector of a neglected interest. Naturally, this expedient is not as good as if the people affected possessed the resources to protect themselves. Those who claim that values are neglected but who are not willing to undertake the political work necessary to give them expression should not be shocked if they do not accomplish much.

Apart from this political activity, however, the demonstration that values of importance are being neglected may be taken as one of the tasks of social scentists. This task is often difficult. Consider the usual claim that the interests of future generations in the realm of natural resources are being sacrificed to the present. Extreme cases have certainly occurred in the past and the depletion of forests and recreation areas has been fought by sportsmen and conservation groups who have succeeded in establishing bureaucracies to protect these values. (This mobilization is itself not without its cost, since such a bureaucracy as the Forest Service comes to develop professional norms that are resistant to such improvements as controlled burning).[11] In many other instances, however, as Milliman has pointed out, conservation proposals may result in penalizing a poorer present in favor of a richer future. Standards of living have been rising and it is not always clear that the present should subsidize the future.[12]

Imagine (for purposes of discussion) that a clear and un-equivocal demonstration could be made that certain values had been neglected. The proof might commend itself to men of good will and steps might be taken to remedy the situation. Yet the required action might carry with it disadvantages for others who would fight to protect themselves. The task would then be one of mobilizing the political support required to overcome their resistance, and part of this task would rest on the demonstration to others that important values had been neglected. Assuming the political system to be democratic, it is difficult to see how any changes, even of a radical kind, could do away with this political requirement. If the President were the only decision maker who counted, it would still be necessary to convince him that he could afford to follow the indicated policy. To maintain the contrary is to suggest that the politicians in a democracy need not be concerned with political costs.[13]

[11] Ashley L. Schiff, *Fire and Water: Scientific Heresy in the Forest Service* (Cambridge, Mass., 1962).

[12] J. W. Milliman, "Can People be Trusted with Natural Resources?" XXXVIII *Land Economics* (August 1962) pp. 199-218.

[13] By "political costs" I refer not only to loss of popularity with segments of the electorate, but also to loss of esteem and effectiveness with other participants in the political system, and to loss of ability to secure policies other than the one immediately under consideration. Those who continually urge the President to go all out—that is, use all his resources on a wide range of issues—rarely stop to consider that the price of success in one area of policy may be defeat in another. If he loses popularity with the electorate, as President Truman did, he may find that Congress turns down virtually his whole domestic program. If he cracks down on the steel industry, as President Kennedy did, he may find himself constrained to lean over backwards in the future to avoid unremitting hos-

This is not to say that improvements in calculating affected values, such as cost-benefit analysis, have no place. Assuming that the method will continue to be improved, and that one accepts the private market as the measure of economic value, it can certainly tell decision makers something about what they will be giving up if they follow a different policy. By using two methods—one based on regional and the other on national factors—an appraisal might be made of the economic costs of federalism. Cost-benefit analysis also has some possible political uses that might be stressed more than they have been. The technique gives the responsible official a good reason for turning down projects together with a public-interest explanation the Congressman can use with his constituents and the interest-group leader with his members. The burden of calculation may be reduced by following cost-benefit analysis for many projects and introducing other values only for a few. To expect, however, that the method itself (which distributes indulgences to some and deprivations to others) would not be subject to manipulation in the political process is to say that we shall be governed by formula and not by men.

Consider the situation in which an agency finds it desirable to achieve a geographical spread in its projects in order to establish a wider base of support. Assume (with good reason) that cost-benefit criteria will not permit projects to be established in some states because the value of the land or water is too low. One can say that this is just too bad and observe the agency seeking ways around the restriction by playing up benefits, playing down costs, or attacking the whole benefit cost concept as inapplicable. Another approach would be to recognize that federalism—meaning, realistically, the distribution of indulgences to state units—represents a political value

tility from the business community. Resources like patronage are strictly limited and use in one case prohibits use in another once the appointment has been made. Political benefits occur when an official gains in popularity, esteem, effectiveness, and resources that he can use in another case.

worth promoting to some extent and that gaining nation-wide support is important. From this viewpoint, a compromise solution would be to except one or two projects in each state or region from meeting the full requirement of the formula, though the projects with the highest benefit-cost ratio would have to be chosen. In return for sacrificing full adherence to the formula in a few instances, one would get enhanced support for it in many others.

Because the cost-benefit formula does not always jibe with political realities—that is, it omits political costs and benefits —we can expect it to be twisted out of shape from time to time. Yet cost-benefit analysis may still be important in getting rid of the worst projects. Avoiding the worst where you can't get the best is no small accomplishment.

Up to this point we have omitted an exceedingly important mechanism for overcoming the difficulties caused by the partial neglect of consequences in making individual budgetary decisions. Let us turn, therefore, to a discussion of the various roles adopted by participants in budgeting, roles that result in the protection of a multitude of different values by different participants.

ROLES

Roles (the expectations of behavior attached to institutional positions) are part of the division of labor. They may, therefore, be viewed as calculating mechanisms. In appraising them, however, it must be understood that no one role exists apart from others. The relationship between the whole complex of roles—the agency as advocate, the Budget Bureau as Presidential servant with a cutting bias, the House Appropriations Committee as guardian of the Treasury, the Senate Appropriations Committee as responsible appeals court— must be considered before the constitutent parts may be evaluated.

The roles fit in with one another and set up a stable pattern of mutual expectations, which do a great deal to reduce the burden of calculations for the participants. The agencies need not consider in great detail how their requests will affect the President's over-all program; they know that such criteria will be introduced in the Budget Bureau. The Appropriations Committees and the Budget Bureau know that the agencies are likely to put forth all the programs for which there is prospect of support and can concentrate on fitting them into the President's program or on paring them down. The Senate Committee operates on the assumption that if important items are left out through House action the agency will carry an appeal. If the agencies suddenly reversed roles and sold themselves short, the entire pattern of mutual expectations might be upset, leaving the participants without a firm anchor in a sea of complexity. This kind of situation sometimes appeared in Weather Bureau appropriations because the agency was exceedingly cautious in putting forth its claims. Hence the following type of questioning arose in House and Senate hearings:

Rep. Thomas. You should have been a little more aggressive, should you not?

Weather Bureau Official. I agree with you . . .

Rep. Thomas. It is no fault of the committee [that the bureau ran out of essential funds]. It is no fault of the Bureau of the Budget.

Senator Smith. Have you requested enough money to permit you to progress as fast as you can?

Weather Bureau Official. Senator Smith, I wonder if there is any agency that ever gets enough money. There are always so many things you can do beyond the budget possibilities. Certainly we could use a great deal more . . .

Senator Smith. My question was prompted because we cannot know what you could use unless you tell us. . . . If you do not ask for it, the point is, the responsibility is yours, is it not?

If the agency refuses the role of advocate, it increases the burden on the Congressmen; they not only have to choose among desirable items placed before them with some fervor, they also have to discover what these items might be. This is a task ordinarily far beyond their limited time, energy, information, and competence. Hence the insistence by Thomas and Smith that they should not be held responsible if the agency does not perform its expected role in the budgetary division of labor.

The roles also appear to be "natural" to the occupants of these institutional positions. A man who has spent many years working in, say, the natural resources area can be expected to believe that his programs are immensely worthy of support. (He may try to eliminate programs he deems unworthy but there are always others to take their place.) Indeed, he would hardly be worth having as a governmental employee if he did not feel this way in his position. One can only imagine what the reaction would be if such a person intimated that soil conservation, reforestation, or recreation might just possibly be all right but that he was more than ready to believe that many, many other things were equally or more important, and that his projects could easily be postponed or eliminated. By serving as advocate in the real world he sees to it that important values in his area are not neglected if he can help it.

Unless one is disposed to argue on political grounds that Presidents should be made less powerful, the existence of a Budget Bureau to overcome his limitations of time, energy, and knowledge seems desirable. And helping him as he wishes to be helped would seem to be the proper role for Bureau staff. Beyond the point of safeguarding the preferences of the Presidential constituency, the Bureau is compelled by agency advocacy to take on a cutting role. Even where the Bureau is disposed to increase a program over the previous year, the chances are that the agency is requesting even more and there is little choice but to wield the knife. The Bureau does on occasion work to help an agency get more funds in areas in which the political process seems negligent. It might be suggested that the Bureau do more of this and constitute itself a guardian of some interests not satisfactorily protected elsewhere, perhaps because appropriations committees find it attractive to cut in such places as administrative expenses and maintenance. How much of this the Bureau could afford to do might best be discovered by doing a little more.

The House Appropriations Committee's role of guarding the Treasury, with its emphasis on reducing requests, makes sense in the context of agency advocacy. If the Congressmen can be reasonably certain that the agency has put its best foot forward, then their decisions may be viewed as choices along the margins of the top percentage of expenditures advocated by the agencies. Guardianship provides the Congressmen with a stance that supplies reasonably clear instructions—cut the estimates—while keeping the area within which they must focus their attention—the largest increases—manageable in terms of their limited time and ability to calculate. Nor need the cuts be stereotyped. By varying the severity and the areas in which cuts are made, and by an occasional increase, committee members can keep administrators responsive. And it should be realized that the total sum of agency appropriations normally increases from year to year; it is the estimates, increased perhaps by the assumption of advocacy, which are cut.

Suppose we imagine that the House Appropriations Committee adopted the role of "attacking the Treasury" by consistently advocating increases in estimates. The orientations of other participants remaining the same, we would have to assume that the role of attacking the Treasury would put Congress in the position of advocating substantially greater expenditures. This event is unlikely, to say the least. A more likely consequence would be a change in roles by one of the other participants. Either the agencies would be compelled to accept artificially low estimates or the Budget Bureau would take over the role of guardianship, systematically reducing requests way below present practice. This, in turn, would depend on the President's willingness to accept a more negative role. One suspects that the game by which administrators make known their preferences to Congressmen would be played with a vengeance and that informal processes would operate to counteract the formal ones.

Barring an unexpected change in the agency role of advocacy, guardianship would seem to be a more appropriate and more viable role for appropriations committee members than one of attacking the Treasury. But "attack" and "guardianship" at least share one virtue; they both provide a firm orientation toward the budget that defines the roles of the participants and establishes a division of labor that reduces the burden of calculation.

An alternative role for the appropriations committee members would be one that could be described as "mixed." The Congressmen would be oriented toward neither cutting nor increasing but to doing both in about equal proportions. Each case would have to be considered on its own merits. To some extent, of course, this balance occurs under the prevailing system. The difference is one of degree but not less important for being such. For where they are in doubt or do not care to inquire in detail, the Congressmen may now follow their prevailing orientation—usually to cut at the margin—expecting to receive feedback if something drastic happens. Under a "mixed" role, however, an exhaustive inquiry into all or most items would be called for. The resulting increase in amounts of calculation required would be immense. And to the extent that other participants adopted a mixed role, the pattern of expectations upon which they are so dependent as a calculating device would no longer prove stable. The calculation of preferences, essential in a democratic system, would become far more burdensome since inquiries would have to be instituted to find out what the various groups wanted in specific cases.

Furthermore, the adoption of a mixed role would be likely to lead to a greater neglect of values (that is, events and objects desired by people) affected by decisions.[14] Unless the ability of each participant to calculate the consequences of his actions is much more impressive than the evidence suggests, he is bound to neglect more if he attempts to do more. Yet this is precisely what a mixed role would force him to do. Instead of concentrating on a limited range of values within his jurisdiction, as his present role requires, he would have to consider the widest possible range of values in order to make a mixed role work. In place of the reasonable certainty that each participant would do a good job of looking after the relatively narrow range of values entrusted to his care, we would have little certainty that any particular value would be protected because no one had been especially directed to look after it. Let us explore this question further as a fundamental problem in normative political theory.

PVPI VERSUS TVPI

Why, it may be asked, should the various participants take a partial view? Why should they not simply decide in accord-

[14] Alain Enthoven and Harry Rowen argue that ". . . One of the most important things any defense allocation mechanism should do is to help prevent gaps from appearing in our capability. . . . [I]t is valuable to have the separate Services 'looking for business,' trying to expand and take on new jobs. . . . Human limitations being what they are, there is good reason to believe that a decentralized competitive system, in which people have incentives to propose alternatives, will usually meet this test more effectively than a highly centralized system." The authors then go on to observe that the Army's tenacity in defending a place for ground forces was useful in helping mitigate an unfortunate tendency to believe that nuclear weapons provided all the capability the nation needed. "Defense Planning and Organization," *Public Finances, Needs, Sources and Utilizations,* National Bureau of Economic Research (Princeton, 1961) pp. 369-371.

ance with what the public interest requires? Actually, this is the principle the participants think they are following now; they all believe that their version of the public interest is correct. It is their differing institutional positions, professional training, and group values that lead to perspectives producing somewhat different interpretations of the public interest. Let us, then, rephrase the question to ask whether it is better for each participant to view the public interest as involved primarily in the achievement of his own goals (including the goals entrusted to him by virtue of his position), or whether he should view the goals of others as of prime or at least equal importance?

I am prepared to argue that the partial-view-of-the-public-interest approach is preferable to the total-view-of-the public-interest approach, which is so often urged as being superior. First, it is much simpler for each participant to calculate his own preferences than for each to try to calculate the preferences of all. It is difficult enough for a participant to calculate how the interests he is protecting might best be served without requiring that he perform the same calculation for many others who might also be affected. The "partial" approach has the virtue of enabling others to accept as an input in their calculations the determination of each participant as to his preferences, which is not possible under the total approach. The danger of omitting important values is much greater when participants neglect the values in their immediate care in favor of what seems to them a broader view. How can anyone know what is being neglected if everyone speaks for someone else and no one for himself? Can we expect participants to act to protect the interests of others (which they believe they should take into account but which are not theirs) as well as those who have these interests?

The partial approach is more efficient for resolving conflicts, a process that lies at the heart of democratic politics. Because the approach is partial, it does not require its practitioners to discover all or most possible conflicts and to work out answers to problems that may never materialize. It permits each participant to go his own way until he discovers that the activities of others interfere. Effort can then be devoted to overcoming the difficulties that do exist. The formation of alliances in a political system that requires them is facilitated by the expression and pursuit of demands by those in closest touch with the social reality from which they issue forth. Then it is not a matter of a kind of *noblesse oblige* that assures that rival demands are considered. It is, rather, that the articulators of these demands insist on being heard and have the political resources to compel a hearing. A partial adversary system in which the various interests compete for control of policy (under agreed-upon rules) seems more likely to result in reasonable decisions—that is, decisions that take account of the multiplicity of values involved—than one in which the best policy is assumed to be discoverable by a well-intentioned search for the public interest for all by everyone.

If it is granted that budgetary practices based on a partial view of the public interest are desirable, then it would appear necessary to accept the use of strategies designed to secure appropriation goals. It is not surprising, however, that critics find something basically underhanded, even undemocratic, in the maneuvering of "special interests" for strategic advantage. Would not a straightforward approach based on the "merits" of each program be preferable? Suppose we proceed to an appraisal of strategies in order to determine whether or not they are desirable in whole or in part.

STRATEGIES

Requiring an individual to commit suicide for the public good may at times have an acceptable rationale; suggesting that it become a common practice can hardly claim as much. I shall take it as understood, then, that asking participants in budgeting consistently to follow practices extremely disadvantageous to themselves and their associates is not reasonable. The participants must be able to maintain themselves in the existing environment. Some strategies may be preferable to others from a moral viewpoint or because they foster changes in response to changes in values and goals. Other strategies may be undesirable because they do not enable certain pressing difficulties to be met. But it would not be helpful to urge strategies which place individuals and programs in the worst possible light or which do not permit the achievement of some success in securing appropriations.

The notion that administrators go around telling each other (or believing in secret) that the purposes for which they request funds are not valid but that they want the money anyway in order to advance themselves and build empires is not worthy of consideration. It would be exceedingly difficult to keep people in an organization if they could not justify its purposes to themselves. Such an attitude would be bound to come to the attention of other participants, who would take appropriate action. It would be bad strategically as well as morally. Attempts to reduce a complex distributive process like budgeting to the terms of a western melodrama—the good men ride white horses and advance on their merits; the bad men wear black masks and rely on strategies—do away with the great problem of deciding upon expenditures advocated by officials who are sincere believers in their proposals, knowing that not all demands can be satisfied.

THE BEST CASE

Budgetary strategies may generally be characterized as proceeding from a standpoint in which requests for appropriations are drawn up in an attempt to make the best case for the agency at the best time. This behavior follows from the role of the agency as advocate. As a practical matter, we would expect any agency head worth his keep to respond to opportunities for increasing appropriations and warding off cuts. Who would want to work for a person who did not give his staff opportunities for achievement by emphasizing the importance of their activities at a time when the reaction is likely to be favorable? The contrary position—making the worst case at the worst time—is not likely to be greeted with enthusiasm.

This orientation need not (and in most cases does not) mean that the estimates are dishonest. The desirability of maintaining confidence over the years suggests, if nothing else, the inadvisability of the slippery statistic and the grossly inaccurate report. What it does mean is that in a world in which there are usually a variety of honest ways to present and compare programs, the approach that experience suggests is likely to make the best impression on the intended audience will be selected. An administrator may have what he considers a dozen good arguments for a program, some more impressive than others, but all valid in some sense. Naturally, he picks and chooses among these for the one with the most appeal at the time.

Take the case of the agency that has several possible bases for estimating how much it will need to spend on a program. It can use an average of the last five years' expenditures; it can use the previous year on the ground that it is closest in time; it can try to make a cost estimate based on an assumed level of services. Now all of these approaches have something to be said for them and all are subject to distortion, although no one can know for certain which will be the most accurate until after the predicted events have occurred. Why, then, should the agency choose the most disadvantageous prediction? In an uncertain world, prudence might dictate leaving an ample margin for error.

Seizing on the opportune moment for advancing the agency's budgetary goals has much to commend it. The nation is served by initiative in meeting the needs of the time. An element of flexibility is generated that helps ensure that opportunities for action will be taken. "Crisis" strategies belong in this category. What is the difference, we may ask, between using a crisis to increase appropriations and acting to meet the nation's requirements in an hour of need? Perhaps some uneasiness results from a fear that a crisis may be created out of whole cloth or exaggerated just to receive funds. The sanctions for deceit being so great we need not concern ourselves unduly with the purely fictional crisis. Exaggeration is the problem. There seems to be no way, however, of avoiding this difficulty other than by intelligent scrutiny of requests at a time when no one may be in a position to assess the magnitude of the danger. The special attention paid to new programs or large increases in old ones under an incremental approach gives some assurance that the proposal will receive considerable scrutiny. On balance, it seems desirable to accept the disabilities flowing from exaggeration in order to reap the benefits of quick response to emergent needs.

The desire to present the agency's requests in the best light can be used in a positive sense to improve the thinking of the operating units. The budget office can play an important role because, though it is in the agency, it is also somewhat outside by virtue of the necessity it faces of justifying actions to the outside world. By playing devil's advocate, by pointing out that justifications are not clear or persuasive, by saying that the program heads have to do better to convince the Budget Bureau or the Appropriations Committee, the Budget office may compel or encourage thinking from diverse perspectives. In this way, a wider range of interests and values receive consideration.

Program people sometimes think they have done enough if they defend their requests as desirable within the agency's own frame of reference. They may become upset, therefore, when the agency head or budget officer insists that this is not enough, that perspectives emanating from the Budget Bureau and Congress also have to be considered, even though the presentation is deemed adequate on its face. The higher one goes in the administrative hierarchy, the more important becomes the task of representing, negotiating, accommodating to the other participants. If this task is done effectively, the prestige of the top official within his agency rises. But in the process he may have to give away some of the things which his people want and which he agrees are justified. Unless one is prepared to argue that what other key participants—other agencies, interest groups, Presidents, Congressmen—want is immaterial, there seems to be no way out of this process of reconciliation of demands. Nor, so long as we accept the separation of powers and democracy, can this process be deemed anything but desirable.

Presenting the best possible case is an aid to calculation for the other participants. They know that if this path is followed they do not have to think about whether or not there are better justifications for the appropriations; they can assume that the best justifications have been made and concentrate on doing their part of the job. It may be that what we want is the best argument on the part of all the agencies so that the worth of the program will be clearly established as a starting point for consideration by others.

SUPPORT

Clientele and confidence strategies are desirable as well as inevitable in a democratic society. The feedback that clientele give to the participants is essential political information about who wants what programs, at what level, and with what degree of intensity. The establishment of confidence provides the trust necessary for living with complexity; the sanctions that follow from lack of confidence represent a great safeguard against duplicity. That morality is to some extent the handmaiden of necessity does not make it any less real or valuable.

Analysis of the principles by which constituencies are formed and cultivated may be used for good purposes. The reader may recall a previous illustration in which the Census Bureau was enabled to get support for a housing census by changing its program from a simple national survey into one in which metropolitan areas were covered, thus increasing greatly the number of interested Congressmen. As long as the essential purpose of the program is not perverted, fitting the activity to the need for widespread constituency support increases an important value in a democratic society—consent. Surely, a program like summer institutes for mathematics teachers is not rendered less desirable by being distributed in a good many constituencies.

The creative arrangement of clientele may be used to alleviate the worst consequences arising out of the need for support. An agency may have to give up some of what it wants in order to receive support for other programs. This bargaining element is woven into the fabric of a democratic system. If the situation becomes untenable, however, so that the agency faces virtual capture by the affected interests, a broader arrangement of constituencies may be in order. The Grazing Service suffered because of its rather complete dependence on stockmen and those who spoke for them in Congress. By merging the Service into an expanded Bureau of Land Management, an act accomplished with the aid of interests adversely affected under the previous arrangement, the new organization has reduced its dependence by being able to appeal to a broader constituency. The Soil Conservation Service, to cite another instance, can afford to incur the wrath of limestone producers, who object to conservation practices that do not use their product, because it gets support from the National Association of Soil Conservation Districts, an interest group it has done much to foster.

The use of strategies is one means by which an agency can try to protect values ordinarily neglected in the political system. Suppose an agency has a marketing program that benefits most people a few dollars a year. Although the total benefits for the whole program are large, it is difficult to gather support for it because no one person receives sufficient benefits to make it worthwhile for him to act. Such a program is a handy target when cuts are made because an active clientele that would protest is lacking. One way in which the agency can protect this less popular program is to adopt a strategy—cutting more popular programs to which funds are likely to be restored—which will leave the less popular program intact. Though the end appears to be justified, the means seem to be suspect. On the surface, a more honest position would seem to require reducing the least valuable program regardless of the consequences for the total budget. One difficulty is that the agency may not be able to rank its programs and may, therefore, see no reason why it should not make the cuts in the places most favorable for its purposes. If the programs with the greatest political popularity are also the least valuable, then no problem arises because the strategy and the moral standard coincide. Cuts will be proposed in the least valuable program. But if the least popular program politically is also least desirable comparatively speaking, and the least desirable is deemed to be valuable in itself, a difficult problem arises. Should we, in the name of honesty, require an agency to sacrifice a program it believes valuable in favor of a more valuable one that is likely to be supported anyway? One could at least argue that total value would be increased by retaining the less popular program, cutting the more popular one, and thus emerging with funds for both. The strategy, of course, is neutral: it could be used to protect poor programs.

DECEIT?

A naked recital of strategies is bound to suggest that a certain amount of trickery or duplicity is involved.[15] Some strategies that appear to be deceitful represent amoral adjustments to an environment that does not give the participants much choice. Consider the kind of duplicity that appears to be involved in the game wherein agency people make believe that they are supporting the President's Budget while actually encouraging Congressmen to ask questions that will permit them to talk about what they would really like to have. Is this behavior immoral or does the immorality belong to the Executive Office directive that tries to compel agency personnel to say things they do not believe in order to support the President? Congress has the power of the purse and it is difficult to argue that it should not have the kind of information—what the people in charge of the program think they ought to get—which may be most helpful in arriving at decisions. If one wants to get rid of Congress, then the problem solves itself. But if one accepts the separation of powers, then it may well be that there is no point in denying to Congress information it would like to have when it is manifestly in the interests of administrators to supply it. The biblical injunction against excessive temptation is appropriate here.

One way to eliminate the element of deceit is to do away with the cause by requiring the publication of what the agency originally asked for from the Budget Bureau. Agencies would still be bound by the President's Budget to the same extent they are now. They just would not have to engage in artful (or not so artful) dodging when the subject is mentioned at hearings. It may be judged that the fiction that the Presi-

[15] Lest anyone receive the mistaken impression that such practices are confined to the government, see the following reference on deceptive practices in industry: Frank Jasinsky, "Use and Misuse of Efficiency Controls," XXXIV *Harvard Business Review* (July and August, 1956) pp. 105-112.

dent's Budget is universally supported is worth maintaining in order to cut down the number of cases in which contrary information reaches Congress. This in itself is a strategic decision. Those who hold this view, however, should not then go on to complain that participants are acting deceitfully when all they are demonstrating is that the Emperor really does not have any clothes after all.

Strategies such as advertising and salesmanship belong in the same category. They are good if one likes the program that is being furthered, and bad if one does not. Scandalous propaganda by power-hungry bureaucrats quickly becomes information for the benefit of the American people depending on whether one approves or disapproves of a Polaris missile, an RS-70 bomber, Mission 66 Park, or even Smokey-the-Bear fire-prevention programs. The idea that the good programs somehow sell themselves runs contrary to experience, and not only in government.

Many of the same things can be said about the strategic wedge. If one approves of the program that was begun by keeping a foot in the budgetary door, then the strategy is an example of courageous foresight. If not, then the strategy is just a blatant raid on the treasury. When the emphasis is on reducing expenditures, a lot of wedging items may seem excessive. When the demand is for speedy action, the fact that a first step has been taken may appear most fortunate.

Taking advantage of the separation of powers and the division of labor in Congress may seem inordinately manipulative until one asks whether or not there is any reasonable alternative. As things stand now, an agency may suffer because it lacks support in one of the Houses of Congress, in the substantive or appropriations committees, in the Conference Committee, or in the Executive Office. The American political system provides many detours, not to say reverses and roadblocks. To ask the agency not to take advantage of an opportunity for using superior strength in one of these centers of power is to consign it to permanent impotence unless it is so fortunate as to be loved equally everywhere. A code of conduct that states that only the disadvantages of the system are acceptable is rather strange.

There are a few strategies that are clearly immoral. In 1957, for example, Secretary of Defense Wilson tried to end the Air Force practice of phased buying. By buying parts for a larger number of weapons, instead of the smaller number indicated in the appropriation request, the Air Force left the President and Congress little alternative but to pay for the remaining parts if any of the material was to be useful. After a public controversy, the Air Force agreed to mend its ways. Eternal vigilance being the price of liberty, such practices should be discouraged, and they are in part through the self-corrective mechanism of the loss of confidence. To the best of my knowledge, few agencies engage in similar strategies.

MERIT

Despite all that has been said, the very idea that strategies are employed may appear disturbing. Why cannot programs be presented on their merits and their merits alone?

The most obvious answer is that the question presupposes an agreement on what merit consists of when the real problem is that people do not agree. That is why we have politics. To lay down and enforce criteria of merit in budgeting would be, in effect, to deny the need for politics by deciding what the government shall do in advance.

Much of what is meant by merit turns out to be "meets my preferences" or "serves my interests" or "the interests of those with whom I identify." It would be most peculiar for a nation calling itself a democracy to announce that only the most meritorious policies were carried out despite the fact that they were not preferred by any significant group in the population.

The degree to which widespread preferences are met not only *is* but *ought* to be *part* of policies deemed meritorious.

We all know that people do not always realize what is good for them. They are occupied with many things and may not recognize the benefits flowing from certain policies. They may find it difficult to support policies that are meritorious but not directly related to individual constituencies. Here is where strategies come in. Where support is lacking, it may be mobilized; where attention is unfocused, it may be directed by advertising; where merits are not obvious, they may be presented in striking form. Ability to devise strategies to advance the recognition of merit is immensely more helpful than cries of indignation that political craftsmanship should be necessary.

Merit consists in part of the effectiveness with which programs are formulated and carried out. No one should doubt that this criterion is recognized in the budgetary process; estimates, justifications, and presentations are directed to this factor. Though effectiveness is indispensable—confidence would be lacking without it, for one thing; clientele would be dissatisfied, for another—agencies find that it does not take them far enough. An agency may be wonderfully effective in formulating and carrying out its programs and yet see its fortunes suffer because of the need to cut that year or to shift funds to some vital area. Defense appropriations are often a function of domestic concerns; stabilization policy may be constrained by military needs; the complexity of a project or the difficulty of demonstrating immediate results may militate against it. Consequently, the agency invariably finds that in some areas its good works and best efforts are not being rewarded. Prizes are simply not distributed for good deeds alone. The agency's mode of adapting to this circumstance is to use demonstration of good works as one among a number of strategies. Forbidding agencies to use strategies designed to give its good requests a better chance, because bad requests can also be dressed up, seems inadvisable as well as unlikely to succeed.

CONCLUSION

In appraising the budgetary process, we must deal with real men in the real world for whom the best they can get is to be preferred to the perfection they cannot achieve. Unwilling or unable to alter the basic features of the political system, they seek to make it work for them in budgeting rather than against them. Following Frank Knight, James Buchanan has observed "To argue that an existing order is 'imperfect' in comparison with an alternative order of affairs that turns out, upon careful inspection, to be unobtainable may not be different from arguing that the existing order is 'perfect.' "[16]

Participants in budgeting not only work within the specified constitutional rules, they also make active use of them. Problems of calculation are mitigated by the division of labor in the separation of powers; morality is enforced by substantial external checks as well as by inner motives; a wider range of preferences is taken into account by making the institutional participants responsible for somewhat different ones. A great deal of informal coordination takes place as participants adjust to their expectation of behavior by others. An incremental approach guards against radical departures most of the time, whereas agency advocacy and strategies designed to take advantage of emergent needs help ensure flexibility. A basic conclusion of this appraisal is that the existing budgetary process works much better than is commonly supposed.

There is, however, no special magic in the *status quo*. Inertia and ignorance as well as experience and wisdom may be responsible for the present state of affairs. Improvements of many kinds are undoubtedly possible and desirable. But the major suggested alternatives to the existing budgetary process such as comprehensive calculation and formal coordination turn out to be unfeasible, undesirable, or both. My view is

[16] James M. Buchanan, "Politics, Policy and the Pigovian Margins," XXIX *Economica* (February 1962) p. 19.

that the process should be taken as far as it will go and then should be corrected for its worst deficiencies. Future proposals for reform should advocate a more thoroughgoing incremental approach rather than a more comprehensive one. There should be greater use of aids to calculation rather than less. Agencies should not be told to give up advocacy but to make their best case even more persuasive.

To say that no strategies should be pursued is to imply that there are no purposes for which it is legitimate to plan (scheme, if you prefer) to secure funds.[17] Indeed, those who are serious about effectuating changes would do well to suggest that the strategies they prefer will prove more successful in securing funds than those currently being practiced. The proponents of change might consider ways and means of structuring the budgetary process so that their preferred strategies will turn out to be those which participants find it advantageous to pursue. I would take my stand with the authors of the *Federalist* (especially the superb fifty-first number) who argue that the good may be most dependably secured by arranging things so "that the private interest of every individual may be a sentinel over the public rights."[18]

[17] It is instructive to observe that one of the outstanding proposals for budgetary reform was given a name with the strategic purpose of gathering support. According to Wilfred McNeil, who served on the Hoover Commission to reorganize the executive branch of the government, "It was Mr. [Herbert] Hoover who put the label on that plan, the word 'performance budget.' He himself said it [the reform] had to have some sales appeal, and the name 'performance' was selected." Committee on Government Operations, Subcommittee Hearings, U.S. House of Representatives, *Improving Federal Budgeting and Appropriations*, 85th Congress, 1st Session, 1957, p. 271.

[18] In discussing changes in accounting procedures, Wilfred McNeil states that "If we can get accounting and human nature to work together, we have got something, but if they are opposing we haven't solved the problem." He cited as an example a circumstance in which the Marine Corps had fairly good radio equipment but needed and wanted better radios. "From my standpoint," McNeil declared, "I could see why the people involved didn't want to cancel [large old contracts]. If they canceled under the annual appropriation system it [the item for procuring radios] was out, but the House and Senate Appropriations

The intimate connection between descriptive and normative statements is never more evident than when policy recommendations are made. For sensible policy depends as much on knowledge of the world as it is, as on knowledge of the world as it ought to be. Knowing more about what the budgetary process actually accomplishes, we are able to suggest more appropriate and less drastic suggestions for change. The more we know about how the process works, the better position we will be in to make recommendations to policy makers that make sense, and that do not fool either the giver or the recipients of this advice.

Committee that year changed their procurement funds to the continuing type. . . . The result was that there was about $300 million worth of materiel that was canceled to be replaced with orders for materiel that was up to date." Committee on Government Operations, Subcommittee Hearings, U.S. House of Representatives, *Budget and Accounting*, 84th Congress, 2nd Session, 1956.

PPB AND ZBB
6

IF THE OLD BUDGETING became anti-analytical because it arrested development at the level of inputs, the new budgeting became irrational by dwelling excessively on outputs. A fixation on what is put in has been replaced by a compulsion over what should be taken out. Objectives replace resources as *the* key to analysis. After decades of discussing effort instead of accomplishment — how hard teachers work but not how well students learn, how much money is spent on police but not how much crime is reduced — the urge to concentrate on results rather than resources is understandable. Unfortunately, the grip on one excess has been loosened only to embrace another; alas, the affair with resources has been replaced by the romance with objectives.

Policy analysis, in contrast to these two extremes, compares programs. Only programs combine the compromises between resources and objectives that make workable alternatives. Resources change objectives — a million dollars might make one think of different things to do than would a thousand — as much as the other way around. Each analysis, as well as every practical application, should teach us as much about what we prefer as about how much we put in. Ends and means are chosen simultaneously, and what life has joined, policy analysis must not rend asunder.

The idea that means alone should change, but never ends, is attractive. It suggests the lone hero, who keeps the faith — a vow to God, a promise to the people, a mandate from the movement. The price paid is rarely recognized; that there is invariably carnage along the way is less important than personal vindication. Rigidity becomes deified into righteousness. But righteousness is no substitute for right action; it is irresponsible to promise what cannot be delivered.

A policy alternative may be defined as a hypothesis: If certain things are done, then others will follow. A program tests this hypothesis in action. One way of thinking about objectives is that they are established before the hypothesis is tested and can be compared to consequences. But without resources there can be no objectives. A hypothesis includes "if" as well as "then"; if in a program specific amounts of resources are combined in certain ways by people possessing particular authority, then and only then does the policy hypothesis exist in a form that can be tested. A policy hypothesis includes both means and ends, not just one or the other.

Policy analysis does not consist in enunciating objectives as if no objective had to be sacrificed to achieve another. It is as easy and useless to make endless lists of objectives as to draw up and ignore New Year's resolutions. How much money for each objective? If the first one or two (an increase in Social Security, say, or a massive medical program) exhaust all available resources, it doesn't matter what the rest are, or in what order. How much for all? Analysts know that how far you go depends on what you've got to get there.

Analysis does not consist of showing that objectives have not been met; anybody can curse the fates. So what? Such evaluations do not help program managers who need to know which resources under their control they can manipulate to do better. Programs can only be countered by other programs. If a bad program is the best available, it may still be good compared to the alternatives. Bad, however, is not yet beautiful. Constraints exist to be overcome. At any one time, however, only the irresponsible promise the loosening of all restraints in a promised land of milk and honey, where no choice is necessary because there is no scarcity. Altering objectives to fit resources, therefore, is as much a part of good analysis as varying resources to accomplish objectives. That is why analysts advise not only on the allocation of resources but on the reformulation of objectives.

Although there has been some scrutiny of budgetary systems, they have never, so far as I know, been compared critically as modes of problem solving. It is assumed that their strength lies in assisting rational choice, their weaknesses in coping with the irrational features that political self-interest unfortunately brings to policymaking. My argument is different. These budgetary systems are defective because they constitute bad advice on what is (and how to get) good policy analysis. Analysis is about action as well as advice; therefore, analysis, judging information good only if organizations actually use it to do better, seeks to embed itself in organizational incentives. Analysis is historically grounded to use conflict creatively, for otherwise, by magnifying disagreement, it becomes its own worst problem. Analysis does not consider alternative objectives or alternative mixes of resources in isolation but rather together as alternative programs.

Before turning to PPB and ZBB, it is useful to say a few words about MBO (Management by Objectives) because it is the epitome of a method for improving choice based on analyzing objectives. The lesson of Management by Objectives is that what may begin as puffery (Look at our wonderful objectives!) often winds up as self-deception — ranking objectives equals analyzing problems.

MANAGEMENT BY OBJECTIVES

The idea behind Management by Objectives is that objectives should be specified and that management and workers should agree on the results by which workers are to be judged in accordance with these objectives. At each level objectives are formulated, discussed, agreed to, and passed up the hierarchy. Minor objectives are stacked like Chinese boxes within major ones. What could possibly be wrong with so appealing an idea? Managers should have objectives for their organizations, and workers should be held to account for achieving results. MBO, in a word, is a restatement of good management based on rational choice for effective decision making. The trouble is that the attempt to formalize procedures for choosing objectives without considering organizational dynamics leads to the opposite of what was intended: irrational choice and ineffective action.

The main product of MBO, as experience in the United States federal government suggests, is literally a series of objectives. Aside from the unnecessary paperwork, such exercises are self-defeating because they become mechanisms for avoiding rather than making choices. Long lists of objectives are useless because rarely do resources exist to carry out more than the first few. The experience of the various federal commissions on national priorities, for instance, is that there is no point in listing 846 or even 79 national objectives because almost all the money is gone after the first three or four are funded. If choosing objectives means abandoning choice, choosing objectives is a bad idea.

The larger the number of objectives, the greater the likelihood that some organizational activity will somehow contribute to at least one, the less the need to give up one thing for another. Public agencies prefer more objectives rather than fewer, so whatever consequences they cause are more likely to fit under one of them. Everyone knows that objectives of public agencies tend to be multiple, conflicting, and vague; multiple and conflicting because different people want different things with varying degrees of intensity, and vague because objectives can thus accommodate disagreement. Reconciling these conflicts is not made easier by telling bureaucrats that their strategic behavior — staking out their own objectives as a prelude to bargaining — has become sanctified as an object of virtue, indeed, as the essence of rationality itself.

The most elaborate evaluation of an MBO operation, "The Case of the Social and Rehabilitation Service," shows that MBO's chief effects are an increase in paperwork and in discussion of objectives and a decrease in time spent on programmatic activity. When asked what they would recommend as improvements beyond MBO, "Both regional and central administrators mention management accountability and responsibility . . . better teamwork . . . coordination . . . a need for clear mission goals and priorities . . . and the development of management information systems" — in other words, exactly what MBO was supposed to accomplish in the first place. Interviews with 159 top administrators reveal that MBO "is generally perceived by managers and supervisors as a system which reinforces such bureaucratic norms as centralized organizational control and decision-making, paperwork, efficiency emphasis and lack of participation." [1]

By putting all the emphasis on objectives, MBO subsumes critical problems of organizational design — how to relate people and activities so that errors become evident and are corrected — under the surface sentimentality of human relations jargon. What MBO does to program objectives, PPB does to organizational incentives.

[1] Jong S. Jun, "Management by Objectives in a Government Agency: The Case of the Social and Rehabilitation Service." Mimeographed. The Social and Rehabilitation Service Department of HEW (August 1973).

On August 25, 1965, President Johnson announced that he was asking the heads of all federal agencies to introduce "a very new and revolutionary system" of budgeting. Staffs of experts set up in each agency would define goals using "modern methods of program analysis." Then the "most effective and the least costly" way to accomplish these goals would be found.[2] The general idea is that budgetary decisions should be made by focusing on output categories like governmental goals, objectives, and end products instead of inputs like personnel, equipment, and maintenance. Once priorities among objectives were established, this budgetary procedure was supposed to determine the best expenditure mix in the annual budget to secure the largest future benefits. Hence it went by the name of Planning, Programming, and Budgeting Systems (PPB), or just program budgeting.

Although there are a few historical precursors of program budgeting,[3] its recent impetus came in the 1960s from the experience of the federal government. From there it spread with amazing speed to numerous American cities and states, foreign governments, and even international agencies. Clearly, from the standpoint of sheer effort and attention, PPB is the major budgetary phenomenon (perhaps cause célèbre would be more accurate) of our time. Hence it requires serious attention. First I shall consider three essential features of PPB — its objectivity, its centralization, and its political content. Then I shall briefly survey experience in implementing PPB and try to account for its difficulties.

[2] David Novick, editor, *Program Budgeting*, 2nd ed. (Cambridge, Mass., Harvard University Press, 1967), pp. v–vi.

[3] See Allen Schick, *Budget Innovation in the States* (Washington, D.C., The Brookings Institution, 1971); and David Novick, *Origin and History of Program Budgeting* (Santa Monica, California, RAND Corporation, October 1966).

Programs are not made in heaven. They must be manufactured by men, and no one can give instructions for making up programs. There are as many ways to conceive of programs as there are of organizing activity,[4] as the comments of the following writers eloquently testify:

It is by no means obvious . . . whether a good program structure should be based on components of specific end objectives (e.g., the accomplishment of certain land reclamation targets), on the principle of cost separation (identifying as a program any activity the costs of which can be readily segregated), on the separation of means and ends (Is education a means or an end in a situation such as skill-retaining courses for workers displaced by automation?), or on some artificially designed pattern that draws from all these and other classification criteria.[5]

Just what categories constitute the most useful programs and program elements is far from obvious. . . . If one puts all educational activities into a broad package of educational programs, he cannot simultaneously include school lunch programs or physical education activities in a Health Program, or include defense educational activities (such as the military academies) in the Defense Program. . . . In short, precisely how to achieve a rational and useful structure for a program budget is not yet evident.[6]

A first question one might ask is whether, given their nature, health activities merit a separate, independent status in a program budget. The question arises because these activities often are constituents of, or inputs into, other activities whose purpose or goal orientation is the dominating one. Outlays by the Department of Defense for hospital care, for example, though they assist in maintaining the health of one segment of the population, are undertaken on

---

[4] A look at the classic work by Luther Gulick and Lyndall Urwick, *Papers on the Science of Administration* (New York, 1937), reveals considerable similarity between their suggested bases of organization and ways of conceptualizing programs.

[5] Melvin Anshen in D. Novick, *op. cit.*, pp. 19–20.

[6] George A. Steiner in *ibid.*, p. 356.

behalf of national defense, and the latter is their justification.[7]

The difficulties with the program concept are illustrated in
the space program. A first glance suggests that space projects
are ideally suited for program budgeting because they are
physical systems designed to accomplish different missions.
Actually, there is a remarkable degree of interdependence
between different missions and objectives — pride, scientific
research, space exploration, military exploration and uses,
etc. — so that it is difficult to apportion costs properly. Consider the problem of a rocket developed for one mission and
useful for others. To apportion costs to each new mission is
purely arbitrary; to allocate the cost to the first mission and
regard the rocket as free for all subsequent missions is ludi-
crous. Making a separate program out of the rocket itself
does violence to the concept of programs as end products.
The difficulty is compounded because facilities that have
multiple uses, like boosters and tracking networks, tend to
be expensive compared to the items that are specific to a
particular mission.[8] Simple concepts of programs evaporate
upon inspection.

CENTRALIZATION

Who should exert power over which programs is a major
question of government. How programs are structured is,
therefore, a crucial political question. Political realities lie
behind the failure to devise principles for defining programs.
Asking if centralization is better than decentralization is
equivalent to asking who will rule. As Melvin Anshen puts
it, "The central issue is, of course, nothing less than the
definition of the ultimate objectives of the Federal govern-

[7] Arthur Smithies in *ibid.*, p. 41.
[8] See the excellent chapter by Milton A. Margolis and Stephen M.
Barro in *ibid.*, pp. 120–145.

ment as they are realized through operational decisions." The arrangement of the programs inevitably affects the specific actions taken to implement them. "Set in this framework," Anshen continues, "the designation of a schedule of programs may be described as building a bridge between a matter of political philosophy (what is government for?) and . . . assigning scarce resources among alternative governmental objectives." [9]

Proponents of program budgeting are markedly ambivalent about the necessity for reorganization of the federal government to centralize authority for wide-ranging programs in order to give PPB a chance to work. The problem is that responsibility for programs is scattered throughout the whole federal establishment and decentralized to state and local authorities as well. In the field of health, for example, expenditures are distributed among at least twelve agencies and six departments outside Health, Education, and Welfare. A far greater number of organizations are concerned with American activities abroad, with natural resources, and with education. The multiple jurisdictions and overlapping responsibilities do violence to the concept of comprehensive and consistent programs. It "causes one to doubt," Marvin Frankel writes, "whether there can exist in the administrative echelons the kind of overall perspective that would seem indispensable if Federal health resources are to be rationally allocated." [10] To G. A. Steiner it is evident that "the present 'chest of drawers' type of organization cannot for long be compatible with program budgeting." [11]

Program budgeting contains an extreme centralizing bias. Power is to be centralized in the Presidency (through the Office of Management and Budget) at the national level, in superdepartments rather than bureaus within the Executive

---

[9] Anshen, *op. cit.*, p. 18.
[10] Marvin Frankel in D. Novick, *op. cit.*, p. 237.
[11] Steiner, *op. cit.*, p. 248.

Branch, and in the federal government as a whole instead of state or local governments. Note how W. Z. Hirsh assumes the desirability of national dominance when he writes: "These methods of analysis can guide Federal officials in the responsibility of bringing local education decisions into closer harmony with national objectives." [12] G. A. Steiner observes that comprehensiveness may be affected by unrestricted federal grants-in-aid to the states because "such a plan would remove a substantial part of Federal expenditures from a program budgeting system of the Federal government." [13] Should there be reluctance on the part of state and local officials to employ the new tools, Anshen states "that the Federal government may employ familiar incentives to accelerate this progress." [14] Summing it up, Hirsch says, "It appears doubtful that a natural resources program budget would have much impact without a good deal of centralization." [15]

Within the great federal organizations designed to encompass the widest range of objectives, there would have to be strong executives. Cutting across the subunits of the organization, as is the case in the Department of Defense, the program budget could be put together only by the top executive. A more useful tool for increasing his power to control his subordinates would be difficult to imagine.

That all decisions ought to be made by the most central person in the most centralized body is a proposition difficult to justify on scientific grounds. In fact, it cannot be justified except as reflecting a distaste of politics — for the more centralized a system, the fewer the decision-makers and the less the need to bargain.

In the literature discussed earlier there appears several

[12] Werner Z. Hirsch in D. Novick, *op. cit.*, p. 370.
[13] Steiner, *op. cit.*, p. 347.
[14] Anshen, *op. cit.*, p. 365.
[15] Hirsch, *op. cit.*, p. 203.

times the proposition that "the program budget is a neutral tool. It has no politics." [16]

How could men make so foolish a statement? Perhaps they identify program budgeting with something good and beautiful, and politics with something bad and ugly. McKean and Anshen speak of politics in terms of "pressure and expedient adjustments," "haphazard acts . . . unresponsive to a planned analysis of the needs of efficient decision design." From the political structure they expect only "resistance and opposition, corresponding to the familiar human disposition to protect established seats of power and procedures made honorable by the mere facts of existence and custom." [17] In other places we hear of "vested interests," "wasteful duplication," "special interest groups," and the "Parkinson syndrome." [18] Somebody doesn't like politics.

POLITICS

Political rationality is the fundamental kind of reason, because it deals with the preservation and improvement of decision structures, and decision structures are the source of all decisions. Unless a decision structure exists, no reasoning and no decisions are possible. . . . There can be no conflict between political rationality and . . . technical, legal, social, or economic rationality, because the solution of political problems makes possible an attack on any other problem, while a serious political deficiency can prevent or undo all other problem solving. . . . Non-political decisions are reached by considering a problem in its own terms, and by evaluating proposals according to how well they solve the problem. The best available proposal should be accepted regardless of who makes it or who opposes it, and a faulty proposal should be rejected or improved no matter who makes it. Compromise is always irrational; the rational procedure is to determine which proposal is the

[16] Anshen, *op. cit.*, p. 370.
[17] R. McKean and M. Anshen, *op. cit.*, p. 289.
[18] *Ibid.*, p. 359.

best, and to accept it. In a political decision, on the other hand, action never is based on the merits of a proposal but always on who makes it and who opposes it. Action should be designed to avoid complete identification with any proposal and any point of view, no matter how good or how popular it might be. The best available proposal should never be accepted just because it is best; it should be deferred, objected to, discussed, until major opposition disappears. Compromise is always a rational procedure, even when the compromise is between a good and bad proposal.[19]

It will be useful to distinguish between policy politics (which policy will be adopted?), partisan politics (which political party will win office?), and system politics (how will decision structures be set up?). Program budgeting is manifestly concerned with policy politics, and not much with partisan politics, although it could have important consequences for issues that divide the nation's parties. My contention is that the thrust of program budgeting makes it an integral part of system politics.

It is hard to find men who take up the cause of political rationality, who plead the case for political man, and who are primarily concerned with the laws that enable the political machinery to keep working. One is driven to a philosopher like Paul Diesing to find the case for the political:

. . . the political problem is always basic and prior to the others. . . . This means that any suggested course of action must be evaluated first by its effects on the political structure. A course of action which corrects economic or social deficiencies but increases political difficulties must be rejected, while an action which contributes to political improvement is desirable even if it is not entirely sound from an economic or social standpoint.[20]

[19] Paul Diesing, *Reason in Society* (Urbana, Ill., 1962) pp. 198, 203–204, 231–232.
[20] *Ibid.*, p. 228.

There is hardly a political scientist who would claim half as much.

A major task of the political system is to specify goals or objectives. It is impermissible to treat goals as if they were known in advance. "Goals" may well be the product of interaction among key participants rather than pronouncements of some deus ex machina or (to use Bentley's term) some "spook" which posits values in advance of our knowledge of them.

Once the political process becomes a focus of attention, it is evident that the principal participants may not be clear about their goals. What we call goals or objectives may, in large part, be operationally determined by the policies we can agree upon. In a political situation, then, the need for support assumes central importance. Not simply the economic but the political costs and benefits turn out to be crucial.

The literature of economics usually treats organizations and institutions as if they were costless entities. The standard procedure is to consider rival alternatives (in consideration of price policy or other criteria), calculate the differences in cost and achievement among them, and show that one is more or less efficient than another. This way of thinking is insufficient. If the costs include getting an agency to change its policies or procedures, then these organizational costs must also be taken into account.

PRACTICE

What happened when efforts were made to implement PPB? Did it change the traditional budgetary process? Did it alter substantive outcomes?

Marvin and Rouse conducted 400 interviews in a large number of agencies and found that even where PPB processes were well developed, their contribution to decision making was minor. "Detailed PPB processes have been developed in . . . [a] group of agencies; for example, Interior. With the exception of the work in an occasional bureau, the materials produced through these processes have not been used extensively by decisionmakers. . . ." [21] In another group of agencies, "well-developed analytic activities have contributed to decision making and did so long before the advent of PPB. . . . The result is that PPB's contribution in restructuring the decision-making process in these agencies has been marginal." [22]

Similar conclusions are found in another study prepared by a practitioner. Jack W. Carlson studied a group of twenty-six agencies and discovered that though program structures had been developed, "the formal structure has been only partially successful." [23] He concluded that the benefits derived from their preparation were mainly educational.[24]

Hard choices (trade-offs among activities devoted to similar ends) can be avoided either by proliferating categories so there is one for every major activity, or by severely limiting the number of categories so they are broad and vague. Both strategies were used in the Department of Agriculture. No important program cut across more than a single bureau; the new program elements essentially renamed old activities.[25]

And the first shall be last. Since 1961, Defense has been held up as the prime example of what PPB can do and how

[21] Keith E. Marvin and Andrew M. Rouse, "The Status of PPB in Federal Agencies: A Comparative Perspective," in R. Haveman and J. Margolis, editors, *Public Policy Expenditures and Policy Analysis* (Chicago, 1970), p. 448.

[22] *Ibid*.

[23] Jack W. Carlson, "The Status and Next Steps for Planning, Programming and Budgeting," in Haveman and Margolis, *op. cit.*, p. 374.

[24] *Ibid*.

[25] Aaron Wildavsky and Jeanne Nienaber, *The Budgeting and Evaluation of Federal Recreation Programs, or Money Doesn't Grow on Trees* (New York, 1973).

well it can succeed.[26] But PPB did not change budgetary decisions in DOD to any significant degree. Programming did not have the anticipated effect on budgeting. Rather, the yearly appropriations placed limitations on programs. John P. Crecine, who has conducted an intensive study of the subject, concluded that, "In spite of the many differences in necessary procedures under PPBS, the methods of arriving at dollar figures for the line items in the appropriations request, consistent with the fiscal constraints on the total . . . are not dissimilar from those utilized during the Truman-Eisenhower administrations." [27] The Department decides on what it will ask for in the same way as it did before PPB. Budget reviewers in DOD, when forecasting the cuts that are going to be made, base their decisions on past budget decisions. "Basically . . . *experience with the decision system* [the "base" in our terms] *is the prime ingredient in the budget review exercise*" (italics in original).[28]

PPB's application to DOD's final budget is insignificant, but within the Department it might be thought to have had an effect. However, this does not appear to have been the case, for two reasons: First, "PPB decisions are always made to conform to appropriations decisions made during the October–December budget crunch"; and second, "The current PPB system does not do what any foreseeable budget decision system has to do if it is to be the primary determinate of DOD resource allocation; it has to adapt to external, fiscal constraints." [29] PPB, apparently, is not only a "has been" in Defense but may well be a "never was."

PPB staffs often claim advances in the area of policy

[26] G. W. Shipp, "Program Budgeting in the Defense Department: A Small Change" (unpublished paper, University of California, Berkeley, 1966), p. 24.

[27] John P. Crecine, *Defense Budgeting: Constraints and Organizational Adaptations*, Discussion Paper No. 6, University of Michigan, Institute of Public Policy Studies (1969), p. 38.

[28] *Ibid.*, p. 49.

[29] *Ibid.*, pp. 54–55.

analysis. To support the claim they point to a number of so-called successful analytical studies. Had implementation really succeeded, of course, there would have been so many analytical studies that referring to one or two would have been a tremendous understatement. The rare analytical study which PPB officials hold out as proof for advancement is praised because it is unique, or as Schick calls it, a "museum piece . . . exuberantly displayed for outsiders but a 'hands off' practice bars their use in actual decisions." [30]

I have not been able to find a single example of successful implementation of PPB. As Harper, Kramer, and Rouse put it, "observers of the budgeting process agree that PPB has had limited influence on the major resource allocation decisions in domestic agencies of the federal government." [31] Even where implementation was seriously carried out and a large investment made, the primary goal — changing budgetary procedures and decisions — was never achieved.

Why? Did ugly old politics beat up nice young PPB? No doubt. But that is not the half of it. Practitioners of program budgeting were never able to define programs or attach costs to them, or make it worthwhile for organizations to figure out how to do so. What is worse, I shall argue, PPB deserved to die because it is an irrational mode of analysis that leads to suppression rather than correction of error.

POLICY

I have previously argued that program budgeting would run up against severe political difficulties. While most of these arguments have been conceded, I have been told that in a better world, without the vulgar intrusion of political factors (such as the consent of the governed), PPB would perform

[30] Schick, *op. cit.*, p. 104.
[31] Edwin L. Harper, Fred A. Kramer, and Andrew M. Rouse, "Implementation and the Use of PPB in Sixteen Federal Agencies," XXIX *Public Administration Review* (November/December 1969) p. 632.

its wonders as advertised. Now it is clear that for the narrow purpose of predicting why program budgeting will not work there is no need to mention political problems at all. It is sufficient to say that the wholesale introduction of PPB presented insuperable difficulties of calculation: *no one knows how to do program budgeting.* Another way of putting it is that many know what program budgeting should be in general, but no one knows what it should be in any particular case. Program budgeting cannot be stated in operational terms. The reason for the difficulty is that telling an agency to adopt program budgeting means telling it to find better policies, and there is no formula for doing that. One can (and should) talk about measuring effectiveness, estimating costs, and comparing alternatives, but that is a far cry from being able to take the creative leap of formulating a better policy.

On the basis of numerous discussions with would-be practitioners of program budgeting at the federal level, I can describe the usual pattern of its application. Instructions come down from the Bureau of the Budget (now the Office of Management and Budget): You must have a program budget. Agency personnel panic; they do not know how to do what they have been asked to do. So they produce a vast amount of inchoate data characterized by premature quantification of irrelevant items. Neither agency heads nor budget examiners can comprehend the material submitted to them. Its very bulk inhibits understanding. It is useless to the Director of the Budget in making his decisions. In an effort to be helpful, the program analysis unit says something like: "Nice try, fellows; we appreciate all that effort. But you have not quite got the idea of program budgeting yet. Remember, you must clarify goals, define objectives, relate these to quantitative indicators, and project costs into the future. Please send a new submission based on this understanding."

Another furious effort takes place. Huge amounts of overtime are put in. Under severe time pressure, even more data is accumulated. No one can say that agency personnel did not try hard. The new presentation makes a little more sense to some people and a little less to others. It just does not hang together as a presentation of agency policies. There are more encouraging words from the Budget Bureau and another sermon about specifying alternative ways of meeting agency objectives, though not, of course, taking the old objectives for granted. By this time agency personnel are desperate. "We would love to do it," they say, "but we cannot figure out the right way. You experts in the Budget Bureau should show us how to do it." Silence. The word from on high is that the Bureau of the Budget does not interfere with agency operations; it is the agency's task to set up its own budget. After a while, cynicism reigns supreme.

Although PPB dredges up data under numerous headings, it says next to nothing about the impact of one program on another. There is data but no information. Agency heads are at once oversupplied with numbers and undersupplied with propositions about the effects of any action they might undertake.

WHY PPB IS IRRATIONAL

To better understand the failure of program budgeting everywhere and at all times, it is helpful to imagine what would be required for its success. Most discussion has been confined to "sufficient" conditions. The critical assumption has been that it is easy to set up PPB but difficult to implement the system. The problems presumably lie, therefore, in rooted interests, recalcitrant politicians, and hidebound bureaucrats. It has been readily acknowledged, in addition, that the implementation of PPB has been hampered by lack of trained manpower, absence of essential data, and even inadequacies in the state of the art. The point is that all these putative defects can be remedied. Unreceptive politicians and bureaucrats can be got around or replaced. Training can be stepped up, better data can surely be collected, and knowledge of analysis will undoubtedly be improved. If these were the only difficulties, it would be difficult to explain why PPB has no successes whatsoever to its credit. For surely somewhere, sometime, the right conditions for PPB to prosper should have existed. Maybe they should have, but they didn't. Why not? To answer that question we have to be prepared to accept the possibility that PPB lacks "necessary" as well as sufficient conditions, that its disabilities occur not merely in program implementation but in policy design — that, in a word, its defects are defects in principle, not in execution. PPB does not work because it cannot work. Failure is built into its very nature because it requires ability to perform cognitive operations that are beyond present human (or mechanical) capacities.

Program budgeting is like the simultaneous equation of governmental intervention in society. If one can state objectives precisely, find quantitative measures for them, specify alternative ways of achieving them by different inputs of resources, and rank them according to desirability, one has solved the social problems for the period. One has only to bring the program budget up to date each year. Is it surprising that program budgeting does not perform this sort of miracle? Planning, Programming, and Budgeting Systems require a structure in which all policies related to common objectives are compared for cost and effectiveness. Not a single theory for a particular area of policy but, rather, a series of interrelated theories for all policies is required. If we barely sense the relation between inputs and outputs in any single area of policy, however, how likely are we to know what these relationships are across the widest realm of policy? As one area of ignorance interacts exponentially with other areas, we get not an arithmetic but a geometric increase in ignorance.[32]

There is no need to blink at the inevitable conclusion: PPB is not an embodiment of rationality; PPB is irrational. If the goal is to alter the allocation of resources in a more productive way, or to generate better analyses than those that are now used, PPB does not (because it cannot) produce these results. PPB is not cost effective. It produces costly rationales for inevitable failures.

But why do seemingly rational procedures produce irrational results? By sacrificing organizational incentives in the name of economic efficiency, program budgeting serves neither. The good organization is interested in discovering and correcting its own mistakes. The higher the cost of errors — not only in terms of money but also in personnel, programs, and prerogatives — the less the chance anything will be done about them. Organizations should be designed, therefore, to make errors visible and correctable, that is, noticeable and reversible, which in turn is to say, cheap and affordable.

Program budgeting increases rather than decreases the cost of correcting error. The great complaint about bureaucracies is their rigidity. As things stand, the object of organizational affection is the bureau as serviced by the usual line-item categories from which people, money, and facilities flow. Viewed from the standpoint of bureau interests, programs to some extent are negotiable; some can be increased and others decreased while keeping the agency on an even keel or, if necessary, adjusting it to less happy times, without calling into question its very existence. Line-item budgeting, precisely because its categories (personnel, maintenance, supplies) do not relate directly to programs, are easier to change. Budgeting by programs, precisely because money flows to objec-

---

[32] Aaron Wildavsky, "Policy Analysis is What Information Systems Are Not," IV *New York Affairs* (Spring 1977) No. 2, p. 16.

tives, makes it difficult to abandon objectives without abandoning the organization that gets its money for them.

Notice I do not say it is inadvisable for analysis to take place at the level of programs and policies. On the contrary, there is every reason to encourage analytical thrusts from different directions and dimensions of policy, provided only that no single one is encased in concrete and be considered the final way. It is better that non-programmatic categories be used in formal budget categories, thus permitting a diversity of analytical perspectives, than that a temporary analytic insight be made the permanent perspective through which money is funneled.[33]

If error is to be altered, it must be relatively easy to correct. But PPB makes it hard. Its "systems" are characterized by their proponents as highly differentiated and tightly linked. The rationale for program budgeting lies in its connectedness — like programs are grouped together. Program structures are meant to replace the confused concatenations of line-items with clearly differentiated, non-overlapping boundaries; only one set of programs to a structure. This means that a change in one element or structure must result in change reverberating throughout every element in the same system. Instead of alerting only neighboring units or central control units, which would make change feasible, all are, so to speak, wired together, so the choice is effectively all or none.

Imagine one of us deciding whether to buy a tie or a kerchief. A simple task, one might think. Suppose, however, that organizational rules require us to keep our entire wardrobe as a unit. If everything must be rearranged when one item is altered, the probability we will do anything is low. The more tightly linked the elements, and the more highly differentiated they are, the greater the probability of error (because the tolerances are so small), and the less the like-

[33] *Ibid.*, p. 17.

lihood error will be reported (because with change, every element has to be recalibrated with every other one that was previously adjusted). Why idealize an information system like PPB that causes many more mistakes than it can correct? Being caught between revolution (change in everything) and resignation (change in nothing) has little to recommend it.

At one time I knew only that program budgeting data was not used; now I believe I know why this superabundance of data was never converted into information: PPB did not provide information relevant to the user at any level. At the bureau level the questions addressed had to do with whether its existing programs should be abolished or replaced by others. This, to be sure, was a question bureaus not only did not want to answer positively but could not even respond to negatively because it was beyond bureau jurisdiction. To take programs from one bureau and place them in another is reserved for higher authorities — the Department, the President, and Congress. Since the advice was for "them" and not for "us," it was either doctored to appear impressive or ignored because nothing could be done about it. Secretaries needed information on how they might better allocate resources within their departments. Instead they got rationalizations of bureau enterprises.

In the past it has been said that PPB might have succeeded if it had produced better analyses. This, as structuralists say, is no accident.[34] By separating policy analysis from organizational power, PPB is simultaneously rendered unintelligent and impotent.

ZERO BASE BUDGETING

Zero Base Budgeting (ZBB) is the newest in a series of attempted budget reforms reacting against the seemingly anti-

[34] *Ibid.*, pp. 17–18.

analytic and fragmented approach of line-item budgeting. President Carter foresees that "by working together under a ZBB system, we can reduce costs and make the federal government more efficient and effective." [35] Carter includes among the benefits of ZBB avoiding overlap between programs, improving information, focusing on analysis and decision making, forcing managers to evaluate the cost effectiveness of their programs, allowing quick budget adjustments during the year, "and most important to me, broadly expanding management participation and training in the planning, budgeting and decision making process." [36]

Zero Base Budgeting was developed by Peter Pyhrr for use at Texas Instruments, an electronic firm, in 1969. In 1972 Governor Carter introduced the system into the state government in Georgia. Other states (as well as businesses) have subsequently experimented with ZBB. President Carter directed the heads of executive departments and agencies to implement ZBB in the fiscal year 1979 federal budget.

ZBB's major declared purpose is to examine simultaneously all programs from the ground up, to ferret out programs continuing through inertia which do not warrant being continued at all or should be continued only at a reduced level of expenditure. Its goal, Pyhrr maintains, is to:

> . . . force us to identify and analyze what we [are] going to do in total, set goals and objectives, make the necessary operating decisions, and evaluate changing responsibilities and work loads . . . as an integral part of the (budget) process.[37]

For the first time, detailed information about programs is to be available for department review in one place at one

[35] Joel Haveman, "Zero-Base Budgeting," IX *National Journal* (April 2, 1977) No. 14, p. 514.

[36] Jimmy Carter, "Jimmy Carter Tells Why He Will Use Zero-Base Budgeting," *Nation's Business* (January 1977) p. 26.

[37] Peter A. Pyhrr, *Zero-Base Budgeting: A Practical Management Tool for Evaluating Expenses* (New York, 1973), p. 10.

time. The process is to be made more effective by assuring that budgets are developed and reviewed in their entirety, not merely in terms of the justification for incremental increases. This focus requires a priority ranking of all programs and activities in increasing levels of performance and funding, starting from the ground up.

Program managers at each level are assumed to be in the best position to make decisions on priorities and trade-offs in the programs for which they are responsible. Managers are additionally responsible for defining the specific objectives and identifying the outputs of their programs. In a document called the "decision package," the basic tool of ZBB, this description of their program is combined with an analysis of the effects of conducting the program at alternative levels of funding. Typically these funding levels include a minimum below which the operation could not function, the current level above the minimum level, and a middle level between these two. Lower-echelon managers are placed in a position of great responsibility in this system, since they compute the marginal utility of changes in funding and assess the difference these changes would make. With respect to a discrete activity referred to as the "decision unit," a manager presents the activity's purpose, the consequences of not performing the activity, measures of its performance at various levels of operation, alternative courses of action at each level, and the costs and benefits of running the program at the current level.

The second stage of ZBB involves ranking the decision packages. Managers send the packages up the bureaucratic ladder to their direct superiors, who rank them according to the priority of that program within the agency. Subsequently, agency priorities are ranked within the overall department. Many different rankings are compiled as the decision packages gradually move toward the department head's desk. Superiors receive groups of ranked decision packages from those directly below them which they in turn rank, until there is one comprehensive ranking of all programs in the department. A cutoff line is drawn to delineate the expected amount of revenues for the year, or the level of "affordability." Packages that fall above the line receive funding while those below the line do not. This flexible cutoff line is reputed to facilitate accommodating late-year budget windfalls or deficits; the response to a change in expected revenues is merely to move the line and accept or reject several more decision packages.

After isolating the objectives of the program, managers are responsible for explaining the consequences of not funding certain activities. To determine these consequences, managers must thoroughly understand the effects their programs have upon other programs with which they do not normally deal in day-to-day operations. How are they to provide this information? No one knows. And, after figuring out the consequences of doing without particular activities, managers must also compute the efficiency of carrying them on at various levels below the current apportionment. They are asked, basically, "How well would this program function at another level?"; but this is a question to which there are an infinite number of possible answers. Managers must therefore decide which funding levels they wish to analyze.

In general, managers have been unable to assess programs' efficiency at that vague "other" level, and states have provided their managers with set increments at which they are to evaluate their programs. Consequently, managers are actually computing from a base above zero. Instead of trying to discover the minimum level at which to carry on a certain activity (a task posing insurmountable problems), they evaluate the program at an arbitrary low proportion of the current level, say 80 per cent. However, this method removes the assumption that there is any possibility of entirely canceling funding and obviates the necessity of determining the consequences of not performing the activity. Managers are now asked, "How would your program function at this specific level of funding?" Nevertheless, managers still require specific data relating announced objectives to program performance at alternative levels of funding.

Department heads face different considerations; they are in charge of the ranking procedure. If the objective of one package in the Department of Agriculture is to increase crop yields and the objective of another to encourage recreation, where is the basis for comparison? A common denominator between packages is necessary. Since one of the benefits of ZBB is to permit comparison between programs in order to weed out overlap and waste, it is especially important to be able to compare similar programs. Comparison is facilitated if common programs fall within the auspices of a single agency. Usually, however, objectives are distributed among several departments. Consequently, ZBB is often associated with governmental reorganization, or, in effect, consolidation. In Georgia Jimmy Carter simultaneously implemented ZBB and reorganized the state's agencies. As President he has announced similar intentions for the federal government.

Since resources affect objectives, is it possible that a department, when faced with a budget cut, would wish to revamp its programs entirely? No, for the only alternative the department has, after the decision packages have been sent up from below, is some ratio of its present operations, since departments faced with a cut in funds can allocate only through previous ranking of project packages. Consequently, even department heads, with their broader view, cannot alter the department's basic orientation. ZBB considers objectives to be immutable or dispensable but not variable. Objectives may be achieved or abandoned but, apparently, not modified, because the only variable is the level of resources — hence the name "Zero Base Budgeting." Department heads are expected to take a comprehensive view of their decision packages, ranked and competing with one another for funding, but they can only act in a marginal fashion.

Yet all programs may not receive funding and the department heads have to come up with some mixture of packages that will make the final ranking deserving of funding. Which programs will have to be administered at lower funding levels? This is the ultimate question facing department heads.

We see that the different management levels involved in ZBB are dependent upon vast amounts of data — for each level of funding from zero to zed, so to speak. But the different management levels also differ vastly in the type of information they use. Lower-level managers use data relating inputs to outputs of their own activities, while upper-level managers need information that cuts across their agencies by actually comparing programs sharing common objectives.

ZBB introduces the view that basic budget formulations should arise from low-level managers, whereas PPB generates initial requests from the very top, the department heads. Budget requests are sent upward in ZBB; in PPB the department heads send their formulation down so that agencies may conform to the overall program structures. Further, ZBB and PPB diverge in the manner in which programs are linked and evaluated. PPB aligns programs toward common objectives. ZBB does away with these program structures. Decision units must justify their own existence vertically, according to their own objectives, rather than horizontally by conforming to similar programs.

PRACTICE

The first semblance of ZBB was implemented in 1964 in the Department of Agriculture, where it was entirely unsuccessful. The Department used a comprehensive method that was

supposed to justify all expenditures from zero but was un-
supported by ZBB's analytic techniques. Members of the
Department were interviewed to discover whether any decisions could in any way be attributed to the Zero Base Budget.
Did the Agency or Department officials recommend different
programs or different amounts for programs, or distribute
funds among programs differently as a result of the Zero
Base approach? Overwhelmingly, the answer was no.

Most statements were variants of "I don't think anyone
would honestly tell you that they changed their budgets."
Agency personnel continually reiterated their doubts that the
Department was adequately staffed to digest such vast
amounts of material. Asked for evidence of change, respon-
dents usually replied that "the figures we put in have never
been referred to as far as I know," or "it [Zero Base Budget
data] was sent across the street [where the Department
offices are located] and we never heard of it again." A couple
of times an exceedingly small change was reported, though
not without qualification. Although there was "no difference
in the overall amounts requested or received from the department, analysis did lead to the transfer of $20,000 among
programs. This analysis was, however, planned before the
zero-base budget." An excess of expenditures for files in one
agency was also mentioned. In one instance a Department
official did say, "I am confident that decisions were made
which would not have been made or even considered in
the absence of a zero-base budget." But even he could give
only one specific change — a reduction of $100,000 in an
obsolete research program. The paucity of changes attributed to the Zero Base Budget is evident in the fact that this
example was brought up repeatedly; many officials said they
had heard of a change somewhere, but it always turned out
to be this same one. Another Department official insisted
that the Zero Base Budget procedure was not useful in
"ferreting out all the sorts of dark and sinister things which

shouldn't be done, which would turn up quickly anyhow." The general conclusion can be stated in the words of a person in a position to get a general view: "Some butterflies were caught, no elephants stopped." [38]

An interesting phenomenon was that Department officials thought ZBB was unnecessary for them but good for the bureaus, and people in the bureaus thought the reverse. Each level viewed ZBB as a message to the other: We're all right Jack, but you shape up! Information systems are not only methods of getting others to do what you want, they are communications saying "Don't bother. Modern science (PPB, ZBB, MBO, etc.) shows we've been inspected and proven pure."

The majority of the eleven states currently using ZBB in their budgeting procedures use some form of priority ranking for the programs, and most of the states make use of decision packages. In attempting to bridge the gap between upper- and lower-level managers, states have sacrificed the zero-based focus of ZBB. No states justify all programs from zero, and many have abandoned alternative funding levels. Instead, they submit budget proposals indicating the costs of the programs at set levels of operations. Arkansas, Illinois, and Texas selected 90 per cent of the base level of the program for the minimum level of operation. Above that comes the current budgeted amount, and then actually a 10 per cent increase over the base figure. Rather than being a Zero Base Budget, justifying from zero, these states have introduced a 90 per cent base budget.

Missouri, Idaho, and California are even further off zero base. Missouri and Idaho rank only proposed increases above the base. Similarly, California "focuses on proposed changes in the budget." [39] Ranking decision packages above the base

[38] Allen Schick and Robert Keith, "Zero-Base Budgeting in the States," Library of Congress Congressional Research Service (August 31, 1976) p. 28.
[39] *Ibid.*, p. 38.

seems indistinguishable from incremental budgeting. Tennessee has pursued another variant: each program must assess its performance at four preordained levels, which are approached in a unique manner. The levels are (1) continuation at current level of funding, (2) continuation at current level of service, (3) improvement to meet new legislative requirements and to replace lost federal aid, and (4) improvements based on departmental estimates of need.[40]

Few states have a long acquaintance with ZBB. For many, ZBB has only been used for one or two years. In these cases it is difficult to draw any definite conclusions. New Jersey encountered a number of difficulties (such as staff resistance and low-quality submissions), although it feels these problems can be overcome as its personnel become more accustomed to ZBB concepts and processes. Idaho reports that 75 per cent of its first-year reports were unsatisfactory.[41] This high failure rate was due largely to budgeters' inadequate understanding of the procedures. Other states complain, as well, of agency and staff resistance to the system, lack of understanding of basic concepts, and deficient quality of data. After two years in Georgia — one year when revenues markedly decreased and one when expenditures sharply increased — ZBB was abandoned and new submissions were requested.[42]

Even where states can definitely identify budgetary successes, it is not absolutely possible to attribute them to ZBB. Jimmy Carter claimed a 50 per cent savings in state administrative costs in Georgia resulting from the implemen-

---

[40] *Ibid.*, p. 14.

[41] *Ibid.*

[42] George S. Nimier and Roger H. Hermanson, "A Look at Zero-Base Budgeting — The Georgia Experience," *Atlanta Economic Review* (July-August 1976) pp. 5–12. In 1974 there was an increase in available funds and in 1975 a decrease.

tation of ZBB.[43] The only examples he has provided to indicate the success of ZBB have been the highway department saving 15 per cent of its budgetary costs by ceasing to mow the divider strips along highways and the mobilization of highway patrolmen who were replaced at desk jobs with handicapped people.[44] Georgia also underwent major government reorganization simultaneously with ZBB's implementation, so it is difficult to differentiate the successes attributable to agency redistribution or to ZBB.

Although there is unsubstantiated evidence for ZBB's ability to restrict spending, there is absolutely no support at all for ZBB's claims to evaluate programs and reallocate funding to those viewed as more efficient and desirable. In Texas, Roy Lee Hogan concludes, "Quite frankly, it is almost impossible to point to a decision and say that it was a better decision because of the utilization of the zero-base budgeting concept." [45] In Georgia, 100 per cent of the subjects surveyed indicated there had been no apparent shifting of financial resources between functions as a direct result of the new budgeting system.

> One of the major selling points of zero-base budgeting is its presumed ability to shift resources to those areas where they are most needed. It is evident that most survey participants believe that a shifting of resources has not occurred, much less a more efficient shifting of financial resources.[46]

Furthermore, in Georgia, during fiscal years 1973, 1974, and 1975, "not a single instance was found where a function

---

[43] Carter, *op. cit.*, p. 5.

[44] "Interview with Jimmy Carter," *Washington Post*, Vol. LXV (December 27, 1976), Sec. E., p. 22.

[45] Roy L. Hogan, "Zero-Base Budgeting: A Rationalistic Attempt to Improve the Texas Budget System" (Masters Thesis, University of Texas at Austin, 1975), p. 92.

[46] George S. Minmier, *An Evaluation of the ZBB System, Governmental Institutions*, Monograph 68, Georgia State University, p. 131.

received less funds than it had in the previous fiscal year budget." [47] Zero Base Budgeting, where are you?

Not only do states focus on only part of ZBB, the part which is used does not seem to produce identifiable results. Why is this? In Texas, again, Hogan indicates shortcomings that may lead ZBB's failure to fulfill its promises.

> Structuring information by program area often requires the accumulation of such data from several different agencies. To the author's knowledge, such questions were infrequently asked if they were ever asked at all. With regard to the ranking of programs and program levels against one another as they relate to the objectives and needs of the agency, this information was rarely displayed. . . .[48]

> Time constraints and other factors that were experienced during initial program structure design hindered the achievement of this objective on a statewide basis. For example, one-half of the examiners interviewed expressed the opinion that existing organizational structures were a major deterrent in the development of agency program structures. . . .[49]

> All nine examiners interviewed expressed the general opinion that the section dealing with the analysis of alternative methods of accomplishing program or activity did not prove useful to them in determining funding recommendations. . . . Such analysis was usually construed in such a manner so as to justify the present method of operation.[50]

ZBB has not been gloriously received in its few trials within the federal government. The Consumer Product Safety Commission (CPSC) and National Aeronautics and Space Administration (NASA) applied ZBB to their budgets in 1977 in response to the House Appropriations Committee's interest in ZBB's relevance to the federal government.

[47] *Ibid.*
[48] Hogan, *op. cit.*, p. 173.
[49] *Ibid.*, p. 105.
[50] *Ibid.*, p. 116.

Thaddeus Garrett, Jr., the Commissioner of CPSC, concluded about the experiment:

> ZBB is not a panacea. It may be impossible to institute a government-wide zero-based review procedure that will work. It could be so time consuming that it reduces rather than enhances the quality of the budget review.[51]

The CPSC's administration of ZBB resembled the states' attempts to design ZBB for their needs. The decision packages were not zero based but rather assessed programs at three different levels of operation: (1) a minimum level of 85 per cent to 90 per cent of the present appropriation, (2) the current level projected into 1978, (3) an improved level incorporating a 10 per cent to 15 per cent increase. However, Chairman Byington confessed "what we have submitted here was really the submission we gave in September, where we did some zero-base analysis on a gross basis, which became our current level document. Then we did the incrementals up and down." [52] Ultimately, the Commission's minimum levels equaled the current levels of funding, despite stern admonishments that minimum levels should be below current levels. CPSC was also unable to rank the final twenty-one decision packages, because it found that too many of the programs were actually interconnected, so it would be impossible to fund one at the expense of the others. Each program was necessary for the proper operation of the others. In a statement resembling pre-ZBB budgeting, the Commissioners declared they would not know what to do if they were faced with a cut of x per cent. NASA was also unable to rank its programs because of the difficulty of finding a basis for comparison between them. Apparently,

[51] Subcommittee of the Committee on Appropriations, U.S. House of Representatives, *Department of Housing and Urban Development — Independent Agencies Appropriations, Part 4: Consumer Product Safety Commission*, 95th Congress, 1st Session, 1977, p. 4.

[52] *Ibid.*

programs are either integral to one another or disconnected.

Like PPB, ZBB's reasons for failure appear to be built into its design. ZBB does not provide better information; better information is actually a prerequisite for ZBB's functioning. ZBB is dependent on the unqualified support of administrators. Such support has not been forthcoming; the managers complain of not thoroughly understanding the process and of inadequate help from their superiors. The ensuing problems are agency and staff resistance to ZBB, lack of understanding of basic concepts, no improvement in the quality of information, and no effect on the department's allocations.

INFORMATION

The difference in information requirements at the different levels of management in ZBB introduces the possibility of contradictions implicit within the system. These contradictions appear at two levels: (1) the data developed within the system is meant to be used for two different purposes; and (2) the department heads attempt to deal holistically with data which is, by its very nature, marginal. Lower-level managers possess an incremental view of their programs; their task is to analyze the effects of marginal changes in funding in order to find an optimum level, presumably below the current level. However, agency heads want an overview of the consolidated packages in order to compare them for overlap and waste. Lower-level managers compute whether Program X is efficient. Their superiors wish to determine whether Program X is better than Program Y. Each level needs different information which is not provided by a single source of data.

For lower-level managers knowledge of the past is necessary in order to assess the probable effects of alternative funding levels. Saying that output would drop 30 per cent with a 10 per cent funding cut is usually based on a historical relationship between funding and outputs. But history is irrelevant for department heads who are interested in the effectiveness of the alternative funding levels right now. At the bureau level, administrators are interested in which activities should be slowed down or speeded up, while at the department level, administrators are concerned with which activities should be replaced.

MOTIVATION

Since the data in ZBB is always produced by the unit below for use by the unit above, an important concern in evaluating the quality of information is the motivation behind the people who furnish it. When you ask, "Charlie, how much is this going to cost? You're the expert in the field," you are dependent upon Charlie's motives in answering the question accurately and truthfully. This leads to problems of discount and motivation. The discount problem is, "Does Charlie know — how expert is his expertise?" If he hasn't done this sort of thing before, anyone's guess may be as good as his. The motivation problem is that agencies soon learn that it is in their best interest at various times to estimate higher or lower than actual cost. If they want the program, they may say it costs less; when they ask for money, they may say it costs more. Since employees are often rewarded for their ability to meet or exceed targets, they have a further interest in biasing their estimates on the high side. How are we to know whether these people really know and whether indeed they are motivated to tell the truth as they know it?

John LaFaver concluded, after studying New Mexico's experiences with ZBB in 1973, that it is "not reasonable to expect an agency to routinely furnish information that might

result in a lower appropriation — no matter what the justification might be." [53] Has experience born out his findings
on negative motivations?

The critical defect of ZBB and PPB is not only inability
to make the required calculations — who can combine all
possible funding levels? — but the irrationality of doing so
— who would want to? It is instructive to compare PPB,
ZBB, and traditional budgeting as modes of rational choice.

ORGANIZATION

The tension between analysis, which seeks out error and
promotes change, and organization, which seeks stability and
promotes its existing activities, is inevitable. The bulk of
analysis is rejected by the organizations for which it is intended.[54] Better information alone will not matter without
incentives for organizations to use it. Struggling with organizational incentives, therefore, is a perennial (perhaps para-
mount) problem of policy analysis.

Ignoring the organizational levels, and the proper approaches to each, is the original sin of new budgetary systems. PPB fails because no organizational level gets information (1) that it is willing to use and (2) that is relevant to
the resources at its disposal. MBO either obfuscates objectives, so higher levels will be unable to understand them,
or overwhelms the upper echelons with objectives, so they
cannot figure out which ones apply. After participating in
a lengthy MBO exercise, as a result of which it was de-

---

[53] John D. LaFaver, "Zero-Base Budgeting in New Mexico," XLVII
State Government (Spring 1974) p. 110.

[54] David H. Stimson and Ruth H. Stimson, *Operations Research in
Hospitals, Diagnosis and Prognosis* (Chicago, Hospital Research and
Education Trust, 1972), which evaluates several hundred analyses of
hospital administration and suggests that a good 90 per cent were ignored or opposed by the sponsoring agency.

cided that the status quo was splendid, a business participant reported: "I suggest this is a conspiracy by the Board
to prove the fruitlessness of deviation from established group
practices." [55] MBO is better seen as a misguided effort to
violate an analytic theorem — treating objectives apart from
resources — than as a mode of analysis.

Clinging to last year's agreements is enormously economical of critical resources (particularly time and good inter-
personal relations), which would be seriously depleted if all
or most past agreements were reexamined yearly. If there is
a mechanism for holding on to adequate solutions and sequentially proceeding to solve remaining problems — which
focus on increases and decreases to the base — knowledge is
more likely to result. Similarly, an agreement-producing
process is more likely to work if past agreements can be
retained while the system works on unresolved issues.

Only poor countries come close to Zero Base Budgeting,
not because they wish to do so but because their uncertain
financial position continually causes them to go back on
old commitments. Because past disputes are part of present
conflicts, their budgets lack predicictive value; little stated
in them is likely to occur.[56] Ahistorical practices, which are a
dire consequence of extreme instability and from which all
who experience them devoutly desire to escape, should not
be considered normative.

Analysis aims to bring information to bear on current decisions which do have future consequences. Taking these
consequences into account — acting now to do better later
— is what all analysis is about. Because prediction comes at
a premium, however, analysis uses history — what has been
tried in the past, how past patterns have led to present

[55] John Brandies, "Managing and Motivating by Objectives in Practice," IV *Management by Objectives* (1974) No. 1, p. 17.
[56] See Aaron Wildavsky, *The Politics of the Budgetary Process*,
2nd edition (Boston, 1974).

problems, where past obligations limit future commitments — as a source of both limits and possibilities.

A promise underlies public policy: if the actions we recommend are undertaken, good (intended) consequences rather than bad (unintended) ones will come about. Since causal connections are strict in designing public policy — if this is done by government, then that result will follow — failure to match promise with performance is likely to be high, as is reluctance to acknowledge error. Objectives are kept vague and multiple to expand the range within which observed behavior fits. Goal substitution takes place as the consequences actually caused by programs replace the objectives originally sought. Goal displacement becomes the norm as an organization seeks to make the variables it can control, its own efforts and processes, the objectives against which it is measured. This is how organizations come to justify error instead of creating knowledge. On all sides theoretical requirements are abandoned, by considering inputs or outputs alone, until there seems to be no error (and hence no truth), and it becomes impossible to learn from experience.

If our society lacks production functions — which is to say, policy relevant theory that purports to connect resources like teaching to objectives like reading — in most areas we wish to affect, how much more profound must be ignorance of the consequences of alternative programs across areas of policy and over time.[57] PPB and ZBB make demands on theory that cannot be met. They require knowledge of relationships between governmental action and social consequences over the broadest range of issues. Who is most misled by this — the proponents who sell these budget-

[57] See Aaron Wildavsky, "Policy as Its Own Cause," in *Speaking Truth to Power: The Art and Craft of Policy Analysis* (Boston, forthcoming).

ary systems or the politicians who buy them — is debatable. But if these systems represent the best in rational analysis, as many surely believe, and if this presumed rationality is doomed to failure, as it certainly is, then the sure loser is policy analysis, with its idea of applying intelligence to policy problems.

LEARNING

There is more than morbid curiosity in the study of Zero Base and program budgeting. Though one has died and the other should, their experiences teach about better budgeting by negative example. Whatever they do, the rule is, should not be done.

ZBB and PPB embody extreme (though different) forms of comprehensive calculation. (True, they can't practice what they preach; the effort either does them in or they lose any distinctive quality.) ZBB insists on making all possible vertical calculations, from zero to base, as it were, until the most efficient ways of achieving objectives are chosen. PPB covers at least all major horizontal relationships between related programs so the most cost-effective combination for achieving objectives is chosen. Ergo, the lesson is that budgeting should not be comprehensive. Since knowledge, time, and manpower are usually in short supply, most policy analysis is concerned with reducing rather than increasing the cost of calculations. Budgeting should not hinder that effort.

PPB is ahistorical in that it is interested in comparing programs in the here and now. The past is an anachronism, a leftover remnant of an outmoded era, and there is no evolution. ZBB doesn't so much ignore as set out to abolish history; the clock is always set at zero. Budgets apparently spring newborn like Minerva from the brow of Jove. The lesson is clear: budgets should be explicitly historical, comparing what is about to be done with what has recently happened. This evolutionary approach brings insight because policies have internal logics of their own — future policies are usually reactions to the defeats of past policies — that can best be appreciated from the inside.[58] In deciding whether policies are desirable, moreover, it is usually not possible to say that a problem has been solved since objectives are multiple and contradictory where they are not vague and resources including knowledge are usually insufficient. It is wiser, instead, to ask how policies of today (including the evils not yet mitigated) compare with those they superseded yesterday. A historical approach, therefore, not only conserves calculations by focusing on increments of change but also suggests the right kinds of calculations to make for purposes of evaluating public policy.

ZBB and PPB share an emphasis on the virtue of objectives. Program budgeting is about relating larger to smaller objectives among different programs, and Zero Base Budgeting promises to do the same within a single program. The policy implications of these methods of budgeting, which distinguish them from existing approaches, derive from their overwhelming concern with having and ranking objectives. Thinking about objectives is one thing, however, and making budget categories out of them is quite another. Of course, if one wants the objectives of today to be the objectives of tomorrow, if one wants no change in objectives, then building the budget around objectives is a brilliant idea. But if one wants flexibility in objectives (sometimes known as learning from experience), it must be possible to change them without simultaneously destroying the organization by withdrawing financial support.

The traditional line-item budget is, of course, uninterested in objectives. Budgeters may have objectives, but the budget itself is organized around activities or functions — personnel, maintenance, etc. One can change objectives, then,

58 *Ibid.*

without challenging organizational survival. Traditional budgeting does not demand analysis of policy, but neither does it inhibit it.

Every criticism of traditional budgeting is undoubtedly correct. It is incremental rather than comprehensive; it does fragment decisions; it is heavily historical and looks backward more than forward; it is indifferent to objectives; and it is concerned about the care and feeding and control of organizations, their personnel, space, maintenance, and all that. Why, then, has traditional budgeting lasted so long? Because it has the virtue of its defects.

Traditional budgeting makes calculations easy precisely because it is not comprehensive. History provides a strong base on which to rest a case. The present is made part of the past, which may be known, instead of the future, which cannot be comprehended. Choices that might cause conflict are fragmented so that not all difficulties need be faced at one time. Because it is neutral in regard to policy, traditional budgeting is compatible with a variety of policies, all of which can be converted into line items. Traditional budgeting lasts, then, because it is simpler, easier, less stressful, and more flexible than modern alternatives like ZBB and PPB.

Needless to say, traditional budgeting also has the defects of its virtues. Though budgets look back, they may not look back far enough to understand how (or why) they got where they are. Comparing this year with last year may not mean much if the past was a mistake and the future likely to be a bigger one. Quick calculation may be worse than none if it is grossly in error. Policy neutrality may degenerate into disinterest in programs. So why has traditional budgeting lasted? So far no one has come up with another budgetary procedure that has the virtues of traditional budgeting but lacks its defects.

CONGRESS
7

THE DAY AFTER CONGRESS adopted spending and revenue limits for fiscal 1976, the *New York Times* predicted in a front page article that Congressional budget reform, if it continued, "could drastically alter the way Congress transacts its business and rearrange its power structure as well." Has Congress established super Budget Committees that will decide national priorities and enforce their will upon the rest of the legislature, as the Cabinet does in Britain? Or is the new Congressional Budget Act a facade behind which business will go on as usual? Congress could use its new process simply to ratify what its committees have already done; or it actually could fulfill the promise of budget reform by relating individual expenditures to total spending and total spending to revenues.

REASONS FOR REFORM

Before we take a look at what is happening, it would be wise to consider why Congress wanted to reform its budget process. A simple way of approaching this complex subject is to say that legislators were unhappy with the collective consequences of their individual choices. They liked voting for spending but not for taxes. They got their way, in a manner of speaking, by riding roughshod over the appropriations committees, by tunneling beneath them through direct drafts on the Treasury ("backdoor spending"), or by getting around them entirely through tax expenditures (spending that allows certain people to reduce their taxes before these taxes get to the Treasury). Individual members of Congress won but Congress as a whole lost; individual and collective rationality were at odds.

Presidential impoundments of funds, often with sub-rosa Congressional support, became common. Through them, members could vote for spending while the President took the blame for cutting. President Nixon, mounting a direct challenge to Congressional control of the purse, bent this practice so far that it broke in his hands. As a result, attention has been diverted from restraint at the source to restraint by impoundment. Indeed, unless the new reform works, we can expect to see members hinting, despite new legal prohibitions against impoundment, that the President should reduce the flow of spending. If presidents take the heat, however, they will also bask in the glow of power.

As Congress grew more divided over the budget, the authorization-appropriations gap rose into the tens of billions. The legislative committees, whose members select themselves for their personal and constituency interests in particular areas of public policy, consistently authorized more spending than the appropriations subcommittees would support. The trend away from multi-year and toward annual authorizations was an effort by the legislative committees to lobby the appropriations committees for increased spending. The more Congressmen fought, the longer it took; the budget process became notorious for delay, delay which made it difficult for administrative agencies to carry out their responsibilities in an effective manner and difficult for state and local governments to fit federal grants into their plans in a timely fashion.

Then came Vietnam, which suggested Congress was negligent in its responsibilities for defense appropriations; Presidential impoundments, which suggested Congress was losing power domestically; and Watergate, which was all too suggestive of excess by the Chief Executive. Congressional power of the purse had to be strengthened. Taxing and spending are the center of Congressional power; if these powers decline, Congress declines as well. All these factors explain why Congress was willing to contemplate reform; they do not necessarily predict that the individual needs of individual legislators will give way to the collective interests of Congress in maintaining its institutional power.

CONGRESSIONAL REALITIES

Past proposals to reform Congressional budget review failed because they did not sufficiently take into account the realities of decision making in Congress. Whatever is recommended must be workable in a large, heterogeneous, and independent body that operates in an environment of fragmented and dispersed power. There is no sense in treating Congress as if it were, or even were led by, a small cohesive group easily able to agree or to impose its will on others. To avoid these traps, it may be helpful to state the characteristics of the Congressional environment in the form of criteria for evaluating alternative budgetary procedures.

Many committees, not one. A Committee that makes a budget that is not then altered by other committees — a committee without rivals, a steering committee of the legislature — can be called a cabinet on the British model. In contrast, Congress is a pluralistic institution; it has many centers of power, depending on the time and the issue. To be effective Congress must exploit rather than fight its pluralistic nature, and a good way to exploit pluralism is to embrace specialization.

More specialization, not less. Without specialization there is no knowledge, and without knowledge there is no power. When executives wish to emasculate legislatures, they break up existing committees and prevent formation of new ones that are specialized enough to look into specific areas of policy and small enough to act with dispatch. Unless the legislature can keep up with the executive, it will become an auditor after the fact rather than a budgeter in advance.

Simplification, not mystification. Rationality is supposed to mean effective action, not pretentious inaction. The rational person is not one who pretends to compare everything to everything else but rather one who manipulates the few variables under his control to good effect. If attention is focused on all or most possible relationships, it will be impossible to single out those most in need of change. However badly the Chief Executive confuses himself, he can always make a last-minute decision with a show of justification. If Congressmen confuse themselves, they will not be able to act at all. They need mechanisms to reduce the number of decisions to be considered at any one time; they need ways of structuring a series of votes so that these are both meaningful and manageable. Before a legislature can act wisely, it must be able to act. If Congressmen do not employ aids to calculation, they will be unable either to arrive at their own preferences or to settle their differences with others. Making calculations manageable lies at the heart of effective legislative decision making.

THE NEW RULES OF THE GAME

The Congressional Budget and Impoundment Control Act of 1974 states as its purpose that:

> The Congress declares that it is essential: to assure effective Congressional control over the budgetary process; to provide for the Congressional determination each year of the appropriate level of federal revenues and expenditures; to provide a system of impoundment control; to establish national budget priorities; and to provide for the furnishing of information by the Executive branch in a manner that will assist the Congress in discharging its duties.[1]

To accomplish these purposes the Act creates three new institutions: the House Budget Committee, the Senate Budget Committee, and the Congressional Budget Office. The Act also provides a new set of budgeting procedures, a timetable for budgetary actions, and a change in the fiscal year. Finally, it includes procedures to control Presidential impoundment.

The statutory authority for both the Senate and the House Budget Committees is the same. They are required to report at least two concurrent resolutions on the budget each year, to analyze the impact of existing and proposed programs on budgetary outlays, and to oversee the operations of the Congressional Budget Office.

The Senate Budget Committee has sixteen members, the House Budget Committee twenty-five. The Senate Budget Committee is selected in the same way as other Senate committees (by the Democratic and Republican Conferences). The House Budget Committee is selected differently from other House committees. Of the twenty-five, five each

---

[1] Public Law 93–344, "Congressional Budget and Impoundment Control Act of 7974," Section 2.

must be drawn from the House Ways and Means Committee and the House Appropriations Committee and one from each party's leadership. The tenure of the members of the Senate Budget Committee is unlimited. No member of the House Budget Committee may serve for more than four of any ten-year period. Traditional seniority rules of the House are suspended for their Budget Committee.[2] In the Senate the Budget Committee is exempted from the reform that no member can serve on more than two major committees.[3]

The House Republicans allow their ranking members on Ways and Means and on Appropriations to choose the Republicans from those committees for the Budget Committee positions. The Republican Caucus chooses the three other Committee positions. All the Republican members serve the same tenure. The Democrats had similar rules, except for the provision of staggering the tenure of their members to allow for continuity. Since the reforms of the 95th Congress Democratic Caucus, these rules have been changed. The nominations of all Democratic members (except the representative of the leadership, who is picked by the leadership), including those who will represent Ways and Means and Appropriations, are made by the Democratic Steering and Policy Committee. The nominees must be ratified by a vote of the entire Caucus. The rules on staggering the membership have been changed to reflect greater control over the Committee by the leadership and Caucus. Eight new members and eight standing members must be nominated at each new Congress by the Steering and Policy Committee. The Chairmanship of the Budget Committee is a self-nominating position open to any mem-

[2] *Ibid.*, Section 101.
[3] Judy Gardner, "Economic Affairs," XXXIV *Congressional Quarterly Weekly* (November 27, 1976) No. 48, p. 3233.

ber of the committee. The nominees must stand for a full Caucus vote for election to the Chair. This vote also must be carried out each new Congress.[4]

The staff of the Senate Budget Committee has fifty-five professionals and thirty support personnel in total. Thirty-four professionals and fifteen support personnel, who act as the core staff of the Senate Committee, are appointed by the Committee Chairman. The rest of the staff are hired by Committee members. The House Budget Committee has a smaller staff of forty professionals and twenty-five support personnel. The House Committee determined that the rotating nature of its membership required expertise in programmatic and budgetary areas. The Senate staff, on the other hand, are more experienced politically than technically.

The third new institution is the Congressional Budget Office, an analytical unit that is to provide a check on information from the Executive Branch. The Director of the CBO is appointed for a four-year term by the Speaker of the House and the President Pro Tem of the Senate on recommendations of the two Budget Committees. The CBO does not generate original information; rather it analyzes budgetary and programmatic issues. It has three basic responsibilities: (1) monitoring the economy and estimating its impact on the budget, (2) improving the flow and quality of budgetary information, and (3) analyzing the costs and effects of alternative budgetary choices.[5]

[4] XXXIV *Congressional Quarterly* (November 27, 1976) No. 48, pp. 3229–3260; (December 18, 1976) No. 51, pp. 3317–3348; XXXV *Congressional Quarterly* (January 1, 1977) No. 1, pp. 1–32; (January 15, 1977) No. 3, pp. 61–100.

[5] John Ellwood and James Thurber, "The New Congressional Budget Process: The House and Ways of House-Senate Differences," in Lawrence C. Dodd and Bruce I. Oppenheim, editors, *Congress Reconsidered* (New York, 1976).

THE NEW TIMETABLE

The Act changed the beginning of the fiscal year from July 1 to October 1. The new timetable is outlined in Table 7–1.

TABLE 7-1

Congressional budget timetable.

Nov. 10	Current services budget received
Jan. 18 *	President's budget received
Mar. 15	Advice and data from all Congressional Committees (submitted to Budget Committees)
Apr. 1	CBO reports to Budget Committees
Apr. 15	Budget Committees report out First Budget Resolution
May 15	Congressional Committees report new authorizing legislation
	Congress completes action on First Budget Resolution
Labor Day + 7 **	Congress completes action on all spending bills
Sept. 15	Congress completes action on Second Budget Resolution
Sept. 25	Congress completes action on reconciliation measures
Oct. 1	Fiscal year begins

Source: Public Law 93–344, "Congressional Budget and Impoundment Control Act of 1974."
* Or 15 days after Congress convenes.
** Seven days after Labor Day.

The Congressional Budget timetable can be thought of as consisting of four distinct stages.[6] These stages are:

Stage 1
Nov. 10–Apr. 15   Information gathering, analysis, preparation, and submission of Congressional Budget by Congressional Budget Office and Budget Committees.

[6] Public Law 93–344.

Stage 2
Apr. 15–May 15   Debate and adoption of Congressional
                        Budget by both Houses; establishment
                        of national spending priorities.

Stage 3
May 15–Early Sept.   Enactment of spending bills.

Stage 4
Sept. 15–Sept. 25   Reassessment of spending, revenue,
                        and debt requirements in the Second
                        Budget Resolution; enactment of rec-
                        onciliation bill.

THE PROCESS OUTLINED

The new budget process begins on November 10 with the
submission by OMB of the Current Services Budget to the
Joint Economic Committee. The Current Services Budget
is defined by the Congressional Budget and Implementation
Control Act as that budget determined as if:

> all programs and activities were carried on during such en-
> suing fiscal year at the same level as the fiscal year in
> progress and without policy changes in such programs and
> activities.[7]

Put simply, it is what this year's budget would be next year
if there were no policy changes.[8] The Joint Economic Committee must report on the economic impact of the CSB and
return it to the two Budget Committees. This report is the
only role the JEC has in the budgetary process. The CSB is
supposed to be a base from which Congress and its committees are to work in the preparation of the budget for the
next fiscal year. In reality only the Senate Budget Commit-

[7] Public Law 93–344, Section 605.
[8] Ellwood and Thurber, *op cit.*, p. 183.

tee uses it in this fashion. The House Budget Committee uses the President's Budget as its base.

After the President's Budget is delivered, the two Budget Committees receive reports from the other committees in their respective houses. These reports contain views on budget authority, outlays, and revenues within the committees' own jurisdictions. This process lasts until March 15.

The next period concerns work prepared for the two Budget Committees by the Congressional Budget Office. In these reports, budget figures and programs presented in the President's Budget are analyzed to allow the Committees to judge the merits of what the Executive Branch has prepared. The CBO also prepares economic reviews of alternative fiscal policies, including the President's, in order to make the Committees aware of the implications of their choices.

Each Budget Committee has a different way of deciding what it will report out as a Budget Resolution, which is due April 1 though the significance of the day has been lost on most people. In order to avoid a jurisdictional fight between the budget and appropriating committees, the Act stipulated that targets and ceilings were to be set at high levels of aggregation, that is, for sixteen functional categories rather than the approximately 1250 appropriation accounts. Each chamber of the legislature, however, is free to reach its results with as much or as little detail as it wishes. The House works at a low level of aggregation in order to emphasize its virtue of specialization. The Senate, on the other hand, works at a high level of aggregation with few specifics on each program within the sixteen broad categories.

The House also differs from the Senate in that the Chairman of the House Budget Committee uses a "Chairman's mark." This is a suggested budget resolution used as a starting point for committee debate at each markup. It is specific and consists of the President's Budget level for each function and any changes recommended by the Chairman.

The fact that the House Budget Committee uses a low level of aggregation and a Chairman's mark at that level means that the Budget Resolutions reported out of HBC can be broken down to the appropriations account level. The Senate Budget Committee, on the other hand, adopts a given spending level for the whole function. Before I describe the report of this First Budget Resolution, let's look at the resolution in more detail.

The First Concurrent Budget Resolution is a document passed by both Houses to act as an agenda in the budgeting process during the next five months. It contains all that follows and more: the appropriate level of total budget outlays and of total new budget authority; an estimate of budget outlays and an appropriate level of new budget authority for each major functional category, and for contingencies; the amount of the surplus or the deficit appropriate in light of economic conditions; the recommended level of federal revenues and the amount by which they should be increased or decreased; and the amount by which the statutory limit on the public debt should be increased or decreased.[9]

After debate in each House, there is a conference in which the differences between the two Houses are hammered out. The Conference Report and a Joint Statement of Managers allocating targets is then adopted by both Houses. This must be completed by May 15, before any authorizing or spending legislation is passed. To take account of what has actually gone on during the period since the First Concurrent Resolution, a Second Concurrent Budget Resolution is proposed. It either reaffirms or revises the first in light of those realities.

A reconciliation process occurs here. Congress adjusts any laws to the intent of the Second Concurrent Budget Resolution. It does this only if the Second Concurrent Budget

[9] Public Law 93–344, Section 301.

Resolution contains directions to one or more committees to determine and recommend changes in specified items.

THE CONTROL OF IMPOUNDMENT

The Congress hopes to limit the Presidential impoundment power by setting up two categories of impoundment, rescissions and deferrals. A deferral is an impoundment of funds not necessary to achieve Congressional intent. A rescission is an impoundment of funds in order to change Congressional intent. The President can defer the spending of appropriated funds until the end of the fiscal year, unless either House by a majority vote passes an impoundment resolution. The President can alter Congressional intent by not spending appropriated funds only if he submits a rescission bill that passes by a majority in both Houses within forty-five days. The Comptroller General has the authority to bring the President to court if he feels that the President is deferring funds that should be rescinded. The Comptroller General can also bring the President to court if he feels the President is not spending funds after a rejection of a rescission bill.

WHOSE BUDGETARY BASE?

Intended by Congress to serve as a base to simplify calculations for next year's budget, the Current Services Budget (CSB) submitted each November 15 by the Office of Management and Budget has been a failure. The CSB is not taken seriously by those preparing it at OMB and is not used in Congress. Efforts are currently under way to change its format and timing to help alleviate some of its problems, but while procedural changes may be necessary, the basic difficulty is deeper: inability to agree on exactly what should constitute the base for analyzing next year's budget.

The Current Services Budget is useless to OMB because OMB is waiting for one more to its liking, the President's Budget, which is submitted only two months later in January. Hence OMB considers a CSB outdated practically as soon as it is prepared. OMB would prefer, moreover, that the first look Congress has at an executive branch plan for the coming year be the President's formal Budget: the more Congressmen look at the President's Budget, the more of it they will incorporate in their own budget.

The treatment accorded the Current Services Budget by Congress does nothing to convince OMB that this is an important document. Congress' decision to send the CSB to the Joint Economic Committee (JEC) is equivalent to giving last rites: it is sending a useless document to a powerless body. This is the only Budget Act duty of the JEC; since the JEC's power to review the CSB contains no legislative directive, OMB would prefer to spend its time on a document more important to the authoritative committees of Congress.

Part of the difficulty comes from the language of the Budget Act itself. The provision stipulating a Current Services Budget is subject to interpretation as to the requirements placed on the President. The Executive must submit a Budget for the ensuing fiscal year as if "all programs and activities were carried on during such ensuing fiscal year at the same level as the fiscal year in progress and without policy changes in such programs and activities." [10] But while the estimates are to be accompanied by economic and programmatic assumptions underlying the numbers, the current services idea means different things to different people. In the science and energy areas, where many programs have relatively short lives and demonstration projects are continually finishing and being replaced by other demonstrations, the current services concept is ineffectual and con-

[10] Public Law 93–344, Section 344, Section 605.

fusing. Are new demonstrations that are expected to be begun during the coming year included in the CSB? Are programs that are winding down this year included at last year's level?

In the social areas the difficulty is no less vexing. Since economic assumptions are prominent in projecting levels of social welfare expenditures, differences in these assumptions between the executive and legislative branches are certain to cause variations in expected program cost. OMB's Current Services Budget does not contain alternative prognostications based on various economic assumptions.

When a similar enterprise was undertaken in Britain, numerous disputes occurred over the meaning of "current" and "services." Is "current" restricted to what is happening now or to the improvements some said were supposed to take place? Does "service" signify the lower level that has (regretfully) been forthcoming or the higher one promised?

Interpolation apart, OMB and department budget officers are concerned about the requirement that the CSB be submitted by individual appropriations accounts. In order for OMB to submit its report to Congress by November, agency and departmental budget officers must use valuable preparation time during the late summer and early fall to break down hundreds of these individual accounts into categories of "present" and "expected" or "desired" budget items. Such a disaggregation was never required before the Budget Act and to OMB officials who must take the several weeks to get through all the minutiae involved, the process is painful. Congress is never in session when the Current Services Budget is sent to the Hill, no one looks at it carefully, and by the time the President's Budget — the culmination of the OMB's work — comes out, current services are long since past.

To OMB budget examiners — the real workhorses on a project of this variety — the Current Services Budget is a technical requirement to be finished quickly "so we can get on and do our work." The OMB examiners' first mission during the late fall is to work for the President, not for Congress. Budget review division supervisors must sometimes push examiners to work for Congress, since the examiners regard Congressional information demands as peripheral to their jobs.

At the same time, OMB must be careful of the information submitted by agencies and departments on their Current Services levels. Because of the simultaneous work requirements placed on examiners, the CSB might be seen by agencies as an opportunity to "end-run" OMB. There are fears that bureaus and departments will pad their current accounts and overestimate their need to continue "current services" in order to expand the base on which their next budget is built. Programs included under the "current services" label may be immune to significant cutbacks.

The failure of the Current Services Budget as presently constituted does not necessarily signify that the idea of a budget base is faulty. Indeed, action taken by the Carter Administration transition team early in 1977 attests to the usefulness of a base budget figure. In the fiscal year 1978 budget submitted by President Ford before leaving office in January 1977, there were a number of pages documenting major policy changes, accompanied by estimates of how they would add or subtract from outlay or budget authority figures of some undefined current policy base. The Carter Campaign and subsequent Transition Staff Chief had been notified by the Senate Budget Committee staff as early as August 1976 that, if Carter won the election, the new Administration would have to make any revisions to the Ford Budget by February or they would be unable to tie into the Congressional Budget's First Concurrent Resolution, due from the Budget Committee in April. Carter submitted the revisions in February.

Obviously, time had not allowed a comprehensive look at the federal budget. Rather, the transition budget team simplified their calculations by looking at the list of policy changes specified by Ford. Without this list, the new Administration itself would have been forced to figure out a base from which to begin policy formulation and change. An incremental look at already proposed changes gave the new President an easy means to define Administration objectives without making overly large investments of resources.

While OMB's Current Services Budget has not lived up to expectations, the need for a base suitable to the Congress in its own budget procedures remains. Neglecting OMB's Current Services Budget completely, the two Houses have taken different approaches to defining a base from which to work. The House Budget Committee under Chairmen Adams (94th Congress) and Giaimo (95th Congress) has been presented with a suggested budget resolution, a "chairman's mark," as a beginning point for Committee markup debate.[11] Chairman Muskie of the Senate Budget Committee has never presented his own "mark" or budget desires explicitly. The Senate markup materials (for the fiscal year 1978 First Concurrent Resolution) list three possible indicators for action on any given budget item: the President's Budget, current policy estimates (as calculated by CBO), and the authorizing committees' recommendation (sometimes called the "wish list"). The range of these figures is often quite large, as shown in Table 7–2.

Unlike OMB's Current Services Budget, CBO is serious about its projections of "current policy." The Senate Budget

[11] John Ellwood and James Thurber, "Some Implications of the Congressional Budget and Impoundment Control Act for the Senate" (paper prepared for the 1976 Annual Meeting of the APSA; U.S. House of Representatives, Committee on the Budget, "Chairman's Recommendations for the Second Concurrent Resolution on the Budget FY1978," July 27, 1977).

TABLE 7-2

Total budget recommendations for fiscal year 1978: the range of
choice for the Senate is quite broad ($ billions).

	Carter budget	Current policy	Senate committees authorizing	Appropriations
Total budget authority	506.2	495.7	534.5	516.2
Total outlays	458.3	460.5	475.1	464.8

Source: Senate Budget Committee Markup Materials for FY1978
First Concurrent Resolution on the Budget.

Committee sees these CBO estimates as the most value-
neutral figures around, and, for purposes of economic management, likes to look at the total level of current expenditures. This distinction follows the trend of House-Senate
differences. The House likes detail and in its budget process
will allow (and expect) the Chairman, the budget expert,
to define appropriate levels of spending, right down to the
appropriations account level. The Senate deals with aggregates and appreciates bipartisan debate which might lead
to discussion of the appropriateness of total government
spending. The House questions the detail of what goes into
the functional areas such as Agriculture. The Senate likes
to think of itself as determining the proper trade-off between revenue and expenditure. What both House and Senate do agree about is that they should control spending.

WHOSE BUDGET?

Opinions as to the effects of the Title X Impoundment
Provisions of the Budget Act are mixed: "where one stands
depends on where one sits." Some OMB officials feel cas-
trated by the changes: OMB's power over programs has
been severely restricted by Congress. Even outside OMB
few are totally satisfied with present arrangements. Im-

poundment control was a necessary response to the excesses of the Nixon Administration. But some now find the solution to be more onerous than the problem it purported to solve.

When President Nixon, claiming a constitutional right to do so, proposed wholesale rescission of Congressionally appropriated funds in early 1973, he was directly challenging the most important power of the legislature. After all, Nixon explained, someone had to control the Budget and obviously Congress wasn't up to the task. This challenge — questioning the fiscal responsibility of the Democratic-controlled Congress — had to be answered. Some impoundment of funds was a mutually beneficial process in the past; Congress could pass programs and please its constituents, the President could quell "runaway spending" and please his. Nixon brought the system out into the open so that it became impossible to continue the charade. But in making the process public, Congress has also made it inflexible.

Impoundments today are subject to a series of complicated provisions. When a President wants to change the flow of money into a given project, he must court the approval of Congress. When a President proposes to reserve obligated budget authority, that is, not to spend (a rescission, Section 1012), he must submit a special message to both Houses of Congress specifying the amount of budget authority to be rescinded; the specific project or governmental function affected by the rescission; the reasons for his actions; the estimated fiscal, economic, and budgetary effect of the rescission; a statement of the circumstances; and the estimated effect of such rescission on a given program. Unless both Houses expressly approve the rescission bill within forty-five days of its submission to Congress, the money must be made available for obligation.

For deferrals (or delay) of funding (Section 1013), a similar message must be sent; the main difference is that the proposal automatically goes into effect unless either House passes an impoundment resolution disapproving the deferral. To reiterate: A rescission proposal must be approved by both Houses within forty-five days or it cannot take effect. Deferrals are allowed except when vetoed by either House.

OMB finds the impoundment features of the Act to be a "paper mill." Officials there feel Congress, and especially the General Accounting Office (GAO), which is charged with overseeing the rescission and deferral processes, is saying, "we've caught you abusing your power, so now we'll take nothing you say seriously." They feel GAO implies some base intent by OMB to stifle the "will of the people" whenever impoundment messages are filed. All parties agree that the mechanisms generate lots of paperwork. There are those who believe the process can be simplified by drawing a distinction between "technical" and "policy" rescissions. OMB officials believe that Congress should trust the work going on at OMB and that only rescissions of a policy nature (and who is to say what that includes?) should require Congressional sanction. But the Johnson and Nixon years have left a lasting mark on relations between Congress and the Presidency, and trust is not something easily restored. The intricacies of impoundment are specifically set up to control the President. There is nothing in the Act that impels Congress to trust the executive branch. Yet as time passes, and rescissions and deferrals lose their ability to generate publicity as they did in Nixon's time, the process may become less heated and more subject to compromise.

Congress has not approved most proposals for rescissions. A House Appropriations Committee study found that Congress approved only $530 million out of $6.7 billion in proposed rescissions by President Ford during fiscal years 1976 and 1977.[12] A potential problem raised by Congress' routine

---

[12] "Budget: 'Congress Shall . . . Pay the Debts.'" VIII *National Journal* (May 29, 1976), p. 743.

failure to approve such requests is that Congress could become so concerned with fiscal policy that it matters less what money is spent on than that it is spent at all. Spending — keeping up a certain level of government outlays — could become more important than what it buys. Carried to an extreme, such an attitude by Congress could mean more difficulty in the future in closing programs that have outlasted their effectiveness. Impounding, after all, is a sort of Sunset Law. In the past, the threat of impoundment was used by the Administration and its Budget Office against administrative branch program managers — shape up or be scuttled. Unless Congress is to replace the Executive Branch, there should remain a greater degree of discretion over spending consigned to the President.

The issues brewing over impoundment are suggestive of a general executive-legislative clash. Part of this clash is over an Executive Branch perception that Congress is trying to deal with specifics too much. Congress is thought to be not only concerning itself with overall policy direction but increasingly dictating program composition and the day-to-day running of government. The Executive views this as impinging upon the flexibility of the Administration, stifling creativity under the guise of control. Congress' general distrust of the Executive and especially the OMB comes at a time when government is getting more complex. A fear inherent in this distrust, voiced by both Congressional and Administrative sources, is that as Congressmen take on an increasingly activist orientation, they will spread themselves too thin and be forced to rely increasingly on staff; the trend would lead to the gradual bureaucratization of Congress.

During the 1976 Presidential campaign, questions were raised about whether the new budget process would be necessary during a Democratic Administration. Clearly the process had been the response of a Congress of one party battling a President of another party, and there were suggestions that a "unified" one-party government would present fewer differences over policy. Such views now appear to have been naïve. The clash is between branches as well as between parties.

Congress has been changing recently and is becoming more assertive with these changes. Many senior members of Congress have retired since 1970. Budget reforms, disclosure laws, and ethics actions have been accompanied by the growth in importance of younger members. Older leaders have lost their power. In the House the solidarity behind committee chairmen has declined. There is a desire in this younger and more assertive Congress to stop what is perceived as the wholesale giveaway of power to the Executive. Because of recent Presidential abuses of power, Congress chooses not to believe Executive Branch submissions without approval from a Congressional source (witness the GAO oversight of impoundment proposals and CBO's scrutiny of recent Presidential proposals). While both parties agree that a degree of trust between branches is necessary, each branch is trying to protect itself from encroachments by the other.

WHOSE INFORMATION?

Unlike the adversary relations engendered by GAO oversight of impoundment, the Administration has had amicable relations with the new boy in town, the Congressional Budget Office. In a short period of time, CBO has developed a budget analysis division that rivals the capabilities of any government agency. Congress has never had or wanted an agency that would collect primary data for program cost estimation. An attempt to duplicate the informational capacity of the Administration would be a staggering investment. However, Congress does want an agency that can scrutinize the work of other sources. While most often using the primary materials coming out of other agencies,

CBO is helping to improve the quality and honesty of the Executive Branch. This competition in cost projection works on two levels. First, there are deficiencies in the quality of estimates. Agencies may often be content with poor techniques when newer and better tools come along. They may have outdated indices or irrelevant data sets that inhibit their "bits" of data from being put to use as relevant "information." The second difficulty is institutional honesty. Before CBO, Congress' analytic ability was strictly limited; neither GAO's accounting divisions nor the Congressional Research Service could provide up-to-date analysis of economic forecasts or program costs. Before, the Council of Economic Advisers and OMB could monopolize numbers with little chance of having their interpretation challenged by Congress, but now CBO can check on them.

For the past two years, CBO has included an elaborate methodological piece on its economic assumptions in its five-year budget projections. Opening the methodology to public inspection, CBO puts OMB and CEA in a quandary. When either of the Executive Branch agencies makes projections that differ from CBO's they are left open to potentially embarassing questions. This is labeled by a CBO source as "healthy competition."

Consider a dispute over program cost estimate done by HEW in support of their Basic Educational Opportunity Grant program. HEW estimates submitted to Congress in an Appropriations hearing did not match previous Administration economic assumptions about income gains in the economy. HEW estimates assumed that program participant's incomes would change differently than the average for the society. Spotting the discrepancy, CBO changed the agency position. Similarly, CBO analysis was able to convince Congress that the President's proposed budget receipts for outer continental shelf oil leases were overoptimistic.

Today Executive agencies are attempting to work out cost estimate differentials with CBO before they are tested in Congress. For consideration of President Carter's welfare reform package, for example, HEW solicited CBO's advice in designing the project's econometric model. Secretary Califano had been worried about the wide range of cost estimates that accompanied President Nixon's Family Assistance Plan in 1969 and which eventually helped scuttle it. Through executive-legislative cooperation in the use and design of the welfare model, if not the program itself, there would be a greater chance of debate on the relative merits of given programs at given costs, rather than a roundabout argument over whose numbers were more accurate.

How has the Congressional budget process changed the amount or extent of information that flows between the Executive Branch and Congress? A common Executive Branch response is that much more information is required but very little is used. In years before the Act, OMB had been forecasting cost estimates on major new or controversial legislation on a regular basis. Now it must make forecasts for all reported legislation. OMB officials feel this work is a nuisance and nuisance work always seems to take longer. Extra information required of OMB under the Act includes mid-year budget reviews, the Current Services Budget, continuous tracking of federal government outlays, and recurring reports on rescissions and deferrals. Congress has also determined that since the OMB and Congress have comparable computerized budget information only at the lowest, most disaggregated account levels, then this is the level at which outlays should be computed. The changes amount to doing more jobs on a regular basis and doing them at a much more specific level of detail.

Yet while the amount of work done by budget examiners has gone up, their numbers have not. OMB as a whole has grown since the budget Act took effect, but the growth has primarily occurred on the management-organizational side of the agency. Cutbacks in OMB staff are imminent,[13] and these are expected to fall on both sides of OMB. Thus the prospect at OMB is for more work with less staff.

The demands placed on OMB for more data may be seen as the result of two separate happenings. The first is the breakdown of the President's Budget by appropriations accounts into spending out of old and new accounts. This distinction, unnecessary for OMB purposes, requires extra effort to give Congress a better indication of the incremental changes being made by the Administration. The second factor is a rise in the number of users of OMB data. As CBO, Budget Committee, and Appropriations staff members increase — and they have grown significantly since passage of the Act — staff members feel the need to justify their existence and so continually ask OMB for more information.

Administrative agencies and Congressional committees have also been affected by new informational requirements. Section 301(C) of the Budget Act requires each Congressional committee to report to its Budget Committee by March 15 its recommendations and estimates of budget authority and outlays for programs within its jurisdiction for the following fiscal year.[14] To put together these reports each committee must rely to some extent on the Administrative agencies under their jurisdiction. Some of these reports are detailed. The report of the Senate Committee on Agriculture, Nutrition, and Forestry, for instance, gives a specific program-by-program breakdown showing outlays and obligations by individual appropriations account for a three-year period. The Department of Agriculture has been required to submit such a detailed report to the Senate Agriculture

[13] CLXXVII *The New Repubic* (Juy 30, 1977) No. 5, Issue 3264.
[14] Richard Schott, "The Congressional Budget Process: Impact on Federal Administrative Agencies" (draft of paper presented at national meeting of APSA, Washington, D.C., April 20, 1976), pp. 1–15.

Committee for two years now, and this procedure involves a great deal of detailed initial work. The fiscal year 1978 Agriculture Committee report stresses the reason for this detail: "If the potential benefits [of the Budget process] are to be realized, there must be full consideration of every program and every recommendation. . . . The size of the program cannot be used as an indicator of importance. Most agricultural programs are relatively small and tend to be forgotten when the budget function totals are 'rounded' to the nearest $100 million." As the size of government grows toward the trillion dollar level, however, a mere $100 million may well seem small.

WHOSE CBO?

CBO is now considered the best source of budget numbers in Washington. This does not mean there is no debate on numbers. "The way the Hill works," as a legislative aide put it, "is to ask a lot of different agencies to do the same job, to see if they come out with the same answers." If they don't, interested legislators know where to probe.

CBO produces score-keeping reports enabling the House and Senate Budget Committees to monitor the rate at which appropriations are being approved so that it is possible to isolate spending proposals that would break the ceilings (assuming other appropriations keep on their current course). Naturally, score keeping does not guarantee Budget Committee action or its success but it does permit knowledgeable intervention.

The strenuous effort of CBO to edit its reports so they are readable increases its potential audience. The community of policy analysts in Washington — private consultants, research corporations, Department and OMB officials, professors from all over — constitutes a retinue of people who know each other and are interested in the CBO's work.

This community and its network have facilitated recruitment of an able professional staff and enhanced communication of ideas within it. Connecting these policy ideas to the interests of Congress is the problem.

Most analyses done by CBO may be broken into two types, program and budget analysis, which parallel the organizational makeup of the office. The program divisions are set up around functional areas and concentrate on long-term, broad policy analysis that tries to lay out a range of alternatives as well as to make sure such studies are relevant to the Congressional timetable. On the other side is the budget analysis group — "the number crunchers" — who report on cost projections of legislation. Generally, the House Budget Committee (HBC) prefers CBO to spend its time on the cost projections, while the Senate Budget Committee (SBC) supports CBO's study of the broader issues. The House in general and the Budget Committee in particular are wary of the large staff at CBO. Rather than use an external staff of policy analysts, HBC prefers to hire its own staff to generate analyses on their own. When the HBC uses CBO cost projections or budgetary assessments during markups, CBO is given no credit. On the other hand, the Senate Budget Committee hides behind CBO numbers by publishing them in such a way as if to say, "If they're wrong, don't blame us." SBC uses CBO staff to aid and testify at markup hearings; HBC does not.

The difference in House and Senate attitudes may come in part from the fact that House members rarely sit on more than one substantive committee and therefore are more specialized. After the decision that HBC membership was to rotate, its Chairman and Director realized the importance of a professional staff to carry the Committee smoothly through membership transitions. The House chose a highly professional staff in a specific technical area. The Senate Committee chose a staff with more political than programmatic experience. Analysts in the White House have greater difficulty dealing with the SBC than HBC, therefore, because the Senate Committee is less likely to contain staff with technical background.

The contrast between the political and technical expertise of the two committees explains their different orientations. The technical staff of the House Budget Committee sees CBO as an instrument to gather data supporting technical positions on a small scale. The more political staff of the Senate looks to CBO for broader policy analysis. Each year the CBO negotiates with the Budget Committees for a series of budget issue papers. True to form, the HBC looks for areas where CBO can concentrate on number crunching, while the Senate pressures CBO to analyze policy.

But why were the staff functions of CBO separated in the first place? The CBO hierarchy originally separated the program divisions staff from the budget analysis staff because the day-to-day material requested by Congress could easily swamp as many staff as were available. Both CBO director Alice Rivlin and Deputy Director Robert Levine had used this two-tiered approach in previous government policy offices (Rivlin as Assistant Secretary for Planning and Evaluation at HEW, Levine in the comparable office at OEO), and because they felt that policy analysis was lacking in Congress, they worked to give it a fair chance to evolve.

As indicated by the House attempt to eliminate the program divisions entirely, the staff breakdown was not initially beneficial to the Budget Office's prestige. Even at the Senate Budget Committee, which has been the major supporter of policy analysis by the CBO, a senior staffer explained that while he understood the reasoning behind the separation, he believed that CBO should have focused initially on day-to-day matters. Doing the mundane and routine tasks well then becomes a means of entrance into longer-term studies. Further, with CBO split up, Congress may have to deal with two different persons at CBO for information on the same topic, one for short-term data and another for long-term investigation. When a Congressman must change analysts in the middle of the policy stream, time and the trust built through a long working relationship are often lost. Since the budget analysis staff has more direct contact with the Congress, its position is enhanced, as is apparent in the fact that it has lost less staff than the program division: access to power is one way to keep staff happy.

There is general agreement within CBO that things are working better as the program divisions drift away from long-term analyses and toward one-to-two month projects which have the potential to feed directly into legislative decisions. Plans are to look for issues each fall that are relevant to legislation coming up early in the next session of Congress. CBO has become more useful to the Congress by adapting to the legislature's time frame and perspective.

WHAT ACCOMPLISHMENTS?

Just what has the budget reform accomplished? Clearly, Congressional knowledge of economic management is much improved since passage of the Act. At the beginning of implementation the economy was in a severe recession. Joel Haveman reports:

> Members of Congress devoted considerable attention to the danger that a large deficit might result in so much borrowing by the federal government that private borrowers might be crowded out of the money markets. They debated what increase in the money supply would be necessary to finance the deficit without letting inflation get out of control. Arnold H. Packer, chief economist for the Senate Budget Committee, said Congress would have paid

little heed to those issues without the budget resolution to focus their attention.[15]

Indeed, before passage of the Act, the only Congressional entity with authority to deal with overall budgetary matters was the Joint Economic Committee, which was not part of the legislative process and therefore could not bring macro-economic propositions to the floor for a vote. In an interview early in her tenure as director of CBO, Alice Rivlin noted that "as Congressmen are actually called upon to vote on the size of a deficit or surplus, they will have to inform themselves better about the implications of these decisions."[16] Congressional understanding of the relationship between the size and makeup of the federal budget and the economy as a whole has become more sophisticated.

The most important thing about a budget is literally that it is made. While keeping to schedule has not been easy, the deadlines have been met, with virtually all appropriations measures now completed before the start of the fiscal year. After years when almost no Executive department was spared the grief of operating day to day on a continuing resolution that prohibited it from exercising newly granted authority, all fiscal year 1977 appropriations measures were enacted before the beginning of the fiscal year on October 1, 1977, the first year since 1951 to earn that distinction.

This outcome was not easy to attain. Yet, as noted in a recent CBO background paper, meeting the schedule has caused adjustments in the way Congress does its business.

> The congestion of appropriations and authorizing bills that require action in the early summer creates a potentially severe problem. The short time period between the May 15 deadline for reporting all authorizing legislation and the

[15] Joel Havemann, "Budget Report: First Fiscal Resolution Sets $367 Billion Target for Congress," VII *National Journal Reports* (May 24, 1975) No. 21, p. 763.

[16] "Interview with Alice Rivlin," *Challenge* (July/August 1975) p. 28.

House's full-time consideration of appropriations bills in mid-June does not permit either House to consider all authorizing bills reported just before the deadline, prior to taking up the appropriations.[17]

There are large projects that may be technically unauthorized while appropriations markups occur. In the House, this lag forced the leadership to either "lay aside items in the appropriations bills for which authorizations were lacking, or seek rules waiving points of order against appropriations without authorizations." [18]

The May 15 deadline for reporting authorizing legislation results in a slew of new bills coming onto the legislative calendar at once. In 1976 nearly forty authorizing bills were reported in the House on May 14 and 15, while in the Senate almost one hundred were added at the deadline. The House Appropriations Committee sensed that any worsening of this condition could cause a breakdown in the system. Bills reported at the May 15 deadline could not be anticipated in Appropriations hearings and markups, which must be concluded by May 7. Chairman Mahon of the House Committee on Appropriations stressed that whenever possible the potential problem should be avoided by authorizing a year ahead or two years at once.[19] Indeed, the traffic jam may lead to consideration of a two-year cycle in which authorizing legislation would be voted on one year and appropriations the next. It is an idea well worth considering.

What has been the substantive effect (which budgetary items and programs have been markedly raised or lowered?) of the Congressional budget reform? This question is more easily asked than answered. The difficulty is due not only to the short history of the reform but also to the requirement of estimating conditions that might have been (what would

17 U.S. Congress Congressional Budget Office, *Advance Budgeting: A Report to the Congress* (March 1977), p. 19.
18 *Ibid.*
19 *Ibid.*

Congress have done without the reform?) but that now can never be. To know whether Congress has decided differently, we have to know what it would have done had there been no reform. And by no means is it certain that everyone agrees on what the reform was supposed to have accomplished. For the precise purposes of the reform are not mere historical curiosities but objects of current contention. To say what the reform was intended to do is also to argue in favor of what it should now be doing.

Before proceeding, then, it would be wise to review the major purposes of the Congressional Budget and Impoundment Act of 1974. Revenue and expenditure were to be related to each other in a more conscious way. No mention is made of size of deficits because this should depend on conditions and because specifying the size would have destroyed the possibility of high and low spenders' reaching agreement. And since Congress votes appropriations, it can always be said that Congress has, in a manner of speaking, given its permission for the deficit. But did Congress do so because it wanted a deficit of a certain size? Yes and no. Yes, it voted the spending, but no, it was not necessarily happy about the size. That the two decisions are related, as we saw in discussing macro- and micro-spending policy in the Executive Branch, need not necessarily mean they are reconciled. All that can be said is that Congress is now more conscious of total expenditures and their implications for the economy.

A second major purpose of the reform was to increase Congressional control of the Budget. But some sophistication is required to determine what control means and, especially, what it does not. Control cannot mean only cutting expenditures; indeed, the success of the impoundment provisions are determined by the extent to which the President is unable to prevent spending authorized and appropriated by Congress. No, the idea is that Congress gets the spending it wants rather than spending at some predetermined level.

Does control mean, then, that Congress is better able to prevail against the Chief Executive? Perhaps. Interaction within and between Congress and the Executive Branch is so strong, however, that parts of each institution are likely to be allied against the other, and simple comparisons are suspect. Besides, the idea is to control the content of budgets, not merely to prevail over others, however foolish they may be.

Can it be said that Congress makes better or wiser decisions about the Budget or, at least, that it bases its actions on better information? There is no doubt that Congress has more independently derived data and spends more time on budgeting. After all, it has two new committees (HBC and SBC) and one new office (CBO) with over four hundred new people devoted to the task. Whether all this means improvement, of course, is another matter. There are more well-reasoned arguments. But is a well-reasoned argument against a program one believes desirable an improvement? It will not be easy to reach agreement on this matter.

Subjectively speaking, to be sure, the feelings of Congressmen matter. Do they feel more in control in the sense that they believe their new budgetary process more worthy of their respect? Their willingness to support their own procedures measures this respect.

The viability of the budget reform is necessarily tied up with the new units that are charged with making it work. Do they make a difference? How much? What kind? The question of whether Congress relates revenue to expenditures or exerts control over the budget reduces to whether the House and Senate Budget Committees, supported by the Congressional Budget Office, perform these tasks and, to the extent they do, whether this power is gained at the expense of other committees.

Congress as a whole cannot control or relate anything to anything else except in a formal manner. A large and heterogeneous body must work through committees from which it gains guidance and to which (by and large) it gives support. Without a central committee that controls all decisions, on the Cabinet model, Congress has to choose which committees it will support. The basic thrust of the Congressional budget reform was that Congress would choose new committees of its own rather than rubber stamping those of the Executive. Whether Congress trusts itself enough to do this or whether, without saying so, budgetary power will pass by default to the Executive Branch is now being determined.

WHOSE TOTAL?

There is concern by some, elation by others, that the budget has kept down the level of spending. Paul O'Neill, deputy director of the Office of Management and Budget under President Ford, felt that the budget process, by focusing Congressional attention on the size of the deficit, probably resulted in fewer programs to combat the recession than Congress otherwise would have enacted. In his view, spending in fiscal year 1977 came closer to the President's recommendations than it would have without the budget process to restrain spending. According to Edmund Muskie, Chairman of the Senate Budget Committee, the new process avoided $15 billion in spending in fiscal year 1977 and forced Congress to exert self-discipline.[20] It is always easy to "save" money that you only thought of spending. As Alice Rivlin put it, "Who knows what the Congress would have done without the process?" Even where Congress comes close to total spending in the First Fiscal Resolution, this may well be because increases in some items cancel decreases in others. Is there control when the total is in the right range but the parts that make it up have been substantially altered? The

[20] VIII *National Journal* (September 18, 1976) No. 38, p. 1300.

answer depends on whether the Budget Committees merely maintain a single figure or determine the composition as well as the size of the budget.

Concentration on a single number (the Budget Committees as committees on totals) has its virtues: less chance of incurring the hostility of other committees, making up in one area what one loses in another, concentrating on fiscal policy and economic management so as to stake out an area of expertise. The defect lies in the triumph of specificity over generality; there are so many ways of adjusting totals that no specific agency or program need fear the burden. Yet once agreements have been bargained on farm or housing or other appropriations, there is naturally deep reluctance to open up all these matters for reconsideration during the Second Budget Resolution. That is why the First Resolution, which sets tentative boundaries, is important, but the Second, which is intended to adjust them, is not.

Like all others who wish to be influential, the budget Committees can afford to lose a few times but not too often, for if it becomes obvious that the Budget Committees are likely to lose, no one need pay attention to them. In order to avoid head-on clashes between Budget and Appropriations Committees, the Act breaks down the budget by sixteen functions — health, income, security, veterans benefits, etc. — instead of the over twelve hundred individual items by which appropriations are actually voted upon by Congress. Should the Budget Committees confine themselves to totals in these sixteen functional areas or should they look into the items that make them up?

Following the tradition of the larger chamber in favor of specialization, the House Budget Committee builds up its functional targets by separating them into appropriations categories. Aside from being subject to the charge of duplication, this approach increases potential conflict with the Appropriations Committee and decreases conflict with Ways and Means and other committees that spend through tax legislation or direct drafts on the Treasury, known as "back door spending." Nevertheless, by avoiding direct confrontation and by generally supporting the Appropriations Committee, HBC has maintained good relations. For one thing, it avoids giving specific instructions to Appropriations, and for another, it supports Appropriations in its jurisdictional struggles against new back-door-spending authority. HBC's difficulties, to no one's surprise, have come from advocates of increased spending. In regard to a bill to extend the benefits of unemployment compensation, for example, the Ways and Means Committee required a waiver of a provision in the Budget Act forbidding passage of spending legislation before a budget resolution has been passed for the year in which spending is to occur. When HBC opposed the waiver, Representative Corman, in charge of the bill, let loose a blast:

> I think the Budget Committee was trying to tell the Ways and Means Comittee that it doesn't have much power any more. The whole game up here is power, and the staff of the Budget Committee would like to see the committee have a veto over all the other congressional committees.[21]

Or consider the case of highway spending, when both the Appropriations and the Budget Committees wanted to put a $2.2 billion cap on state spending. Although the Chairman of the Public Works and Transportation Subcommittee on Surface Transportation offered a successful amendment on the House floor to remove the ceiling, the Budget Committee tried to reinstate the ceiling in the final version in conference committee. No one would accuse Chairman Howard of undue restraint when he vented his feelings:

> The Committee on the Budget, through its chairman and ranking minority member, has taken it upon itself to ad-

[21] VIII *National Journal* (September 25, 1976) No. 39, pp. 1349–1350.

vise the House conferees to run up the white flag and surrender — or perhaps betray might be a more appropriate word — the expressed will of the House. In all my years in the House of Representatives, I cannot recall a more arrogant reach for power than this attempt to sell out our own conference stand and reverse the majority decision of the House.[22]

Controlling expenditure will not necessarily matter much unless revenue also is adjusted. Bringing resource allocation together with resource mobilization is, after all, the major purpose of the reform. This requires the cooperation (read, to some extent, subordination) of the revenue committees. Tax reform, therefore, is part of budget reform. A decline in tax expenditures, for example, would suggest the budget reform is working, whereas attempts to short-circuit the budget process would imply that it is not.

It is in the Senate that the clash between the Budget and Finance Committees has been most severe. Chairman Muskie of SBC is interested in the big picture. As he told the Senate, "The congressional budget process is not a line-item process and the Budget Committee is not a line-item committee." [23] But expenditures going through the tax process are so large, Muskie feels, that to ignore them would be to nullify efforts at budget control. In colorful language, he raised and answered the rhetorical question:

> Are we supposed to meet each March to propose a congressional budget and then retire to the cloakroom until the fall, when it is too late to advise the Senate of the implications of its tax and spending decisions? And then pop back out like some unwelcome jack-in-the-box each fall to shout, "Surprise! You've blown the budget."? Hardly.[24]

Not to be outdone, Senator Russell Long, Chairman of the Committee on Finance, retorted, "The chairman of the Bud-

22 *Ibid.*, p. 1350.
23 *Ibid.*, pp. 1348–1349.
24 *Ibid.*, p. 1347.

get Committee cannot find anything small enough for the Finance Committee to decide anything about." [25] Back at the House, an HBC staff member expressed his dismay at such direct confrontation saying, "We're aware that we'll get killed if we take on other committees head to head. All we have to work with is the good will of other committees." [26]

This was 1976. The following year witnessed an intensification of the dispute between the two Senate committees. Muskie maintained that the Budget Resolution not only contained a target but also the route by which certain revenues should be reached to maintain the relationship between revenue and expenditure. Senator Long insisted that there was only a grand total; otherwise, SBC would be writing tax legislation. This difference erupted over the important energy bill. "Whatever the merits of this bill as energy legislation," Muskie said, "it is irresponsible as fiscal action." [27] He claimed the bill would cost $4 billion in lost revenues. Long said, "We will take care of it" in conference. He wanted a free hand in horse-trading. Muskie, who had described the energy tax bill "not as a Christmas tree bill — it's too early in the year for that — but as a 'Thanksgiving turkey,'" went on to warn that "from here on we can expect similar provision in revenue laws that would make them completely outside the budget process." Long won.

Now that we are aware of the difficulties facing the Budget Committees, it should be easier to understand the results. Has the new budget process altered substantive outcomes? Not likely. It would be more accurate to say the Budget Committees have succeeded more in predicting outcomes than in influencing them. From the beginning, the Budget Committees saw they were entering an already established Congressional arena with prearranged power structures.

[25] *Ibid.*, p. 1348.
[26] *Ibid.*, p. 1348.
[27] IX *National Journal* (November 5, 1977) No. 45, p. 1733.

Their early efforts have been to measure the way Congressional action would proceed. The recommendations for the First Concurrent Resolution on the budget each spring tend to be educated guesses about future Congressional action. The Budget Committees sense the realities of Capitol Hill; they know that other committees will not accept budget directives that change priorities radically. What the Committees can do, however, is try to create a sense of limits.

A recent example of restraint that could be tied to the budget process and its reliance on spending targets came in the form of an amendment to the 1977 Food Stamp Act in the Senate. The bill eliminated the purchase requirement for food stamps (households would receive a given amount of stamps without having to put up the rest of the minimum allocation in cash); critics claimed the move would open the floodgates to a whole new group of previously non-participating eligibles. Senator Talmadge proposed and the Senate accepted a provision that put a cap on the level of food stamps. While the expenditure ceiling of $5.8 billion was not really restrictive, it indicates the desire of some legislators to anticipate and hold down the level of expenditures on new or revised programs to avoid the unanticipated spending increases that occurred during the late 1960's and early 1970's. Whether this desire will be translated into majority action no one can say.

The budget reform is designed to help Congress relate obligations to income by setting targets for total expenditures. Senator Muskie says of legislators' voting for more spending and lower budget deficits simultaneously, "we just can't make the system work with that kind of a philosophy." [28] Yet Joel Havemann has reported several instances of Con-

28 See Aaron Wildavsky, "Ask Not What Budgeting Does to Society but What Society Does to Budgeting," Introduction to the second edition of *National Journal Reprints* (Washington, D.C., Government Research Corporation, 1977), p. 4.

gressmen engaging in this sort of behavior on the grounds, as one put it, "That's the beauty of the budget process. You can vote for all your favorite programs, and then vote against the deficit." [29]

If nothing else, the budget process has proven a political success. The enactment of budget targets and resolutions by Congress has neutralized spending as a political issue and left charges that a spendthrift Congress was responsible for inflation without a solid base to stand on. The Washington press continues editorially to praise the budget process. And the process has lasted because Congressmen somehow feel it's good for them.

But the seeming size of the budget deficit lies like a land-mine for unwary Congressmen. One reason for support of more accurate estimates is that Congressmen dislike having to vote on deficits by raising the debt limit. When the executive branch agencies mis-estimate a budget item, the President has to go to Congress for a supplemental appropriation; and he gets one of his budget advisors to hold a technical press conference that no one understands. Increase in spending by the Executive gets little, if any, press coverage. Hence Presidents bear little of the public burden for overspending. If Congress does not have accurate estimates on costs during the passage of the Budget Resolutions, however, appropriations bills coming to the floor may be in excess of Resolution figures and thereby out of order. Thus Congress has to vote on raising the budget ceiling. Whenever a supplemental appropriation comes through so that the aggregate budget totals are exceeded, Congress has to vote to specifically raise the deficit and often incurs wide press coverage. So Congress is now more open to criticism on the budget than is the President.

I sympathize with the Congressman whose opponent ran against him saying, "not only did he vote for a $60 billion

29 *Ibid.*, p. 4.

deficit, he went back three months later to raise it to a $65 billion deficit." Such fears may prompt Congress to pad all budget resolutions to be sure estimates come out lower rather than higher.

Though the Budget Committee may doubt its influence, spending agencies can't afford to be half safe. A major result of the Congressional budget process has been to complicate the legislative political environment within which federal agencies operate.[30] Decisions made by the Budget Committees regarding budget targets may ultimately influence the decisions of the authorizing and appropriations committees and thus bear directly on the agencies. Congressional committees appreciate stability at their contact points with agencies. The agencies feel as strongly about this stability in the committees with whom they must deal. But the membership of the House Budget Committee is intentionally unstable; HBC members can only serve four of every ten years.

And despite its youth, the stakes are real in this "new game in town."

> The significance of the process appears to have been brought home to the majority of agencies, aided perhaps by (FY 76's) defeat of the Department of Defense in its request for a higher level of appropriations than allowed by the first resolution. One agency Congressional liaison officer, asked whether the agency was taking the new process seriously, responded, "You betcha," and quoted one staffer of a budget committee as saying, "We'll remember our friends." This same official suggested that the budget committees were less likely to recommend a relative low functional target if they enjoyed good rapport with the agency and thought highly of its activities.[31]

People learn to play any system. The budget reform enables Congressmen to make intelligent decisions. There is a base; departures are identified; calculations are possible; votes

---

[30] Richard Schott, *op. cit.*
[31] *Ibid.*

are large enough in number to be discriminatory but not so large as to be overwhelming. Beyond this point, procedures can be permissive but they cannot be compelling. If the House and Senate Budget Committees stick to totals, they wonder if they are predicting rather than controlling expenditures. If they try to alter the character or composition of expenditures within totals, they threaten all power of other committees. Fiscal conservatives are unhappy because $60 to $100 billion deficits are not their idea of control. Liberal spenders complain because the Budget Committees are another obstacle to their desires. So it is not surprising that before Congress has totally tested this reform, new reforms to improve it are being proposed.

HOW MANY YEARS?

For at least five decades, multi-year budgeting has been proposed as a reform to aid rational choice by viewing resource allocation in a long-term perspective. Considering only one year, it has been argued, leads to short-sightedness (only the next year's expenditures are reviewed), overspending (huge disbursements in future years are hidden), conservatism (incremental changes do not open up larger future vistas), and parochialism (programs tend to be viewed in isolation rather than in comparison to their future costs in relation to expected revenue). Extending the time span of budgeting to three or five years, it is argued, would enable long-range planning to overtake short-term reaction and substitute financial control for merely muddling through.

Recent remarkable British experience with just such a budgetary procedure, known as the Public Expenditure Survey (PES), should make us aware of how dependent governmental processes are upon trends in the society at large that, in extraordinary periods, lay bare the usually implicit assumptions on which actions are premised. By looking at what is occurring in American society and government, we may also get a better idea of what is likely to happen to the most important effort in our time to change budgeting — the new congressional reform.

In British central government, under the cabinet system, which may roughly be considered a federation of departments, the ranking finance officers undertook to agree upon the cost of carrying out existing policies not only for the next year but for the succeeding four. This attempt enabled the Treasury to look at projected outlays for five years, compare them with economic forecasts, and decide how much more (it was never less) they wanted to do. As expected, it became more difficult to get new programs accepted on the basis that they would not be too expensive in the next year, when everyone could see costs would increase rapidly in the next few years. In return for help in mitigating future uncertainties, the Treasury agreed to cost-proposed expenditures in constant prices so that departments were, in effect, guaranteed a certain level of service (whatever the cost) for several years. Departments could plan ahead knowing what they would be able to buy. Thus PES was a pact between central controllers and spending departments to sustain mutual stability.

A decade later, amidst huge deficits, PES is in a shambles. Under furious attack for financial laxity, all but one of the top Treasury civil servants concerned with public expenditure have left. PES has been trimmed to three years, with the last two years' expenditures left vague and placed on a cash (current price) basis. A more battered and beleaguered budgetary institution would be hard to find. What happened?

Rampaging inflation, running into the high twenties, coupled with low rates of economic growth, led to vast increases in expenditures without offsetting additions to revenue. The commitment of government to maintain social services (often in the form of mandatory entitlements) left the Treasury with little more to do than add up the totals. Hence the Treasury renegotiated its agreement by saying that if the rate of inflation exceeded current estimates, it would not automatically absorb the difference but would compel the departments to do so. Instead of the controllers and the spenders agreeing to reduce their uncertainties, they wound up fighting over who would suffer the most.

An implicit assumption of PES was monetary stability coupled with economic growth. When these collapsed, PES collapsed. PES was premised on the very stability it promised to create.

What is this new Treasury doctrine of imposing "cash limits"? Nothing other than our ancient and much maligned friend the annual budget. In practice, it is more (or less) than that because, as uncertainty has increased, the budget has increasingly been altered during the year. When even a year is too long to see ahead accurately, numerous "mini-budgets" appear to cope with the latest events. Instead of budgeting from three to five years, the British have found it difficult to budget for three to five months. Budgeting in a turbulent period cannot be the same as in an era of stability.

The seemingly arcane question of whether a budget should be done on a cash or a volume basis will assume importance if the United States adopts multi-year budgeting. The longer the term of the budget, the more important inflation becomes. To the degree that price changes are automatically absorbed into budgets, a certain volume of activity is guaranteed. To the degree agencies have to absorb inflation, their real level of activity declines. The debate is over the relative shares of the public and private sectors — which will be asked to absorb inflation and which, because the total size of the economy is limited, will be encouraged to expand into the economic domain now occupied by the other.

A similar issue of relative shares is created within government by proposals to budget in some sectors for several years and in others for only one. Which sectors of policy will be exposed to the vicissitudes of the short term and which will be protected from them? The ideal self-protecting sector is funded by entitlements indexed against inflation. Whatever adjustments are to be made for price changes or economic management, therefore, must be taken out on others. Should everyone get a fixed share, the United States would have a government of all constants and no variables.

The evident reply to these considerations is that a multi-year budget would be a rolling budget, with adjustments made every year according to circumstances. Aside from the difficulty of tampering with what would then appear to be a commitment to fund for several years, changes across the board leave everyone unhinged. That is why Presidents are reluctant to make extensive changes in the fall. Yet continuing with a fiscal policy derived years earlier leaves much to be desired. As things stand now, the eighteen to twenty-four month lapse between decisions on economic management and their realization might be overcome by substantial adjustments every year. But then that method wouldn't be very different from the annual budget we have now.

The rationale for multi-year budgeting is precisely to extend the time horizon of decision making.[32] Instead of considering effects in the next year, these considerations would extend several years. Now the main reasons for limited time horizons are the short span of the electoral cycle and lack of knowledge of future effects. Neither of these would be changed by multi-year budgeting. The conclusion, so often expressed, that this or that procedure will "force" people to act contrary to clearly perceived interests is doomed by universal experience.

[32] See statement of Alice M. Rivlin, Director, Congressional Budget Office, before the Committee on the Budget, United States Senate, July 1, 1977.

The idea that it is ipso facto desirable to plan ahead is an ancient fallacy. The opposite would be more nearly correct: never plan ahead unless you can't avoid it. Why make decisions today that could be made with better information several years from now? The necessity for planning comes from projects that take years to build, like sewer and water facilities, that force one to imagine what life will be like later on, no matter how wrong one is likely to be. Effects of policies do go on into the future, of course, but such decisions must always be made at some point in time with whatever knowledge we have of them. To be sure, guarantees of future funding are nice to have, but one wonders whether (and under what conditions) they are good for government to give.

Nevertheless, there is a case to be made for a two-year appropriations cycle. Congress and the Executive are kept awfully busy meeting deadlines for the annual Budget. Too much time, effort, and paper are devoted to the minutiae of budgeting. The glacial but inexorable movement of the beginning of the fiscal year from January at the country's beginning to October now is suggestive of overload. With a two-year cycle, substantive authorization could be considered one year and appropriations the next. This might result in less legislation, but new laws don't appear to be in short supply. The real difficulty lies in making a volatile world hold still long enough for decisions made two years before to have some validity. Otherwise, events will compel so many readjustments — rescissions, supplementals, what have you — that a two-year budget will become one in name only. Weighing the advantages of a modicum of stability and order against the disadvantages of failing to keep up with events, one might consider a two-year cycle worth trying. Much depends on external events, but even the annual budget, a time span more hallowed by tradition than justified by principle, is at the mercy of forces it cannot control.

EXTERNAL FORCES

Congressional budget reform is also premised on certain implicit understandings. It too depends on agreements that may not remain as valid as they once were and that may have to be renegotiated with the passage of time. The reform was welded out of the furnace of Vietnam and Watergate. Its financial sword was forged when a disgraced President abused the impoundment of funds to the point of refusing to spend even after Congress passed appropriation bills over his veto. Thus the reform yoked Republicans and Democrats, liberals and conservatives, and big and little spenders in joint defense of Congressional prerogatives against the Chief Executive. If the new budget process were viewed largely in partisan terms, the present party structure might not be able to sustain it. If legislators who advocate or oppose large new spending felt consistently disadvantaged, they might undermine the reform. If the reform were seen as a vehicle for usurping the will of Presidents or bureaucrats, their support could become problematic. And if conditions in the country changed so that sharply higher or lower expenditures were indicated, it would remain to be seen whether the new process would serve for all seasons.

Consider partisanship. The United States today might best be described as having a modified one-party system. Democrats are dominant in the vast majority of state legislatures and governorships. They are so strong in Congress it is difficult in the near term to imagine their losing control of either the Senate or House of Representatives. Only in the Presidency (so far, one must add) does strong party competition remain. Elsewhere, incumbents are regularly re-elected and they are overwhelmingly Democratic. At the same time, however, party ties are weakening not only among the electorate but within Congress itself as recent organizational changes increase the ability of individual members to express themselves and weaken the power of the leadership.

How might this basic change in our parties affect the budgetary process? As Republicans become fewer in number and
more conservative, they may become more cohesive against
higher spending and more partisan against Democratic
spenders. As Democrats increase and become more diverse,
they could become less cohesive — less likely, that is, to vote
in a bloc or to follow Congressional or Presidential leadership. Thus their sense of institutional stakes in maintaining
the power of the purse in Congress by exerting self-discipline
may decline.

Regional cleavages show signs of displacing party. Uneven
rates of development around the country are leading the de-
clining areas of the Midwest and Northeast to stand together
against the growing sunbelt states of the South, Southwest,
and West. The struggle is over federal spending. As efforts
are made to move military bases north and defense contractors to the Midwest and more importantly, to alter the formulas for distribution of social benefits, it will become difficult to take from some areas to give to others. The most
likely outcome is an expanded pie in which some will share
more equally than others. The renegotiation of regional benefits will strain relations among the finance committees,
which have jurisdiction over social services and tax expenditures; the appropriations committees, which would like their
imprint on these billions; and the Budget Committees, which
can see their totals breached by changes in formulas for welfare, transportation, or whatever. These relations are the reason the Chairman of the Senate Budget Committee works
so hard to keep the Finance Committee in line and the
Chairman of the House Budget Committee has his difficulties with Ways and Means. What these finance committees
will get out of the reform, except a loss in power, has not yet
been made clear.

The same is true for the Chief Executive. Presidents must

be ambivalent. They cannot exactly welcome a rival budget, even (perhaps especially) when it comes from their own party. In periods when they wish to reduce the level of future spending, they should continue to recognize Budget Committees as natural allies. But when they wish to do more, they are likely to feel they know best. Permanent party predominance, in which one party controls the executive and the legislative branches, cannot be good for an independent Congressional budget.

Other societal circumstances could work in the opposite direction by creating downward pressure on spending. Much more than President Carter's promise of a balanced budget rides on his triple hopes for lower inflation, lower unemployment, and higher growth rates. Should inflation become more serious, all new policy initiatives are likely to be cast aside in order to pump less money into the economy. Whether this is right or wrong as economic policy, it will strengthen all those who are financial controllers — the President's Office of Management and Budget and Congressional appropriations and budget committees — against liberals concerned with reducing unemployment and expanding social programs. Budget procedures may be enhanced at the expense of becoming identified as a conservative force. No doubt this premise was always implied: What is the point of strengthening financial control unless one means to exercise it?

Nevertheless, it is important not to overemphasize the modest beginnings of this new effort at Congressional control of budgeting. All we have seen are the first offshoots, not a firmly rooted plant. Saying no or arguing for less may not be the most exciting posture for legislators. A good test will be the willingness of legislators to give up other committee assignments in order to serve on the budget committees. The latest evidence suggests something less than a stampede. The rule in the Senate is that members can serve only on two major committees, which means senators might have to resign from one to get on or stay on the Budget Committee. For some reason, volunteers have been scarce. To overcome this difficulty Senators have amended their rules to allow themselves to sit on two committees in addition to their Budget Committee without formally changing its designation as a major committee. According to a staff member, Senators wouldn't give up their other assignments because the Budget Committee "is seen as performing a largely negative function in limiting federal spending and because its members cannot become expert or powerful in any particular area." [33] Perhaps the passage of the anti-property-tax proposition 13 in California will help make cutting expenditures an area worth knowing about. Here again the future of an institutional innovation is dependent not only on its intrinsic merits but on external events.

[33] *National Journal*, No. 27 (July 8, 1978) p. 1105, no author.

APPENDIX

THE FOLLOWING CHARTS are a chronological and graphic representation of the budgetary cycle. They were redrawn from publications of the Executive Office of the President/ Office of Management and Budget, January 1977.

APPENDIX

MAJOR STEPS IN THE BUDGET PROCESS

PERIOD BEFORE THE FISCAL YEAR	FISCAL YEAR	BEYOND FISCAL YEAR
MARCH · · · NOV. JAN. · · · OCT.	SEPT. 30	NOV. 15

FORMULATION of President's Budget
(beginning 19 months before fiscal year)[1]

CONGRESSIONAL BUDGET PROCESS,
including action on appropriations and
revenue measures (beginning 10½ months
before fiscal year)[2]

EXECUTION of Enacted Budget
(during fiscal year)

Final
Data
Available

[1] The President's budget is transmitted to Congress within fifteen days after Congress convenes.

[2] If appropriation action is not completed by September 30, Congress enacts temporary appropriation (i.e., continuing resolution).

FORMULATION OF PRESIDENT'S BUDGET

APPROXIMATE TIMING	AGENCY	OFFICE OF MANAGEMENT AND BUDGET	THE PRESIDENT
BUDGET POLICY DEVELOPMENT			
MARCH (or earlier in some agencies)	Reviews current operations, program objectives, issues, and future plans in relation to upcoming annual budget. Submits projections of requirements that reflect current operations and future plans, supporting memoranda and related analytic studies that identify major issues, alternatives for resolving issues, and comparisons of costs and effectiveness.	Develops economic assumptions. Obtains forecasts of international and domestic situations. Prepares fiscal projections.*	
			Discusses budgetary outlook and policies with the Director of the Office of Management and Budget, and with the Cabinet as appropriate.
APRIL MAY		Issues policy guidance on material to be developed for Spring planning review.	
MAY		Discusses program developments and management issues, and resulting budgetary effects, with agencies. Compiles total outlay estimates for comparison with revenue estimates. Develops recommendations for President on fiscal policy,* program issues, and budget levels.	
			Discusses with the Director of the Office of Management and Budget and others as necessary, general budget policy, major program issues, budgetary planning targets, and projections. Establishes general guidelines and agency planning targets for annual budget.
JUNE	Issues internal instructions on preparation of annual budget estimates.	Issues technical instructions for preparation of annual budget estimates.	

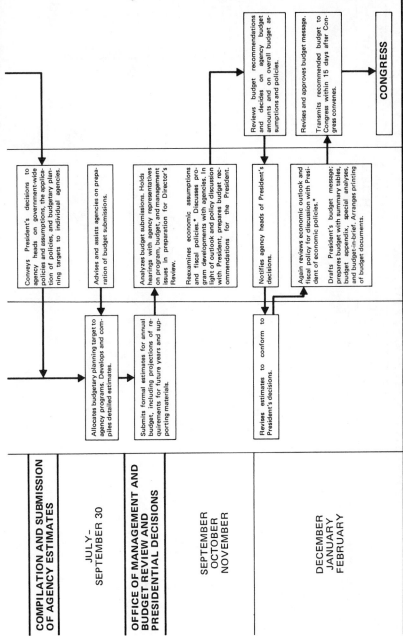

*In cooperation with the Treasury Department and Council of Economic Advisers.

CONGRESSIONAL BUDGET PROCESS

APPROXIMATE TIMING	BUDGET COMMITTEES	CONGRESS	APPROPRIATIONS HOUSE	COMMITTEES SENATE
DEVELOPMENT OF BUDGET TARGETS				
NOVEMBER		Receives current services estimates from the President. (Nov. 10)		
DECEMBER	Receive Joint Economic Committee analysis of current services estimates. (Dec. 31)			
JANUARY	Hold hearings in preparation for drafting 1st concurrent resolution on the budget.	Receives President's budget within fifteen days after Congress convenes.	Hold special hearings on budget overview with Director of Office of Management and Budget, Secretary of the Treasury, and Chairman of the Council of Economic Advisers.	
FEBRUARY	Receive views and estimates of all committees (March 15) and begin drafting 1st concurrent resolution on the budget.			
MARCH			Subcommittees hold hearings, review and draft appropriation bills and reports.	Subcommittees hold hearings and review justifications from each agency.
APRIL	Report 1st concurrent resolution, which sets spending, revenue, and other budget targets for the upcoming fiscal year.	Receives first Presidential update of the budget estimates. (April 10)		
ACTION ON INDIVIDUAL BILLS		Adopts 1st concurrent resolution on the budget. (May 15)	Full Committee reviews actions of subcommittees and adopts or revises bills and reports.	
MAY	Review and evaluate the effect of Congressional action on the budget targets, in preparation for drafting the 2nd concurrent resolution on the budget.	Shall not consider any bill authorizing new budget authority for the upcoming year unless bills are reported by May 15.		
		House debates and passes appropriation bills, with or without amendments.	Completes committee action on all regular appropriation bills, to the extent practicable, and submits a summary report of its actions to House Budget Committee, before reporting the first appropriation bill.	
JUNE-AUGUST		Senate receives House-passed version of appropriation bills and refers to Senate Appropriations Committee.		Subcommittees draft revisions to House bills and reports.
		Receives mid-year Presidential update of the budget estimates. (July 15)		

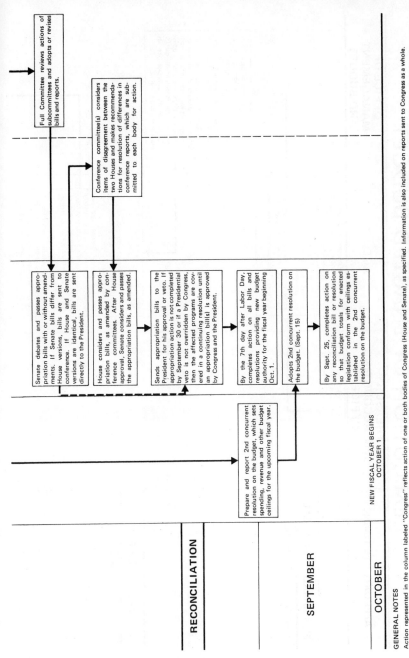

GENERAL NOTES

Action represented in the column labeled "Congress" reflects action of one or both bodies of Congress (House and Senate), as specified. Information is also included on reports sent to Congress as a whole.

Action on revenue measures follows the same general procedure as action on appropriation bills, except that revenue measures are reported by the Ways and Means Committee in the House and by the Finance Committee in the Senate.

Full Committee reviews actions of subcommittees and adopts or revises bills and reports.

Conference committee(s) considers items of disagreement between the two Houses and makes recommendations for resolution of differences in conference reports, which are submitted to each body for action.

Senate debates and passes appropriation bills with or without amendments. If Senate bills differ from House versions, bills are sent to conference. If House and Senate versions are identical, bills are sent directly to the President.

House considers and passes appropriation bills, as amended by conference committees. After House approval, Senate considers and passes the appropriation bills, as amended.

Sends appropriation bills to the President for his approval or veto. If appropriation action is not completed by September 30 or if a Presidential veto is not overridden by Congress, then the affected programs are covered in a continuing resolution until an appropriation bill(s) is approved by Congress and the President.

By the 7th day after Labor Day, completes action on all bills and resolutions providing new budget authority for the fiscal year beginning Oct. 1.

Adopts 2nd concurrent resolution on the budget. (Sept. 15)

By Sept. 25, completes action on any reconciliation bill or resolution so that budget totals for enacted legislation conform with ceilings established in the 2nd concurrent resolution on the budget.

Prepare and report 2nd concurrent resolution on the budget, which sets spending, revenue and other budget ceilings for the upcoming fiscal year.

RECONCILIATION

SEPTEMBER

NEW FISCAL YEAR BEGINS OCTOBER 1

OCTOBER

EXECUTION OF ENACTED BUDGET

APPROXIMATE TIMING	TREASURY-GEN. ACCOUNTING OFFICE	AGENCY	OFFICE OF MANAGEMENT AND BUDGET
		Revenues are assessed, collected, and deposited by the agencies concerned as prescribed by law.	
FUNDS MADE AVAILABLE	On approval of appropriation bill, appropriation warrant is drawn by Treasury and is forwarded to agency.	Revises operating budget in view of approved appropriations and program developments.	
AUGUST–SEPTEMBER		Prepares requests for apportionment by Aug. 21 or within 10 days after approval of appropriations, whichever is later.	Makes apportionment by Sept. 10 or within 30 days after approval of appropriations, whichever is later.
			May reapportion at any time, on own initiative or on agency request.
			May withhold funds through the apportionment process as a deferral or as an amount withheld pending rescission. Such withholding requires transmittal by the President of special messages to the Congress for its approval or disapproval.
CONTROL OVER FUNDS		Allots apportioned funds to various programs or activities.	
Continuous		Restricts obligations through administrative controls to apportioned and allotted amounts.	
		Obligates money. Receives and uses goods and services. Makes monthly or quarterly reports to Office of Management and Budget on status of funds and use of resources in relation to program plans.	
		Reports periodically to Office of Management and Budget on management improvement and actions affecting personnel requirements and costs.	

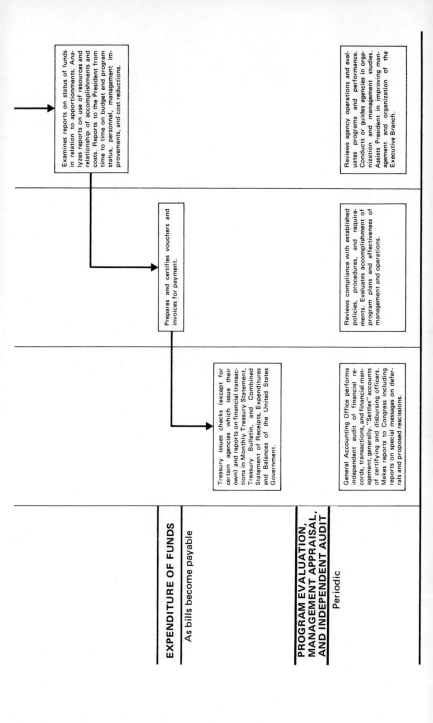

Examines reports on status of funds in relation to apportionments. Analyzes reports on use of resources and relationship of accomplishments and costs. Reports to the President from time to time on budget and program status, personnel, management improvements, and cost reductions.

Reviews agency operations and evaluates programs and performance. Conducts or guides agencies in organization and management studies. Assists President in improving management and organization of the Executive Branch.

Prepares and certifies vouchers and invoices for payment.

Reviews compliance with established policies, procedures, and requirements. Evaluates accomplishment of program plans and effectiveness of management and operations.

Treasury issues checks (except for certain agencies which issue their own) and reports on financial transactions in Monthly Treasury Statement, Treasury Bulletin, and Combined Statement of Receipts, Expenditures and Balances of the United States Government.

General Accounting Office performs independent audit of financial records, transactions, and financial management, generally. "Settles" accounts of certifying and disbursing officers. Makes reports to Congress including reports on special messages on deferrals and proposed rescissions.

EXPENDITURE OF FUNDS

As bills become payable

PROGRAM EVALUATION, MANAGEMENT APPRAISAL, AND INDEPENDENT AUDIT

Periodic

A GUIDE TO BUDGET TERMS AND CONCEPTS

APPORTIONMENT: Under this authority, the Director distributes appropriations and other budgetary resources by time periods (usually quarterly) or by particular projects or activities. The apportionment system is intended to achieve an effective and orderly use of available funds. It is a violation of law for an agency to incur obligations or make expenditures in excess of the apportioned amounts.

APPROPRIATION: An act of Congress that allows Federal agencies to incur obligations and to make payments out of the Treasury for specified purposes. This is the most common form of budget authority.

AUTHORIZATION: Basic substantive legislation enacted by the Congress that sets up a Federal program or agency either indefinitely or for a given period of time. Such legislation is a prerequisite for the subsequent enactment of budget authority and may set limits on the amount that can be appropriated.

BACKDOOR AUTHORITY: Legislative authority to obligate funds provided outside the normal appropriation process. The most common forms of backdoor authority are borrowing authority and contract authority. In other cases, a permanent appropriation is provided that becomes available without current action by the Congress.

BACKDOOR SPENDING: Backdoor authority as well as mandatory

Prepared by and adapted from the Office of Management and Budget.

spending legislation, i.e., legislation that mandates the payment of benefits or entitlements, such as increases in veterans' compensation or pensions. Such mandatory legislation requires the subsequent enactment of appropriations.

BALANCES OF BUDGET AUTHORITY: The amount of budget authority that is unspent at the end of the fiscal year and that is still available for conversion into outlays in the future. Such amounts are called "unexpended" or "undisbursed" balances.

Balances of budget authority result from the fact that not all budget authority enacted in a fiscal year is obligated and paid out in that same year.

BUDGET AMENDMENT: A proposal, submitted by the President after his formal budget transmittal, that increases or decreases the amount of budget authority previously requested in the budget. Amendments are transmitted prior to completion of appropriation action by both Houses of Congress.

BUDGET AUTHORITY: Authority provided by law that permits Government agencies to incur obligations, requiring either immediate or future payment of money. The amount authorized by the Congress to become available for obligation in a given fiscal year is called budget authority for that year.

There are three basic kinds of budget authority — appropriations, contract authority, and authority to spend debt receipts.

BUDGET DEFICIT: For any given year, an excess of budget outlays over budget receipts. The amount of the deficit is the difference between outlays and receipts. Deficits are financed primarily by borrowing from the public.

BUDGET SURPLUS: For any given year, an excess of budget receipts over outlays. The amount of the surplus is the difference between receipts and outlays.

CONTINUING RESOLUTION: Legislation enacted by the Congress to provide authority for agencies to continue operations until their regular appropriations are enacted. Continuing resolutions are enacted when action on appropriations is not completed by the beginning of a fiscal year.

CONTRACT AUTHORITY: A type of budget authority that permits an agency to incur specific obligations in advance of an appropriation. Contract authority does not provide the money to pay the obligation; therefore, it must be followed by an "appropriation to liquidate" (pay) any obligations incurred.

CONTROLLABILITY: The ability of the Congress and the President to increase or decrease outlays in the year in question, generally the current or budget year. "Relatively uncontrollable" refers to spending that the Government cannot increase or decrease without changing existing substantive law. Such spending is usually the result of open-ended programs and fixed costs (e.g., social security, veterans' benefits) and payments coming due under commitments made earlier.

CURRENT SERVICES BUDGET: Information required by the Congressional Budget and Impoundment Control Act of 1974 (P. L. 93–344) to be transmitted by the President to the Congress, by November 10 of each year. The current services budget is required to show the estimated outlays and proposed appropriations that would be necessary to continue existing programs at their current operating levels (without policy changes) in the ensuing fiscal year, together with the economic and programmatic assumptions underlying them.

DEFERRAL: Any executive branch action or inaction — including the establishment of reserves under the Antideficiency Act — that delays the availability of funds. Pursuant to the Congressional Budget and Impoundment Control Act (P. L. 93–344, Title X), the President is required to report each deferral to the Congress in a special message published in the *Federal Register*.

FISCAL YEAR: Beginning with fiscal year 1977, it will be defined as the year running from October 1 to September 30 and will be designated by the calendar year in which it ends. Before FY 1977, it was the year running from July 1 to June 30 and designated by the calendar year in which it ended.

FULL-EMPLOYMENT BUDGET: The estimated receipts, outlays, and surplus or deficit that would occur if the economy were continually operating at full capacity (conventionally defined as a 4% unemployment rate for the civilian labor force).

FUNCTIONAL CLASSIFICATION: A means of presenting budgetary data in terms of the major purposes being served. Each program or activity is placed in the single category (e.g., national defense, health, agriculture) that best represents its major purpose, regardless of the spending agency or department.

IMPOUNDMENT: A term used to characterize any executive branch action that precludes the obligation of funds appropriated by the Congress. (See Deferral and Rescission).

LAPSED FUNDS: Budget authority that, by law, ceases to be available for obligation.

MANDATORY SPENDING LEGISLATION: See Backdoor spending.

MULTIPLE-YEAR APPROPRIATION: An appropriation that is available for a specified number of years.

NO-YEAR APPROPRIATION: An appropriation made available for obligation until the objectives have been obtained (e.g., appropriations for major construction, procurement, research and development.) Accordingly, there is no time limit set on the availability of the funds for obligation.

OBJECT CLASSIFICATION: A means of analyzing the obligations incurred by the Federal Government in terms of the nature of the goods or services purchased (e.g., personnel compensation, supplies and materials, equipment, etc.), regardless of the agency involved or purpose of the programs for which they are used.

OBLIGATIONS: Contracts or other binding commitments made by Federal agencies to pay out money for products, services, or other purposes — as distinct from actual payments. Obligations incurred may not be larger than available budget authority.

OFF-BUDGET AGENCIES: Federally owned and controllable agencies whose transactions have been excluded from the budget totals under provisions of law (e.g., Rural Telephone Bank, Postal Service, Federal Financing Bank). The fiscal activities of these agencies are not reflected in either budget outlays or the budget surplus or deficit, and the appropriation requests for their off-budget activities are not included in the totals of budget authority.

OFFSETTING RECEIPTS: Composed of (1) proprietary receipts from the public derived from Government activities of a business-type or market-oriented nature that are offset against related budget authority and outlays; and (2) intragovernmental transactions. Intragovernmental transactions are payments from governmental accounts to budgetary receipt accounts. Since they are payments from the Government to itself, they are offset against outlays rather than being counted as budget receipts.

ONE-YEAR APPROPRIATION: An appropriation made available for obligation for one year.

OPEN-ENDED PROGRAMS: Programs for which the law places no limit on the amount of obligations that may be incurred. They are programs for which eligibility standards are established by law, and outlays are determined by the number of eligible persons who apply for benefits. Thus, for example, veterans' benefits programs and Medicaid are open-ended programs.

OUTLAYS: Checks issued, interest accrued on the public debt, or other payments made, offset by refunds and reimbursements.

PERMANENT AUTHORITY: See Budget authority.

PUBLIC DEBT: The total of all direct borrowings of the United States Treasury, as opposed to borrowings of other Federal agencies.

RESCISSION: Enacted legislation that cancels (rescinds) budget authority previously granted by the Congress that otherwise would remain unused and available for obligation. Pursuant to the Congressional Budget and Impoundment Control Act (P. L. 93–344, Title X), the President is required to transmit a special message to the Congress whenever he proposes rescission of budget authority. These special messages are also required to be published in the *Federal Register*.

SPENDING AUTHORITY: See Backdoor authority.

SUPPLEMENTAL APPROPRIATIONS: Appropriations made by the Congress, after an initial appropriation, to cover expenditures beyond original estimates.

TAX EXPENDITURE: Tax revenue losses attributable to laws of the United States which provide tax exclusions, tax deductions, preferential tax rates, or tax deferrals.

TRUST FUNDS: Funds collected and used by the Federal Government for specified purposes in accordance with the terms of a trust agreement or statute (e.g., social security and unemployment trust funds). Receipts held in trust are not available for the general purposes of the Government. Trust fund receipts that are not anticipated to be used in the immediate future are generally invested in Government securities and earn interest.

UNIFIED BUDGET: The budget of the Federal Government. In the Federal Budget, the receipts and outlays for Federal funds and trust funds are combined, and the various interfund transactions that occur between them are deducted before arriving at the totals.

UNOBLIGATED BALANCE: See Balances of budget authority.

BIBLIOGRAPHY

Anton, Thomas J., *The Politics of State Expenditure in Illinois* (Urbana, 1966).

Arnow, Kathryn Smul, *The Department of Commerce Field Offices*, The Inter-University Case Program, ICP Case Series, No. 21, February 1954.

Banfield, Edward C., "Congress and the Budget; a Planner's Criticism," XLIII *The American Political Science Review* (December 1949) pp. 1217–1227.

Braybrooke, David, and Charles E. Lindblom, *A Strategy of Decision* (New York, 1963).

Brown, David S., "The Staff Man Looks in the Mirror," XXIII *Public Administration Review* (June 1963) pp. 67–73.

Brown, William H., and Charles E. Gilbert, *Planning Municipal Investment: A Case Study of Philadelphia* (Philadelphia, 1961).

Browning, Rufus P., "Innovative and Non-Innovative Decision Processes in Government Budgeting (Mimeo., 1963).

Bruner, Jerome S., Jacqueline Goodnow, and George Austin, *A Study of Thinking* (New York, 1956).

Buchanan, James M., "Politics, Policy and the Pigovian Margins," XXIX *Economica* (February 1962) pp. 17–28.

Buck, Arthur E., *The Budget in Governments of Today* (New York, 1934).

————, *Municipal Finance* (New York, 1926).

————, *Public Budgeting* (New York, 1929).

Burkhead, Jesse, *Government Budgeting* (New York, 1956).

Caiden, Naomi, and Aaron Wildavsky, *Planning and Budgeting in Poor Countries* (New York, 1974).

Campbell, John Creighton, *Contemporary Japanese Budget Politics* (Ph.D. Dissertation, Columbia University, 1973).

Carlson, Jack W., "The Status and Next Steps for Planning, Programming, and Budgeting," in *Public Policy Expenditures and Policy Analysis*, Robert Haveman and Julius Margolis, editors (Chicago, 1970) pp. 367–412.

Cleveland, Frederick A., "Evolution of the Budget Idea in the United States," LXII *Annals of the American Academy of Political and Social Science* (November 1915) pp. 15–35.

————, and Arthur E. Buck, *The Budget and Responsible Government* (New York, 1920).

Colm, G. and M. Helzner, "The Structure of Governmental Revenue and Expenditure in the United States" (*L'Importance et la Structure des Recettes et des Dépenses Publiques*), International Institute of Public Finance (Brussels, 1960).

Commission on Economy and Efficiency, *The Need for a National Budget*, 62nd Congress, 2nd Session, 1912, House Document No. 854.

Committee on Appropriations, Subcommittee on Agriculture Appropriations, U.S. House of Representatives, *Hearings on Agriculture Department Appropriations Bill for 1947*, 79th Congress, 2nd Session, 1946.

Committee on Government Operations, Subcommittee on National Policy Machinery, U.S. Senate, *Organizing for National Security; The Budget and the Policy Process*, 87th Congress, 1st Session, 1961.

————, Subcommittee Hearings, U.S. House of Representatives,

Improving Federal Budgeting and Appropriations, 85th Congress, 1st Session, 1957.

————, Subcommittee Hearings, U.S. House of Representatives, *Budget and Accounting*, 84th Congress, 2nd Session, 1956.

Committee on Rules, U.S. House of Representatives, *To Create a Joint Committee on the Budget*, 82nd Congress, 2nd Session, 1952.

Crecine, John P., "Coordination of Federal Fiscal and Budgetary Policy Processes: Research Strategies for Complex Decision Systems" (paper presented at the Annual Meeting of the American Political Science Association, Washington, D.C., 1977).

————, *Defense Budgeting: Constraints and Organizational Adaptation*, Discussion Paper No. 6, University of Michigan, Institute of Public Policy Studies (1969) p. 38.

————, *Governmental Problem Solving: A Computer Simulation of Municipal Budgeting* (Chicago, 1969).

————, and Gregory Fischer, "On Resource Allocation Processes in the U.S. Department of Defense," Discussion Paper, University of Michigan, Institute of Public Policy Studies (October 1971).

Cyert, Richard and James March, *A Behavioral Theory of the Firm* (Englewood Cliffs, N.J., 1963).

Dahl, Robert A. and Charles E. Lindblom, "Variation in Public Expenditure," in *Income Stabilization for a Developing Democracy*, Max F. Millikan, editor (New Haven, 1953), pp. 347–396.

Davis, Otto A., M. A. H. Dempster, and Aaron Wildavsky, "A Theory of the Budgetary Process," LX *The American Political Science Review* (September 1966) pp. 529–547.

————, "On the Process of Budgeting II: An Empirical Study of Congressional Appropriations," in *Studies in Budgeting*,

Byrne, Charnes, Cooper, Davis, Gilford, editors (Amsterdam and London, 1971) pp. 292–375.

———, "Toward a Predictive Theory of the Federal Budgetary Process," IV *The British Journal of Political Science* (1974) pp. 419–452.

Dexter, Lewis A., "The Representative and His District," XVI *Human Organization* (Spring 1957) pp. 2–13.

Diesing, Paul, *Reason in Society* (Urbana, 1962) pp. 198, 203–204, 231–232.

Downs, Anthony, *An Economic Theory of Democracy* (New York, 1957).

———, "Why the Government Budget Is Too Small in a Democracy," XII *World Politics* (July 1960) pp. 541–563.

Enthoven, Alain and Harry S. Rowen, "Defense Planning and Organization," in *Public Finances: Needs, Sources and Utilizations*, National Bureau of Economic Research (Princeton, 1961) pp. 365–420.

Fenno, Richard F., Jr., "The House Appropriations Committee as a Political System: The Problem of Integration," LVI *The American Political Science Review* (June 1962) pp. 310–324.

———, *The Power of the Purse: Appropriations Politics in Congress* (Boston, 1966).

Fisher, Louis, "Impoundment of Funds: Uses and Abuses," XXIII *University of Buffalo Law Review* (Fall 1973) pp. 141–200.

———, "Presidential Spending Discretion and Congressional Controls," XXXVII *Law and Contemporary Problems* (Winter 1972) pp. 135–172.

———, "Reprogramming of Funds by the Defense Department," *Journal of Politics* (February 1974).

Fitzpatrick, Edward A., *Budget Making in a Democracy* (New York, 1918).

Froman, Lewis A., Jr., "Why the Senate Is More Liberal Than the House," in his *Congressmen and Their Constituencies* (New York, 1963) pp. 69–97.

Gabis, Stanley T., *Mental Health and Financial Management: Some Dilemmas of Program Budgeting,* Public Administration Program, Department of Political Science Research Report, No. 3 (East Lansing, Mich., 1960).

Gilmour, Robert, "Central Legislative Clearance: A Revised Perspective," XXXI *Public Administration Review* (March/April 1971) pp. 150–158.

Gulick, Luther, and Lyndall Urwick, *Papers on the Science of Administration* (New York, 1937).

Hammond, Thomas H., and Jack H. Knott, *A Zero-Based Look at Zero-Base Budgeting; Or, Why Its Failures in State Government are Being Duplicated in Washington* (New Brunswick, 1979).

Harper, Edwin L., Fred A. Kramer, and Andrew M. Rouse, "Implementation and the Use of PPB in Sixteen Federal Agencies," XXIX *Public Administration Review* (November/December 1969).

Heclo, Hugh, "OMB and the Presidency," *The Public Interest* No. 38 (Winter 1975) pp. 80–98.

———, and Aaron Wildavsky, *The Private Government of Public Money: Community and Policy Inside British Political Administration* (London and Berkeley, 1974).

Hitch, Charles J., "Management of the Defense Dollar," XI *The Federal Accountant* (June 1962) pp. 33–44.

———, and Roland N. McKean, *The Economics of Defense in the Nuclear Age* (Cambridge, Mass., 1960).

Hood, Ronald C., "Reorganizing the Council of Economic Advisers," LXIX *Political Science Quarterly* (September 1954) pp. 413–437.

Hoover Commission on the Organization of the Executive Branch of the Government, *Budgeting and Accounting* (Washington, D.C., 1949).

Horn, Stephen, *Unused Power: The Work of the Senate Committee on Appropriations* (Washington, D.C., 1970).

Huntington, Samuel P., *The Common Defense* (New York, 1961).

Huzar, Elias, *The Purse and the Sword* (Ithaca, N.Y., 1950).

Inter-University Case Program, "The Impounding of Funds by the Bureau of the Budget," ICP Case Series: No. 28, November 1955.

Jasinsky, Frank, "Use and Misuse of Efficiency Controls," XXXIV *Harvard Business Review* (July, August 1956) pp. 105–112.

Jones, Charles O., "Representation in Congress: The Case of the House Agriculture Committee," LV *The American Political Science Review* (June 1961) pp. 358–367.

Jump, W. A., "Budgetary and Financial Administration in an Operating Department of the Federal Government," (Mimeo.) paper delivered at the conference of the Governmental Research Association, September 8, 1939.

Kahn, Herman, *On Thermonuclear War* (Princeton, 1960).

Kammerer, Gladys M., *Program Budgeting: An Aid to Understanding* (Gainesville, Fla., 1959), Public Administration Clearing Service of the University of Florida, Civic Information Series No. 38.

Key, V. O., Jr., "The Lack of a Budgetary Theory," XXXIV *The American Political Science Review* (December 1940) pp. 1137–1144.

Kolodzicj, Edward A., "Congressional Responsibility for the Common Defense: The Money Problem," XVI *The Western Political Quarterly* (March 1963) pp. 149–160.

Lawton, Frederick J., "Legislative-Executive Relationships in Budgeting as Viewed by the Executive," XIII *Public Administration Review* (Summer 1953) pp. 169–176.

Leiserson, Avery, "Coordination of Federal Budgetary and Appropriations Procedures Under the Legislative Reorganization Act of 1946," I *National Tax Journal* (June 1948) pp. 118–126.

LeLoup, Lance T., *Budgetary Politics: Dollars, Deficits, Decisions* (Brunswick, Ohio, 1977).

Lewis, Verne B., "Toward a Theory of Budgeting," XII *Public Administration Review* (Winter 1952) pp. 42–54.

[Rear Admiral] Leydon, John K., "Review of *The Politics of the Budgetary Process*," *U.S. Naval Institute Proceedings* (February 1966) p. 115.

Lindblom, Charles E., "Decision-Making in Taxation and Expenditure," in *Public Finances: Needs, Sources and Utilization*, National Bureau of Economic Research (Princeton, 1961) pp. 295–336.

———, "Policy Analysis," XLVIII *American Economic Review* (June 1958) pp. 298–312.

———, "The Science of 'Muddling Through,'" XIX *Public Administration Review* (Spring 1959) pp. 79–88.

Long, Norton, "Power and Administration," IX *Public Administration Review* (Autumn 1949) pp. 257–264.

Lord, Guy, *The French Budgetary Process* (Berkeley, 1973).

Maas, Arthur, "In Accord with the Program of the President?" Carl Friedrich and Kenneth Galbraith, editors, IV *Public Policy* (Cambridge, Mass., 1954) pp. 77–93.

MacMahon, Arthur, "Congressional Oversight of Administration," LVIII *Political Science Quarterly* (June and September, 1943) pp. 161–190 and 380–414.

Marvick, L. Dwaine, *Congressional Appropriation Politics: A*

Study of Institutional Conditions for Expressing Supply Intent (Ph.D. Dissertation, Columbia University, 1952).

Marvin, Keith E., and Andrew M. Rouse, "The Status of PPB in Federal Agencies: A Comparative Perspective," in *Public Policy Expenditures and Policy Analysis*, Robert Haveman and Julius Margolis, editors (Chicago, 1970) pp. 444–460.

Marx, Fritz Morstein, "The Bureau of the Budget: Its Evolution and Present Role, I and II," XXXIX *The American Political Science Review* (August and October 1945) pp. 653–684 and 869–898.

Masters, Nicholas, "Committee Assignments in the House of Representatives," LV *The American Political Science Review* (June 1961) pp. 345–357.

Meltsner, Arnold, *The Politics of City Revenue* (Berkeley and Los Angeles, 1971).

Merewitz, Leonard, and Stephen H. Sosnick, *The Budget's New Clothes: A Critique of Planning-Programming-Budgeting and Benefit-Cost Analysis*, Series on Public Analysis (Chicago, 1971).

Milliman, J. W., "Can People Be Trusted with National Resources?" XXXVIII *Land Economics* (August 1962) pp. 199–218.

Mosher, Frederick C., *Program Budgeting: Theory and Practice, with Particular Reference to the U.S. Department of the Army*, Public Administration Service (Chicago, 1954).

———, and Orville F. Poland, *The Cost of Governments in The United States: Facts, Trends, Myths* (Mimeo., August 1963).

———, and John Harr, *Programming Systems and Foreign Affairs Leadership: An Attempted Innovation* (New York, 1970) pp. 68–69.

Mueller, Eva, "Public Attitudes Toward Fiscal Programs," LXXVII *The Quarterly Journal of Economics* (May 1963) pp. 210–235.

Musgrave, R. A. and J. M. Culbertson, "The Growth of Public Expenditures in the United States, 1890–1948," VI *National Tax Journal* (June 1953) pp. 97–115.

Nelson, Dalmas H., "The Omnibus Appropriations Act of 1950," XV *Journal of Politics* (May 1953) pp. 274–288.

Neustadt, Richard E., "Presidency and Legislation: The Growth of Central Clearance," XLVIII *The American Political Science Review* (September 1954) pp. 641–671.

———, "Presidency and Legislation: Planning the President's Program," XLIX *American Political Science Review* (December 1955) pp. 980–1021.

Nienaber, Jeanne, and Aaron Wildavsky, *The Budgeting and Evaluation of Federal Recreation Programs, or, Money Doesn't Grow on Trees* (New York, 1973) pp. 116–142.

Niskanen, William A., *Structural Reform of the Federal Budget Process* (Washington, D.C., 1973).

Nourse, Edwin G., *Economics in the Public Service: Administrative Aspects of the Employment Act* (New York, 1953).

Novick, David, *Origin and History of Program Budgeting* (Santa Monica, California, October 1966).

———, editor, *Program Budgeting* (Cambridge, Mass., 1965) p. vi.

Paulson, Robert I., "Poverty, Uncertainty, and Goal Dissensus: The Causes of Underspending in the Model Cities Program" (paper submitted to Aaron Wildavsky's seminar, "Budgets as Political Instruments." Political Science Department, University of California, Berkeley, Spring 1973).

Peacock, Alan T. and Jack Wiseman, *The Growth of Public Expenditures in the United Kingdom* (Princeton, 1961).

Pecham, Joseph A., editor, *Setting National Priorities, the 1979 Budget* (Washington, D.C., 1978).

————, editor, *The 1978 Budget: Setting National Priorities* (Washington, D.C., 1977).

Phillips, John, "The Hadacol of the Budget Makers," IV *National Tax Journal* (September 1951) pp. 255–268.

Pierce, Lawrence, *The Politics of Fiscal Policy Formation* (Englewood Cliffs, N.J., 1971).

Pondy, Louis R., "A Mathematical Model of Budgeting," (Mimeo., Carnegie Institute of Technology, January 24, 1962).

Pressman, Jeffrey, and Aaron Wildavsky, *Implementation* (Berkeley and Los Angeles, 1973).

Prest, A. R., and R. Turvey, "Cost-Benefit Analysis: A Survey," LXXV *The Economic Journal* (December 1965) pp. 683–735.

Pyhrr, Peter A., *Zero-Base Budgeting: A Practical Management Tool for Evaluating Expenses* (New York, 1973).

Rawson, Robert H., "The Formulation of the Federal Budget," I *Public Policy* (Cambridge, Mass., 1941), C. J. Friedrich and E. S. Mason, editors, pp. 78–135.

Riggs, Fred, "Prismatic Society and Financial Administration," V *Administrative Science Quarterly* (June 1960) pp. 1–46.

Sayre, Wallace S. and Herbert Kaufman, *Governing New York City* (New York, 1960).

Schelling, T. C., *The Strategy of Conflict* (Cambridge, Mass., 1960).

Schick, Allen, *Budget Innovation in the States* (Washington, D.C., 1971).

————, "The Road to PPB: The Stages of Budget Reform," XXVI *Public Administration Review* (December 1966) pp. 243–258.

————, "The Budget Bureau that Was: Thoughts on the Rise,

Decline, and Future of a Presidential Agency," XXXV *Law and Contemporary Problems* (Summer 1970) pp. 519–539.

Schiff, Ashley L., *Fire and Water: Scientific Heresy in the Forest Service* (Cambridge, Mass., 1962).

Schilling, Warner R., Paul V. Hammond, and Glenn H. Snyder, *Strategy, Politics and Defense Budgets* (New York, 1962).

Schultze, Charles L., *The Politics and Economics of Public Spending* (Washington, D.C., 1968).

———, Edward L. Fried, Alice M. Rivlin, and Nancy H. Teeters, *Setting National Priorities: The 1973 Budget* (Washington, D.C., 1972) p. 11.

———, *Setting National Priorities: The 1974 Budget* (Washington, D.C., 1973) p. 8.

Seligman, Lester, "Presidential Leadership: The Inner Circle and Institutionalization," XVIII *Journal of Politics* (August 1956) pp. 410–426.

Sharkansky, Ira, *The Politics of Taxing and Spending* (Indianapolis, Ind., 1969).

Shipp, G. W., "Program Budgeting in the Defense Department: A Small Change," (Unpublished paper, Political Science Department, University of California, Berkeley, 1966).

Simon, Herbert A., *Administrative Behavior*, 2nd edition (New York, 1957).

———, *Models of Man* (New York, 1957).

———, Donald Smithburg, and Victor Thompson, *Public Administration* (New York, 1950).

Smithies, Arthur, *The Budgetary Process in the United States* (New York, 1955).

Staats, Elmer B., "Evaluating Program Effectiveness," in *Selected Papers on Public Administration*, D. L. Bowen and L. K. Caldwell, editors, Institute of Training for Public Service, Department of Government, Indiana University (Bloomington, Ind., 1960).

Stourm, René, *The Budget*, translated by Thaddeus Plazinski (New York, 1917).

Sundelson, Jacob Wilner, *Budgetary Methods in National and State Governments* (Albany, N.Y., 1938).

Symposium on Budget Theory, X *Public Administration Review* (Winter 1950) pp. 20–31.

Symposium, "Performance Budgeting: Has the Theory Worked?" XX *Public Administration Review* (Spring 1960) pp. 63–85.

Van Gunsteren, Herman R., *The Quest for Control* (New York, 1976).

Waldo, Dwight, *The Administrative State* (New York, 1948).

Walker, Robert, "William A. Jump: The Staff Officer As a Personality," XIV *Public Administration Review* (Autumn 1954) pp. 233–246.

Wallace, Robert Ash, "Congressional Control of the Budget," III *Midwest Journal of Political Science* (May 1959) pp. 151–167.

Weisbrod, Burton A., *The Economics of Public Health; Measuring the Economic Impact of Diseases* (Philadelphia, 1961).

Wildavsky, Aaron, "The Annual Expenditure Increment," XXXIII *The Public Interest* (Fall 1973) pp. 84–108.

———, *Budgeting* (Boston, 1975).

———, *Dixon-Yates: A Study in Power Politics* (New Haven, 1962).

———, "The Political Economy of Efficiency: Cost-Benefit Analysis, Systems Analysis, and Program Budgeting," XXVI *Public Administration Review* (December 1966) pp. 292–310.

————, "Political Implications of Budgetary Reform," XXI *Public Administration Review* (Autumn, 1961) pp. 183–190.

————, "Rescuing Policy Analysis from PPBS," XXIX *Public Administration Review* (March/April 1969) pp. 189–202.

————, "The Self-Evaluating Organization," XXXII *Public Administration Review* (September/October 1972) pp. 509–520.

————, "TVA and Power Politics," LV *The American Political Science Review* (September 1961) pp. 576–590.

————, and Arthur Hammond, "Comprehensive Versus Incremental Budgeting in the Department of Agriculture," X *Administrative Science Quarterly* (December 1965) pp. 321–346.

Willoughby, William Franklin, "The Budget," *Encyclopedia of the Social Sciences*, Vol. III (New York, 1930) pp. 38–44.

————, *The Movement for Budgetary Reform in the States* (New York, 1918).

————, *The National Budget System* (Baltimore, 1927).

————, *The Problem of a National Budget* (New York, 1918).

Wilmerding, Lucius, Jr., *The Spending Power* (New Haven, 1943).

Wyden, Peter, "The Man Who Frightens Bureaucrats," *Saturday Evening Post* (January 31, 1959) pp. 27, 87–89.

INDEX

Across-the-board cuts, 148
Administrative expenses, 110
    cuts in, 103
Advertising as a strategy, 120
Advisory committees, 70
Agencies
    clientele, 65
    goals of department heads,
        19
    mobilizing to avoid cuts,
        108
    roles and perspectives, 18
Agency officials, problems of,
    102
Aids to calculation, 171
    experience, 11
    incremental method, 13
    lowering goals, 12
    objectives of, 184–185
    parallels, 147
    simplification, 12
    vs. organization, 216–218
Analysts, policy, 246–249
Anshen, Melvin, 188–189,
    190, 191
Appeals, budgetary, 58
Appropriations Committees,
    155, 227, 240, 255–256,
    269
    apprenticeship of members,
        58

at center of Congressional
    system, 57
deciding size of appropria-
    tions, 56
most recommendations ac-
    cepted, 54
relations between legislative
    committees and, xv
roles and perspectives, 47
Arkansas, 209
Authorization legislation, 112

"Back door spending," 256
Balanced budget, 72
Bargaining, 131
    "Base" of budget, 16, 102,
        108–109
Budget
    balancing, 72
    Bureau of the (see Bureau
        of the Budget)
    complexity, 74, 93
    comprehensiveness, 146
    as a contract, 2
    control, 219
    defined and described, 1,
        128
    effect of political changes
        on, 132
    efficiency, 133
    form of, as strategy, 104

Budget (*cont.*)
  and human purposes, 1
  increase in size of, xviii
  influencing, 132
  lack of flexibility in, 13
  as political thing, 4
  precedent and, 3
  priorities, 73, 105
  a product of experience, 24
  purposes of men and, 4
  restoring Congressional control of, x
Budgetary calculation, improvements in, 152
Budgetary incrementalism, xix, 210, 213, 214, 221
  relation between organizational learning and, xii
Budgetary models, 126
Budgetary process
  alternative to, 145
  coordination, 152
  general criticisms, 145
  ignorance of, 143
  means-ends analysis, 147
  rejection of more data for, 231
  simplification, 147
Budgetary reform, 123, 222–224, 229–231, 254–262
  formidable nature, 132
  politics, 131
Budget Director, relationship with President, 37
Budgeting
  "adding-machine" approach, 29
  complexity, 8
  conflicts in (*see* Conflict in budgeting)
  coordination, 152

  coordination, lack of, 153
  cycle, 123
  defense, xii
  efficiency, 142
  environmental conditions, 7
  existential situation in, 144
  and foreign aid, 141
  fragmenting, 59
  general theory, 123
  historical nature, 58
  human aspect, 102
  incremental approach, 136, 150, 210, 213, 214, 221
  long-term upward trend, 123
  neglected groups, 157
  neglected interests, 156
  non-programmatic nature, 60
  normative theory, 128
  partial adversary system, 167
  problem of distributing shares, 143
  program package approach, 141
  reducing conflict in (*see* Conflict in budgeting)
  reforms, 127, 222–224, 229–231, 254–262
  repetitive nature, 60
  roles of participants, 6, 160
  sampling techniques, 151
  sequential nature, 60
  short cuts, 147
  specialization, 57
  as study of politics, 126
  theory, 128, 218–219
Budget Office as devil's advocate, 170
Budget officials, 75
  as guardians of the Treasury, 75

integrity, 78
Budget requests, deciding on size of, 21
Burden of calculation, reduction of, 130, 136
Bureaucrats and the budget, 74
Bureau of the Budget, 23, 134, 151. *See also* Office of Management and Budget
advocacy function, 35
and agencies, mutual dependence, 56
Congressional action is its guide, 41
Congressional attitudes toward, 38
a necessary evil, 38
pre-eminence hurt by Congress, 41
and program budgeting, 186–202, 216, 218
recommendations not guaranteed, 40
relationships of agency with, 39
as roadblock in governmental process, 41
role, 160, 162
roles and perspectives, 35
size of recommendations, 42
support of agencies, 40
weakness, 42
Bureau of the Census, 75, 98
Byington, Rep., 213

Cabinet on the British model, 134
Caiden, Naomi, xv
Calculation
aids to (*see* Aids to calculation)

of budgetary systems, 219, 220–221
defined and described, 7
and legislative decision making, 225
methods, general description, 8
restrictions on, 10
Califano, Joseph, 244
California, 209, 270
Carlson, Jack W., 194
Carryover, 31
Carter, James E., 203, 206, 210–212, 236, 244, 269
"Case of the Social and Rehabilitation Service, The," 185
"Cash limits," 264
CBO. *See* Congressional Budget Office
Census Bureau, 75, 98
Centralization, government, 188–190
"Chairman's mark," 231–232, 237
Chronology of budget procedures, 229–230
Coercive deficiency as strategy, 31
Commitment strategy, 101
Complexity of budgeting, 8, 74, 93
comparisons, 10
reasons for, examples, 8
Comprehensive budgeting, 149, 221
Compromise, political, 191–192
Comptroller General, 233
Conference Committees, 61, 100

Conference Committees
(*cont.*)
as added level of decision,
100
Conference Report and Joint
Statement of Managers,
Congressional, 232
Confidence as requisite in
budgeting, 74
Conflict in budgeting, 136
desirability of, 138
reduction of, 136
Congress
consideration of budgetary
reforms, ix
dependence on appropria-
tions committees, 57
Congressional Budget and Impoundment Control Act
of 1974, 222, 226, 229–
230, 231, 235, 238–240,
252, 255
Congressional Budget Office
(CBO), 226, 228, 231,
237–238, 242–244, 246–
249, 253
Congressional Budget Resolutions, 232–233, 236, 254–
255, 260
Congressional committee hearings, 84
Congressional contacts, 26
Congressmen
and the budget, 102
integrity, 82
relationships with administrators, 82
relationships with agency
officials, 80
Consumer Product Safety

Commission (CPSC),
212–213
Contingency and calculation,
101
Corman, Rep., 256
Cost-benefit analysis, 46, 159
Cost-benefit ratios, 43
Costs and budgetary programs,
187, 193, 199, 200, 214
Council of Economic Advisers,
134
Counter-strategies, 103, 105
Country program packages,
141
CPSC (Consumer Product
Safety Commission),
212–213
Crecine, John P., xii, 195
Crisis, strategy of, 118
CSB. *See* Current Services
Budget
Current Services Budget
(CSB), 230, 233–237,
244
Cuts
across-the-board, 148
administrative expenses, 103
elimination of program, 104
made without blame, 35
percentage, 148
in promotional activities,
103
shifting the blame, 105
turned into increases, 108
Cyclical nature of budgeting,
123

Deadlines, budgetary, 250–251
Deceit in strategies, 174
Deciding how much to spend,
31

Decision making
and calculation, 225, 253, 261
and ZBB, 208
Decision packages, 204–207, 209–210, 213, 214
Deferral of funds, 233, 239–240
Deficiency hearings, 32
Deficits, 260–261
Democratic party, 239, 267–268
Democratic Steering and Policy Committee, 227–228
Department(s)
vs. bureaus, 32, 209
heads of, 205–207, 214, 215
Department of Agriculture, 194, 206, 207–209, 245–246
Department of Defense, ix, 138, 190, 194–195
Department of Health, Education, and Welfare, 243, 244
Department of Treasury, 223, 256, 264
Devil's advocate role of BOB, 170
Diesing, Paul, 192
Director of the Budget, 197
Dixon-Yates case, 73
Dual authorities, 99

Efficiency in budgeting, 142
Emergency appropriations, 113
Environmental conditions of budgeting, 7, 224–226, 261–262
Estimates
and appropriations compared, 40
honesty of, 169
importance of, in budget requests, 64
Executive branch of government, Federal, 225, 240–242, 243–244, 248, 252. *See also* President
Existential situation in budgeting, 144
Expanding the base, 111
Expected level of appropriations, 43
Expenditures, governmental, 123, 255–257
Experience as calculation factor, 11

"Fair share" of budget, 16, 154
Federalist, 179
Feedback of information, 67, 171
Fenno, Richard F., Jr., 11, 14, 19, 27, 41, 47, 55, 143
Fischer, Gregory, xii
Flexibility, lack of, in budget, 13
Food Stamp Act of 1977, 259
Ford, Gerald R., 236, 237, 240, 254
Foreign aid budgeting, 97, 141
Fragmentation
of budget, 59
of power, 98, 100
France, 222
budget practices of, xi
Frankel, Marvin, 189
Funding and ZBB, 204, 205–206, 208, 211–212, 215, 216

Funds, impounding of, xiv, 37, 223, 224, 226, 233, 238–241, 252, 267

Garrett, Thaddeus, Jr., 213
General Accounting Office, xx, 151, 240, 243
Georgia, 210–211
Gerrymandering, 53
Goals, policy. *See* Objectives, policy
Governmental expenditures, rising trend in, 123
Great Britain, xi, 262–264

Harper, Edwin L., 196
Haveman, Joel, 249, 259–260
HBC. *See* House Budget Committee
Hearings
  of Congressional committees, 84
  psychology, 88
Heclo, Hugh, xvi
Hidden costs of programs, 151
Hirsch, W. Z., 190
Historical approach to budgeting, 219–220, 221
Historical nature of budgeting, 58
Hogan, Roy Lee, 211, 212
House Appropriations Committee, 11, 19, 47, 73, 137, 151, 227, 240, 255–256
  "mixed" role, 164
  pre-eminence in appropriations, 52
  role in budgeting, 160
House Budget Committee (HBC), 226–228, 231–232, 238, 246, 247–248, 253, 255–257, 258–259, 261, 262, 268, 269
House Ways and Means Committee, 227, 255–256, 268
Howard, Rep., 256–257
Hypotheses, policy, 181

Idaho, 209, 210
Illinois, 209
Impounding of funds, xiv, 37, 223, 224, 226, 233, 238–241, 252, 267
Incremental method of calculation, 15
Incrementalism, budgetary, xix, 210 ,213, 214, 221
  relation between organizational learning and, xii
Indicators, 24
Inflation, 263–264, 269
Influence, 33
Information
  costs of, 156
  and ZBB, 214–215
Internal contract, 2
Irrationality of PPB, 198–200

JEC. *See* Joint Economic Committee
Johnson, Lyndon B., 186, 240
Joint Committee on the Legislative Budget, 134
Joint Economic Committee (JEC), 230, 234, 250
Jump, William A., 18, 23, 34

Kramer, Fred A., 196

LaFaver, John, 215–216

Learning from budgetary systems, 219–221
Legislation, financial implications of, 100
Legislators, counter-strategies of, 103
Levine, Robert, 248
Leydon, John K., xii
Limitation on agency funds, 32
Lindblom, Charles E., 131, 148, 156
Line-item budgeting form, 59, 135
Logrolling, 136, 138
Long, Russel, 257–258

McKean, R. N., 191
McNeil, Wilfred, 11, 179
Mahon, Rep., 251
Management by Objectives (MBO), 183–185, 216–217
Managers
  and MBO, 184, 185
  and ZBB, 204, 205–206, 207, 214–215
  Man-years, 117
Marvin, Keith E., 193
Maximizing budgetary benefits, 129, 142
MBO. *See* Management by Objectives
Means-ends analysis, 147, 187, 188
Merit of programs
  as basis of presentation, 176
  effectiveness as criterion, 177
Mission, 66, 121
Missouri, 209

Models of budgeting, 126
Moods, spending and cutting, 72
Motivation and ZBB, 215–216
Multi-year budgets, 262–266
Muskie, Edmund, 237, 254, 257, 258, 259

NASA (National Aeronautics and Space Administration), 212, 213
National Institutes of Health, 33, 43, 48, 70, 71, 87, 92, 103, 111, 115, 119
Neustadt, Richard, xvii
New Jersey, 210
New Mexico, 215–216
New programs, getting appropriations for, 108
New York Times, 222
Nixon, Richard M., 223, 239, 240, 244
Normative theory of budgeting, 128

Objectives, policy
  and budgetary systems, 220–221
  and PPB, 186, 187, 188, 190, 193, 199–202
  and resources, 181–185
  and theory, 218
  and traditional line-item budgeting, 220–221
  and ZBB, 205–207
Office of Management and Budget (OMB), 230, 233–236, 240, 241, 242, 244–245, 269. *See also* Bureau of the Budget
O'Neill, Paul, 254

"Operation Outdoors," 121
Organization vs. analysis, 216–218
Organizational learning, relation between budgetary incrementalism and, xii

Packages, program, 137, 141
Packer, Arnold H., 249–250
Padding, 23
Partial adversary system of budgeting, 167
Partisanship
  in budgeting, 137
  in politics, 267–268
Paulson, Robert, xv
Percentage cut, 148
Percentage increase, 148
"Peter Rabbit" presentations, 121
Planning, Programming, and Budgeting Systems. *See* Program budgeting
Plateaus in cycle of expenditures, 123
Pluralism of Congress, 224–225
Polaris missile program, 70, 76
Policy
  and PPB, 196–202
  and traditional line-item budgeting, 221
Policy analysis, 181–183
Political rationality, 189
Politics in budget reform, 131, 191–196
PPBS. (*See* Program budgeting)
Practical budgeting, 143
Practice, PPB in, 193–196

President, 225, 236, 267
  vs. Congressional budgetary power, 253–254, 268–269
  and deficits, 260
  and impoundment of funds, xiv, 37, 223, 224, 226, 233, 238–241, 252, 267
  and multi-year budgets, 265, 266
  and program budgeting, 189–190
President's Budget, 231, 234, 245
Priorities, 23, 73, 105, 186
  and ZBB, 204–205
Profit making as strategy, 117
Program budgeting (Planning, Programming, and Budgeting Systems; PPBS), x, xii, 186–202, 216, 218
  calculations in, 201
  consequences of, 137
  definition, 135,
  in Department of Defense, 138
  learning from, 219–220, 221
  vs. traditional budgeting, 135
  vs. ZBB, 207, 216
Program packages, 137, 141
Promotional activities cuts, 103
Psychology of hearings, 88
Public Expenditure Survey (PES), 262–264
Publicity, 68
PVPI vs. TVPI, 165
Pyhrr, Peter, 203

Quantification, 116

Reciprocal expectations of House and Senate, 53
Reform, budgetary, 123, 127
  Congressional consideration of, ix
  and Congressional timetable, 229–231
  reasons for, 222–224
  reasons for failure, 131
  and spending, 254–262
  typical example, 133
Regional cleavages, 268
Repetitive nature of budgeting, 60
Republican Caucus, 227
Republican party, 267–268
Rescission of funds, 233, 239, 240–241
Resources and policy objectives, 181–183, 184
Rivlin, Alice, 248, 250, 254
Roles
  of budgeting participants, 6, 160
  defined, 160
Rooney, John, 22, 47, 49, 54, 61, 76, 77, 78, 88, 93, 96, 100, 107, 112, 120
Rounding off figures, 109
Rouse, Andrew M., 193, 196

Salesmanship as a strategy, 120
Sampling techniques in budgeting, 151
"Satisfice," lowering goals to, 12
SBC. *See* Senate Budget Committee
Schick, Allen, 196

Schott, Richard, 261
Senate
  appeals procedure, 58
  budgetary practice of, 16
  more liberal than House, 53
  role as responsible appeals court, 52
Senate Appropriations Committee: and House Committee, differences in perspectives, 51
  role of, in budgeting, 160
Senate Budget Committee (SBC), 226, 228, 230–231, 236, 237–238, 246, 247–248, 253, 255, 257–259, 262, 268, 269–270
Senate Finance Committee, 257, 268
Sequential calculation, 61
Sequential nature of budgeting, 60
Shocks in budgetary process, 126
Short cuts in budgeting, 147
Signals. *See* Indicators
Simplification in calculation, 12
Slippery statistic, the, 169
Smithies, Arthur, 133
Specialization
  of budgeting, 57
  policy, 225
Stans, Maurice, Budget Director, 13, 25, 36, 149
Steiner, G. A., 189, 190
Strategies
  "absorb it if it is so small," 114
  advertising and salesmanship, 120, 175

Strategies (*cont.*)
  advisors, multiple uses of,
    71
  advisory committees, 70
  appearance is vital, 104
  balanced budget, 72
  being a good politician, 64
  coercive deficiency, 31
  commitment, 101
  "commitment or no choice,"
    115
  compensation, 98
  compromise, 81
  concentrate on constituen-
    cies, 67
  constituency support, 73
  the crisis, 118
  deceitful, 174
  "the defense motif," 121
  defined, 63
  developing personal rela-
    tionships, 79
  "educating" Congressmen,
    92
  evading responsibility for
    cuts, 107
  exaggerated claims, 96
  exaggeration, 170
  expanding clientele, 66
  feedback of information, 67
  gaining support, 171
  good and bad, 167
  hiding behind the BOB, 108
  honesty, 76
  "if this then that," 115
  image, 87
  immoral, 176
  increasing the base, 108
  "insignificant" increase, 113
  intangible results, 94
  "it makes a profit," 117

  keep categories but increase
    content, 110
  knowledge, 87
  making best case at best
    time, 168
  "nobody loves a backlog,"
    115
  "overselling," 122
  planted questions, 86
  preparation, 85
  presentation, 85
  publicity, 68
  resisting cuts, 102
  results as favorable evi-
    dence, 90
  rounding off figures, 109
  service to clientele, 66
  "spend to save," 118
  statistics, relevant and other-
    wise, 95
  subdividing, 70
  temporary means perma-
    nent, 113
  transfer between categories,
    110
  turning cuts into increases,
    108
  types of, 65
  ubiquitous and contingent,
    64
  varying annual requests, 109
  the wedge, 111, 175
  work-load data, 116
  "work loads and work
    loads," 116
Subcommittees, relations with
    agency personnel, 83
Supplemental appropriations,
    21, 23

Talmadge, Herman E., 259

Taxation, 223, 257, 258
Tax policy, treatment of, as a process of strategic interaction, xvi
"Tell us what you really want," 34
Tennessee, 210
Texas, 209, 211, 212
Theory and budgeting systems, 218–219
Traditional budgeting, 220–221
  vs. program budgeting, 135
Transfer of appropriations expenditures, 110
TVA, 73, 119
"Twelfths," 57

Ubiquitous and contingent strategies, 64

"Underspending," phenomenon of, xiv
Understaffing, danger of, 24
United States Information Agency, 17, 61, 66, 94, 107, 119
United States Weather Bureau, 27, 69, 70, 97, 114, 121

Wilson, Paul, xxii
Work-load data, 46
  as strategy, 116

Zero Base Budgeting (ZBB), 202–216, 217, 218, 219–220, 221